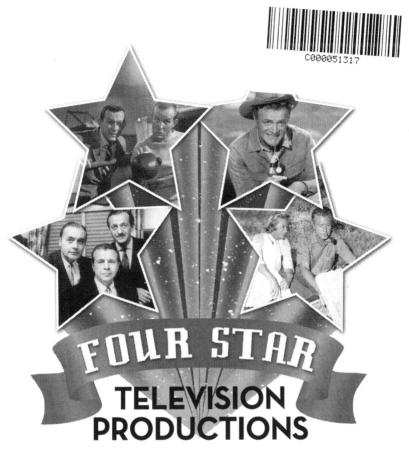

# FOUR STAR

## TELEVISION
## PRODUCTIONS

A History of the Business,
Series, and Pilots of the
Iconic Television Production
Company: 1952-1989

# Richard Irvin

Four Star Television Productions
Richard Irvin

Published in the USA by:
BearManor Media
P O Box 71426
Albany, Georgia 31708
www.bearmanormedia.com

ISBN: 978-1-62933-416-5
BearManor Media, Albany, Georgia
Printed in the United States of America
Book design by Robbie Adkins, www.adkinsconsult.com

# Table of Contents

# Acknowledgements

I wish to acknowledge the following institutions for their contributions to this work: staff at the Rauner Special Collections Library, Dartmouth College for material from the Frank Gilroy Papers; Ned Comstock with the Cinematic Arts Library at the University of California for his tremendous help in providing information about Four Star's pilots; Margaret Herrick Library, Academy of Motion Picture Arts and Sciences for details from the Paul Henreid Papers and the Sam Peckinpah Papers; Jeannette M. Berard for her assistance in summarizing material from the Broadcasting Collections at the Thousand Oaks Library in California; Lilly Library, Indiana University for access to the McGreevey Papers; the Wisconsin Center for Film and Theater Research for scripts from the Walter Mirisch Papers and the NBC Television Collection; American Heritage Center for material from the Christopher Knopf Papers and the Marc Brandel Papers; The New York Public Library for information from the Tad Mosel Collection; University of California Los Angeles for material from their television archives and from the Martin Berkeley Papers, Mort Fine Papers, Shirley Jones Papers, Alan Le May Papers, and the Norman Lessing Papers; University of Chicago Library for information from the Mortimer Adler Papers; Payson Library, Pepperdine University for access to the Don Ingalls Papers; and Syracuse University Libraries for material from the Gertrude Berg Papers.

I would also like to thank the following for their help with this book: Jonathan Ballak, John Eimen, Stephen Kandel, Marlyn Mason, Joey Paige, George Segal, Sherry Van Meter, and Garry Settimi.

# Preface

In Tim Brooks and Earle Marsh's *The Complete Directory to Prime Time Network and Cable TV Shows*, the authors define the different eras of prime-time programming from "Vaudeo" (1948-1957) to the "Reality Era" in the 2000s. The history of Four Star Productions in the 1950s and 1960s mirrored, for the most part, the first three eras described by Brooks and Marsh.

While the authors labeled the first era "Vaudeo" referring to the plethora of variety shows in the early days of television, they also pointed out that during the early fifties, "'Serious' television was represented mainly by dramatic anthology series, which offered a different play with a new cast each week."[1] Four Star Productions was originally formed by agent Don Sharpe and actors Dick Powell, David Niven, and Charles Boyer to produce the anthology *Four Star Playhouse*. The production company continued to produce anthology series through the late fifties and into the early sixties and used these vehicles to introduce several pilots for potential new shows.

The next era of programming delineated by Brooks and Marsh was the "Adult Western" era from 1957 to the early 1960s. This era was Four Star's heyday using the Dick Powell Western anthology *Zane Grey Theatre* to pilot many adult Westerns such as *Trackdown*, *The Rifleman*, and *Johnny Ringo*. Those series in turn were used as launching pads for other Westerns like *Wanted: Dead or Alive* and *The Law of the Plainsman*.

Four Star innovated the use of the "planted spin-off" or "back-door pilot" on its continuing character series, in particular its Westerns. Such spin-offs introduced new characters interacting with the stars of an established series in the hope that the new characters could be spun-off into their own series. Back-door pilots allowed the company to spend less on producing a pilot while also gauging audience reaction to it.

The subsequent era of programming from the early to late 1960s – the "Idiot Sitcom" era, was the youth decade with TV shows aimed at young people. That era was the beginning of the end for Four Star. While the company had multiple successes with dramatic anthologies and Westerns, it was never able to launch a really popular situation comedy. During that period, Four Star had comedies like *McKeever and the Colonel*, *Ensign O'Toole*, and *The Smothers Brothers Show* that fit the definition of comedies targeted at youth but none of those series lasted for more than one season. The production company also attempted to mimic the secret agent fad exemplified by *The Man from U.N.C.L.E.* and *I Spy* with shows like *Amos Burke, Secret Agent* and *Honey West*, a rare drama featuring a female in the lead. But again those series failed to generate much excitement.

In the late sixties and through the next seventeen years, Four Star was a mere shadow of itself in producing network television series. It spent most of those years syndicating shows to local TV stations – a few dramas, many game and variety shows as well as reality-type documentaries.

This book covers the business side of Four Star Productions which, through the years, changed its name to Four Star Films and then Four Star Television and finally Four Star International. The book also describes the many television series and other projects made by the company. Although Four Star produced and distributed some motion pictures and was involved, to some extent, in the music business, this work's primary focus is on Four Star's television series and pilots.

Television series and pilots are organized according to their genre and the time period in which they were made. Within each chapter, series are listed by their premiere dates; pilots are described after the series to which they were related or, if not a potential "spinoff" from a series, they are listed in a separate chapter section by the dates in which they were considered as projects and/or produced.

# Chapter 1:
# Three Stars and an Agent

One of the most prolific agent-packagers in 1950s television was a man named Don Sharpe. Sharpe had the knack of coming up with ideas and knowing how to carry them out. He would present his concepts for television series to potential sponsors and then oversee the series to ensure that the results were what he expected.

Born in Livingston, Montana, Don Sharpe attended Northwestern University and acted in little theater plays. Subsequently, he traveled to Hollywood and, at age twenty-two, became an actor at the Pasadena Community Playhouse.

Sharpe began his broadcasting career in radio initially preparing dramatic spots for the *Kate Smith Show* and writing scripts for *Cavalcade of America*. Later, he packaged radio shows featuring major movie stars. Based on the movie *Mr. Blandings Builds His Dream House*, Sharpe had star Cary Grant reprise his role as Blandings on a radio series. He also had actor Brian Donlevy star in the radio series, *Dangerous Assignment*, Charles Boyer in the *Adventures of Marcel*, Dick Powell in *Richard Diamond*, Frank Lovejoy in *Nightbeat*, and Lucille Ball in *My Favorite Husband*.

With the advent of television, Mr. Sharpe sought to transfer many of his radio shows to the new medium as well as to develop new TV programs working mainly with Official Films – a firm that distributed syndicated programs to television stations. Sharpe managed a deal with CBS to air *I Love Lucy*. He became the exclusive representative for Desilu Productions and was essential in having Desilu produce, in addition to the *Lucy* series, *Our Miss Brooks* with Eve Arden. Sharpe was instrumental in helping Douglas Fairbanks, Jr. form his own production company, Dougfair. For actor Robert Cummings, he developed a TV comedy called *My Hero* which began airing on NBC in 1952.

*The three star owners of Four Star Productions – Charles Boyer, Dick Powell, and David Niven*

Sharpe was key in recruiting Dick Powell, Charles Boyer, and David Niven for his television version of *Four Star Playhouse* and forming Four Star Productions with the three stars.

Born Richard Ewing Powell in Mountain View, Arkansas on November 14, 1904, Dick Powell began a singing career in college and performed with several orchestras after graduation. Acting as master of ceremonies and singing at a theater in Pittsburgh, Pennsylvania in 1932, he was spotted by a talent scout who brought him to Hollywood were he began starring in movie musicals like *Forty-Second Street* and *Shipmates Forever*. His involvement in show business would be marked by several changes in his career. Tiring of singing, Powell got the chance to star in a non-singing role in the film noir *Murder, My Sweet* which launched his career as a dramatic actor. He would later become a movie producer and director helming features like *Split Second* in 1953, a remake of *It Happened One Night* called *You Can't Run Away from It* (1956), *The Conqueror* with John Wayne (1956), *The Enemy Below* (1957), and *The Hunters* (1958).

Powell was the one star out of the triumvirate who was interested in the business side of making television shows and not just in acting. He once said that, "I started out with two assets, a voice that didn't drive audiences into the streets and a determination to make money. I've always worked like a dog. If you don't keep working hard in this business, you're dead."[2]

Dick Powell passed away in January 1963 from stomach cancer.

Charles Boyer, born in Figeac, Lot, France on August 28, 1899, is probably best known for his starring roles in movies including *Algiers* (1938), *Love Affair* (1939), and *Gaslight* (1944). He was nominated four times for the Academy Award as Best Actor but never won. While in France, he appeared in plays and movies. His first leading role in America was in the musical *Caravan* in 1934. In addition to roles on *Four Star Playhouse*, he appeared on Four Star's *Alcoa-Goodyear Award Theatre* and *The Rogues*. For his acting on *Four Star Playhouse*, he was nominated for an Emmy for Best Continuing Performance by an Actor in a Dramatic Series. Thanks to his association with Don Sharpe, he guest starred on *I Love Lucy* in 1956. Two days after his wife's death from cancer in 1978, Charles Boyer committed suicide with an overdose of Seconal.

Boyer served on the board of Four Star until the company was sold in 1967 and became Four Star International. As his biographer described:

> The early betting among the Hollywood gentry had been that the triumvirate of president Powell and vice-presidents Boyer and Niven would never make a go of it: their egos were too gigantic, their temperaments too volatile. Boyer reasoned that they must have solved the problem nicely "just by never getting together." Occasionally they could manage their obligatory annual meeting over lunch, but more often the three partners were scattered around the world and had to manage their meeting by phone.[3]

James David Graham Niven was born on March 1, 1910 in London, England and died on July 29, 1983 of amyotrophic lateral sclerosis (ALS). Niven is probably better known for his movie roles than for his acting on television or his part ownership of Four Star Productions. He arrived in Hollywood in 1934 and was featured in motion pictures like *The Dawn Patrol* (1938), *Raffles* (1939), and *The Bishop's Wife* (1947). However, his biggest feature film successes came after his hosting and acting duties on *Four Star Playhouse*. In 1956, he starred as Phileas Fogg in Mike Todd's *Around the World in Eight Days*. Niven won the Oscar for Best Actor for the film *Separate Tables* (1958) and had memorable roles in *Please Don't' Eat the Daises* (1960), The *Guns of Navarone* (1961), and *The Pink Panther* (1963).

Reflecting in 1955 on the formation of Four Star Productions, Niven remarked, "We formed the company in 1952 because of the picture business slump. We took a terrific gamble in going into TV, because at the time everyone advised against it. We were the first names to go into TV film wholeheartedly . . . If I never get a cent out of Four Star, I've more than broken even."[4]

In the first year of operation, Four Star lost $160,000 even though none of the partners collected a salary.

Supposedly, Dick Powell once said that he insured Four Star Productions of mental equilibrium ". . . by going into partnership with someone who could never be serious (Niven) and someone who could never be anything else (Boyer). Anyway, they never fought, and Niven attributed that to their being actors – 'The only voice we pay attention to is our own.'"[5]

The three-way partnership lasted until Powell's death in 1963. After that, Niven and Boyer continued as officers of the company until 1967 when they sold their stock shares to an investment group headed by David Charnay. After several changes in management and ownership through the seventies and eighties, Four Star ceased existence in the late 1980s becoming part of New World Entertainment in 1989.

# Chapter 2:
## *Four Star Playhouse*, 1952-56

Producer Don Sharpe developed *The Four Star Playhouse* originally as a radio series for NBC beginning on July 3, 1949. Stories,
built around a strong central character, were adapted from ones in
*Cosmopolitan* magazine. The original four stars headlining the radio
anthology were Fred MacMurray, Loretta Young, Rosalind Russell,
and Robert Cummings. Each actor would appear in one episode
per month. The radio show lasted until September 11, 1949.

In forming the television version of the series, Cummings, Young,
and MacMurray were not available as hosts or actors. Robert Cummings was already involved with his new sitcom, *My Hero*. Fred
MacMurray had no interest in doing a television series until producer Don Fedderson worked out an arrangement with the actor
to star on *My Three Sons* beginning in 1960, and Loretta Young
was about to develop her own anthology series with her husband
as one of the producers. Having worked with both Dick Powell
and Charles Boyer on radio, Sharpe invited each of them to host
the television version of *Four Star Playhouse* along with Rosalind
Russell and Joel McCrea. According to Dick Powell, "Roz and
Joel took one look at themselves in the kinescopes and they said,
'This stuff will never make it. Besides, the work is too hard.' So
they backed out. . ."[6] While that may have been true of Rosalind
Russell, at the time Joel McCrea was also involved in attempting a
TV version of his radio series, *Tales of the Texas Rangers* – another
radio program produced by Don Sharpe. That project may have
contributed to McCrea declining the Four Star offer. David Niven
replaced Joel McCrea as a host of the series and as a partner in Four
Star Productions. As Niven related, "I ran into Charles (Boyer) in
San Francisco, where we were both appearing, had dinner with
him, heard the story that Joel (McCrea) wanted out. Also I was
asked if I knew of anyone who might want to take over his part in
the venture. I kicked him so hard under the table he had no other

choice but to ask me. That's how I got into it."[7] The fourth host spot was left open for various guest stars like Ronald Coleman until Ida Lupino officially became the fourth star in 1955, although her first appearance as an actress on the series was in 1953. As William Hawes describes in his book, *Filmed Television Drama, 1952-1958*, "While directing *The Bigamist*, 1953, England, Ida Lupino got a call from her old friend, David Niven: 'Lupy, Kupy, I know you're against television, but come over and do a guest shot on our show anyway.' I said, 'Oh, Niv, I can't. The whole thing scares me.' He said, 'Come and do just one.'"[8] Unlike Powell, Boyer, and Niven, Ida Lupino never had an ownership interest in Four Star.

Singer Sewing Machine Company first sponsored *Four Star Playhouse* series on CBS which initially alternated with the comedy *Amos 'n Andy*. After its first season, *Four Star Playhouse* became a weekly series and ran for a total of four seasons. The cost of each episode, including the star's fee of $5000 per show, was $30,000, but Singer budgeted only $25,000 per episode. The network would not make up the deficit. In addition to the actor's fee, Boyer, Powell, and Niven had a 30% profit participation fee and Official Films had a70% profit participation.[9] The stars agreed to defer their $5000 fee and Official Films decided to reduce their profit participation to 30% and give Boyer, Powell, and Niven 70%. Out of this grew Four Star Productions with Powell, Boyer, and Niven each with a 25% ownership interest in the company and with Don Sharpe as president controlling part of the remaining 25% along with other stockholders.

*Four Star Playhouse* featured both comedies and dramas. The first episode starred Charles Boyer in a story written by Larry Marcus. Boyer played a man who created a fictitious wife named Geraldine Graham in order to obtain employment with a toy company whose boss would only hire people with a stable family life. The Boyer character rents a new house and buys clothes and other items for his fictional wife and convinces Rose (Una Merkel), the manager of the housing development, and his neighbors that his wife really exists. However, when he is hospitalized after a slight accident and people try to contact Geraldine to no avail, neighbors jump to the conclusion that she has been murdered by her husband. His boss hires a private detective to find out what happened to her. When Mr. Graham is released from the hospital, he confesses to Rose that Geraldine doesn't really exist. Rose poses as Mrs. Graham when a detective comes by wanting to see Geraldine.

About acting on this anthology, Boyer remarked, "... on our show, which is filmed on a three-day schedule, it is necessary to learn at least ten times as much dialogue for each day's shooting as on the most rapidly filmed motion pictures."[10]

Dick Powell's first episode was "Dante's Inferno" by Blake Edwards where the actor played Willie Dante, proprietor of the club, Dante's Inferno, which included a gambling casino. A woman at the club discloses that her husband is going to kill her because she learned of his shady business dealings of cheating his partner out of money. Her husband is afraid that she'll inform on him. Later, the police advise Dante that the woman is dead, but he can't identify her because of the beating she suffered. The husband is arrested for murder. But the woman Dante met at his club was actually posing as the wife of the newly incarcerated husband. The partner who was being cheated, a gambler at Dante's Inferno, had his partner's real wife killed to frame her husband, as revenge for taking money from the business.

David Niven's initial appearance on the anthology was in an installment titled "The Island" where he played a doctor treating the natives on an island owned by his employer, a soap company. The company's owner arrives with his wife and, suspicious of the doctor's background, tells him to leave. However, when the owner has an appendicitis attack, the doctor has to operate. The owner eventually apologizes to the doctor and allows him to stay. After the owner leaves the island, the doctor confesses to the company's manager that he really never got his medical degree. He had only spent some years in medical school before the war. The doctor decides to leave the island and obtain his degree.

On a 1953 episode titled "House for Sale," Ida Lupino made her first appearance on *Four Star Playhouse* as Mrs. McIntyre, a woman looking to buy a new house. She sees a listing for a home in a remote section of town and visits it encountering a morose-looking man whom she thinks is the real estate agent. However, he is an escaped mental patient who has murdered the agent. After seeing the body of the dead agent in the fireplace, Mrs. McIntyre attempts to flee but is stopped by the killer. When another realtor and his female client stop by to look at the property, Mrs. McIntyre tries to warn them about the killer, but they don't believe her and leave. Finally, the female client returns with a police man who shoots the maniac. Turns out that the client wanted her husband to look at the house, and he happened to be a policeman.

*Four Star Playhouse* was nominated for an Emmy as best dramatic series in 1954. That same year David Niven was nominated as best actor in a drama. He repeated that nomination in 1956 along with Charles Boyer and Ida Lupino both being recognized for their acting on the series. Ironically, Dick Powell never received an Emmy nomination.

On November 10, 1954, *Variety* reported that Powell would step away from working on television if the feature film he was making at the time, *The Conqueror* with John Wayne, turned out to be a hit. Presumably he would have devoted himself to directing full-time. While the movie did respectable business at the box office, it was a critical flop, and Mr. Powell continued his involvement with television for the rest of his life.

In spring 1956, thinking that *Four Star Playhouse* would be renewed for another season, both Charles Boyer and David Niven sought to establish recurring characters for themselves to play in future episodes like Dick Powell had done with the Willie Dante character. Powell had planned to continue portraying Dante on at least eight episodes during the 1956-57 season.

Charles Boyer commissioned at least five scripts about a worldly playwright and novelist named Paul Bergere. Boyer did appear as that character on a March 22, 1956 installment of *Four Star Playhouse* titled "Desert Encounter." When Bergere's chauffeur is ill, Paul has to drive himself from a town in Mexico to a conference in Los Angeles. Along the way, he encounters Anita (Susan Kohner), a young woman who asks him to drive her to her father's ranch. When the two arrive, Anita's father and brothers think that Bergere is Anita's boyfriend whom she has to marry since she had spent the night with her real boyfriend, Bob (Stuart Whitman). After the priest arrives for the wedding ceremony, Bob shows up as well, and the couple explains who Bob is.

If *Four Star Playhouse* had been renewed beyond the 1955-56 broadcast year, Mr. Boyer may have appeared as the character Paul Bergere on future episodes. There was also some discussion that Boyer would play Paul Bergere on his own series titled *Charles Boyer Presents* during the 1956-57 television season, but that series never happened.

For the anticipated 1956-57 season, David Niven considered making three episodes of *Four Star Playhouse* playing Lord Peter Wimsey created by mystery writer Dorothy Sayers. The shows were to be filmed in London.

Since the series ended after the 1955-56 season, none of these continuing character episodes were made. When CBS canceled *Four Star Playhouse* to make way for its own ninety-minute anthology, *Playhouse 90*, Dick Powell accused the network of monopoly practices. However, the feud with CBS was resolved when the network picked up *Dick Powell's Zane Grey Theatre* for the 1956-57 season.

In 1970, there was word that Four Star would revive *Four Star Playhouse* with a new set of motion picture actors. By then, actor Anthony Quinn had signed a deal with the company to develop TV shows and movies. Quinn along with Audrey Hepburn and Burt Lancaster were reportedly to be the new hosts of the reboot. The new *Four Star Playhouse*, which never materialized, would have been a one-hour series.

*Four Star Playhouse* started the practice by its production company of airing episodes that directly or indirectly were pilots for potential series.

## Dante

In addition to the first season episode noted above, Dick Powell played the Willie Dante character on at least seven other *Four Star Playhouse* installments over the series run. Most of the stories dealt with the gambling aspect of Dante's nightclub. For instance, in season two, "The Squeeze," the District Attorney's son, a secret gambler, loses big at Dante's Inferno and pays his debt with a check which a gangster, appearing before the grand jury, wants to obtain in order to blackmail the DA. Powell also played Dante on a November 19, 1953 installment, "The Hard Way" which featured the story of Willie unwittingly using counterfeit money to pay a jackpot winner.

In season three, "The House Always Wins" (April 28, 1955) focused on a woman familiar to Dante showing up at the club with another man and a couple. She informs Willie that the people accompanying her are planning to rob the place.

On the final season of *Four Star Playhouse*, Powell appeared in four episodes as Dante. In "High Stakes" (January 26, 1955), Dante is a target for murder due to his latest flame. "No Limit" (February 16, 1956) had Willie rebuffing the attempts of a gangster to take over his casino. In "A Long Way from Texas" (May 3, 1956), a young bride wants to learn how to gamble so she can share her new husband's interest in the sport. The final installment of Dante on *Four Star Playhouse*, titled "The Stacked Deck" (June 28, 1956) had blackmailers wanting to use the nightclub as the location for a payoff.

In May 1955, Four Star announced that its first theatrical feature would be a full-length film based on the Dante character with Dick Powell in the lead. Character actors Herb Vigran, Regis Toomey, and Alan Mowbray who had appeared in the *Four Star Playhouse* episodes of Dante would be in the movie. Dick Powell was reported to be singing six numbers in the planned film. However, as with other Four Star announcements of proposed motion pictures, this one was never produced.

Later in 1955, Powell thought of playing Willie Dante on a weekly basis in a series of his own, but he never went through with the idea. *Dante* did premiere as its own series produced by Four Star in 1960 with Howard Duff as the lead character.

### Jonas Gentry, M.D.

David Niven contemplated starring on his own comedy series playing a pediatrician who also has to deal with the problems of his three kids at home. This unsold pilot, titled "A Matter of Advice" written by Norman Paul, aired in October 1953 on *Four Star Play-*

*house*. Starring with Niven were Fay Baker as his wife Eve, Sally Fraser as his oldest daughter Trudy, Sheila James as daughter Luana, and Freddy Ridgeway as his son Mike. The story line involved Dr. Gentry planning to attend the play *Romeo and Juliet* starring Trudy as Juliet, but being continually interrupted by phone calls from Mrs. Carter, a mother who just brought her first baby home from the hospital. Meanwhile, Luana wants to attend the play with her parents, but her father says she cannot stay up that late. Even though she is told to remain home, she comes to the play anyway dressed in her mother's hat and stole. During the performance, Dr. Gentry receives another call from Mrs. Carter concerned that her baby hasn't burped after being fed. The audience overhears the doctor berating the mother for the phone call which interrupts Trudy's best scene. However, Trudy is not upset because the director complimented her on not letting the conversation interrupt her performance, and Gentry learns that Luana is maturing as a young woman.

### Nightbeat

*Nightbeat*, about a newspaper reporter played by Frank Lovejoy, had been a series on radio starting in 1950 and lasting until 1952. A pilot for the television version of the series aired as an episode of *Four Star Playhouse* on November 5, 1953. The episode, titled "Search in the Night," starred Lovejoy as reporter Randy Stone working for a Chicago newspaper. He comes upon the scene of a diver hired to search for a woman's purse that was dropped into the Chicago River. After the diver locates the pocketbook and returns it to the woman, he informs Stone that it contained a gun and a wad of cash. He also says that he saw a dead body in the river. Stone finds the dead man's coat containing a photo of the woman who had lost her purse. The reporter visits her and learns that the dead man was the woman's husband who had previously been reported as deceased and so she had remarried. When her first husband reappeared, he began extorting money from her and her new husband. She was taking another payoff to him when her pocketbook fell into the water. He dived in after it and drowned.

If *Nightbeat* had become a TV series, the show would have been similar to an anthology with rotating stars. However, each star would have played the same character on each of their episodes. While Frank Lovejoy would have been the night beat reporter in Chicago, MacDonald Carey would have played such a reporter in New York City and Ronald Reagan would have appeared as a journalist covering Los Angeles.

Four Star would use the same technique of different leads headlining the same series as a way to reduce each star's workload on a weekly program. For example, the company did this on the mid-1960s series *The Rogues* with lead actors Gig Young, David Niven, and Charles Boyer starring on different episodes.

## Meet McGraw

Later during the 1953-54 season, *Four Star Playhouse* aired another pilot with Frank Lovejoy as the main character. Titled "Meet McGraw," the episode concerned a man who would do anything, short of murder, if the price was right. McGraw is hired by a woman who says her husband, a gangster, threatens to kill her if she divorces him. Reluctant at first to take the case, McGraw relents after someone fires a gun at her. McGraw learns that her husband couldn't have been the shooter since he was imprisoned in Texas for income tax problems after someone informed the authorities. From the woman's maid, McGraw discovers that the woman is having an affair with another man. The woman had her lover try to shot McGraw – not her as McGraw had thought. The woman's real motive was to incriminate her paramour in McGraw's death as retaliation for him informing on her husband's tax fraud. McGraw turns the woman and her lover over to the police.

Frank Lovejoy reprised the McGraw character in a 1957 to 1958 NBC series. However, the series was not produced by Four Star. By then, Don Sharpe, no longer president of the company, had formed Sharpe-Lewis Productions with Warren Lewis, a producer for *Four Star Playhouse*, and that company made the series, *Meet McGraw*.

## Ronald Coleman T.V.

Frequent host of *Four Star Playhouse* before Ida Lupino became a regular, Ronald Coleman together with Don Sharpe developed an anthology series that Coleman would host based on stories by W. Somerset Maugham. The pilot for this projected series, made in

1953, aired in January 1954 as an installment of *Four Star Playhouse*. Titled "String of Beads," Mr. Coleman, as the storyteller, related the tale of Joan Robinson (Angela Lansbury), a governess, who is asked to attend an exclusive party by her employer when one of the invited guests bows out. Guests begin making snide remarks about Joan being just a governess which prompts Count Borselli (George Macready), a jewelry connoisseur, on a whim, to remark that the pearls Joan is wearing are worth 60,000 pounds even though Joan knows she purchased them for a few shillings. Joan begins receiving several invitations to upper class functions and starts dating a handsome man she met at the party named Peter Jeffries (Ron Randell). When her employer, Edythe Livingstone (Brenda Forbes), discovers the truth about the pearl necklace, she fires Joan and threatens to expose her. After Joan informs Peter that she has been discharged and that the pearls are not as valuable as he thought they were, he leaves her. In the end, Joan marries Count Borselli who is enchanted by her.

When Ronald Coleman's radio series, *Halls of Ivy*, was adapted for television, he was not able to host this anthology. However, the stories by Somerset Maugham were used by Four Star for many episodes of another anthology titled *The Star and the Story*.

# Chapter 3:
# Clones of *Four Star Playhouse*, 1953-56

The big news for Four Star in late 1955 was that president Don Sharpe was asked to leave his post by Powell, Boyer, and Niven because they felt that the company was not growing as fast as it should and that Sharpe was spread too thin with all of his outside interests including heading his own talent agency, representing Desilu, and handling chores for Douglas Fairbanks Jr.'s production company. There was also thought among the three stars of doing work on outside packages, and Sharpe considered himself a packager and not a professional manager. Four Star's attorney William Cruikshank became the acting president. Mr. Sharpe continued to have stock in Four Star and remained on the Board of Directors, but he gave up his responsibilities as exclusive sales representative for any of the company's new projects. Nevertheless, Sharpe remained the representative for current contracts and would still develop new packages for Four Star. The company retained the William Morris Agency to act as its sales representative for new undertakings and used that agency to lure several major movie stars to appear on Four Star's television series.

Commenting on the change in leadership, new president Cruikshank said that planned additional activities for the company, including entering the field of motion pictures, "would place an impossible burden on Mr. Sharpe because of his outside activities. That is why the mutual decision was made regarding his resignation."[11]

In February 1956, Four Star sold all the assets of Four Star Productions and Four Star Television to Official Films in a stock swap deal. The assets in question were rights to rerun all episodes of *Four Star Playhouse*, *Star and the Story*, *Stage 7*, and *DuPont Cavalcade Theatre*. From that point, Four Star Productions ceased to exist. New series produced by Four Star would come under the Four Star Films designation still owned by Powell, Boyer, and Niven. As a result of the deal, Four Star Films owned 26% of the outstanding stock of Official Films but had voting rights for only about 10% of Official's stock.

Official Films organized the shows it bought from Four Star into four packages for syndication: three each consisting of those in which David Niven, Dick Powell, and Charles Boyer starred and a fourth package of other actors and actresses who had been the main star on various anthology series episodes.

Four Star developed the following anthologies in the early to mid-1950s.

## *The Star and the Story*

This first-run syndicated anthology was a joint production of Four Star, Sharpe-Lewis Productions, and Official Films and premiered in most of the country in 1955. The program first appeared on ten TV stations in the West in June, 1954 sponsored by Liebmann Breweries. Actor Henry Fonda introduced each episode, but he hosted only those episodes sponsored by Liebmann.

When *The Star and the Story* was syndicated to the rest of the country through Official Films, the lead actor on each episode handled the introduction. The show's title was based on the idea that each week's star chose the teleplay in which he or she was featured.

Four Star had purchased the rights to Somerset Maugham's short stories for a possible Ronald Coleman anthology described in Chapter 2. When that project failed to become a series, the tales were used as the basis for twelve episodes of *The Star and the Story* including "Louise" with Judith Anderson playing the role of a woman who attempts to destroy her daughter's romance by pretending to be an invalid and "The Round Dozen" where a writer, staying at an inn in Europe, encounters a bigamist courting an unsuspecting woman.

The first show of the series, "The Thin Line" featured David Niven and Joan Camden as husband and wife. A musician, Johnny Marlin (Niven), is released from a mental institution where he was confined after trying to kill his wife Kathy and then himself with a razor. He can't remember anything about his past in general and the incident specifically. A friendly attendant at the institution named Red (Chuck Connors) counsels him about his past so he can be released. After discharge, he goes to his apartment where his wife informs him that his music came between them and that she is now happy that they can do anything that she wants. When one of his recordings is played, he remembers how she hated his music and that she actually slashed her husband's wrists, and, after he blacked out, she drew the razor across her throat just enough to open a cut but not kill her. He promises to help her regain mental stability.

On an installment titled "Dark Stranger," Edmund O'Brien played novelist Ray Ericson who falls in love with a female character from his novel but then he finds that she may actually exist. The book Ericson wrote, *Dark Stranger*, is about a man hired to kill a girl, but the man begins falling in love with her. The female character, Jill Andrews (Joanne Woodward) that Ericson created, comes to life in his eyes, and he tries to prevent her from being murdered as he attempts to revise his completed book. After she professes love for him, Ray decides to marry her so she will no longer be "Jill Andrews" but "Jill Ericson." However, she buys his novel and understands who she is. The end reveals that Ericson had been hit by a car when running after a woman who looked like Jill. He had been in a coma for five weeks fantasizing about her.

Another somewhat unique episode featured Edmund Gwenn as Paddy Faneen. Set in Ireland, Faneen insists he saw a flying saucer much to the consternation of his wife and granddaughter. Furthermore, he says that passengers departed from the saucer. Taking a walk with a friend, he sees the shining light again and encounters one of the "passengers" who turns out to be a journalist from Dublin wanting to do a story about his sightings. Instead of recanting his story, he relates his sightings to the reporter thinking the article will make him famous.

## *Stage 7* and Its Pilots

When it first premiered on CBS on December 12, 1954, this anthology was called *Your Favorite Playhouse* comprised of reruns from other anthologies. However, beginning on January 30, 1955, the series title changed to *Stage 7*, and it began to feature new episodes produced by Four Star and sponsored by Bristol-Myers.

The first episode, "Deceiving Eye," featured Frank Lovejoy as a criminology professor who is accused of murder. The professor researches the validity of eyewitness accounts of crime. Pursuant to this, he appears in a police line-up dressed as a bum and ends up as a murder suspect because his name appeared in the victim's diary and because the manager of his apartment building identified him as being near the murder scene in clothes he wore at the line-up. The witness's husband is in the process of divorcing her and planned to marry the girl who was killed. The witness framed the professor for the murder. She is found to be the perpetrator when the professor questions her about the victim's hair color. The victim was a brunette but on the night she was murdered, she was bleaching her hair blonde. Only the murderer would have said the murdered girl's hair was blonde.

Lovejoy also appeared in another episode of this anthology on March 27, 1955 as McGraw. The second *Meet McGraw* episode had previously aired on February 25, 1954 on *Four Star Playhouse*. In "The Long Count," McGraw becomes involved with beautiful girls, a prizefighter, and disreputable fight promoters.

As with *Four Star Playhouse*, *Stage 7* also aired pilots for possible series.

### "The Magic Hat"

An April 24, 1955 episode titled "The Magic Hat" starred George Brent as Professor Michael X. Balsam, a widower, raising a nine-year-old daughter Jody (Lydia Reed). Nora Marlowe appeared as Mrs. Kakoonis, their part-time housekeeper. Filmed in 1954, this story was a pilot for a comedy series to be called *Jody and Me*. Written by Irving Gaynor Neiman, the story line had the former, now retired, Columbia University professor, as a cabinet maker in a small town, allowing his daughter to buy a hat intended for an older girl. Jody wants the hat to wear to a reception for the new school principal. She purchases a large hat with feathers on the top and wears it in public for the first time. When she returns, she puts the hat back in its box and says she is not going to the principal's party. Mrs. Kakoonis informs Jody's dad that kids made fun of the hat when they saw Jody wearing it. However, after her dad relates a story about a prince looking for a princess who chose the only girl who wore clothes different from everyone else's, Jody decides to go to the party wearing her new hat. She becomes the star of the party.

This episode of *Stage 7* was not the first attempt at launching *Jody and Me*. Talent Associates, a company headed by David Susskind, produced the same story which aired on *Armstrong Circle Theatre* in fall 1954 with actor James Dunn as the professor along with child actress Patty McCormack as Jody. The *Stage 7* production was the second attempt at a pilot for this intended series.

### "The Hayfield"

This pilot for a proposed series titled *Blandings' Way*, based on the books and movie about Jim Blandings, a New York ad executive who buys a home in Connecticut, starred MacDonald Carey as Blandings, Phyllis Thaxter as his wife Muriel, and Dick Foran as their friend and lawyer, Bill Cole. "The Hayfield," airing September 18, 1955 on *Stage 7*, had Blandings thinking of harvesting hay from his ten acres and selling it for a profit after he sees a newspaper report about a farmer who sold his hay. After Blandings places an ad in the local paper, several people respond, but they all want to sell Jim machinery for cutting the field. One person, who does express interest in the hay, looks at the field and says that it is mostly weeds and should be burned. He wants $200 to burn off the weeds. Blandings decides to burn the field himself with predictable results. The wind direction changes with the fire threatening his house. He calls the fire department, which puts out the blaze but charges Blandings for its efforts. Jim also has to pay a fine for failure to obtain a permit for the burning.

### "The Fox Hunt"

"The Fox Hunt" was the final episode of *Stage 7* airing September 25, 1955. It was also a pilot for a series based on the exploits of a Texas Ranger. Actor George Montgomery was offered the lead in the pilot but declined. Dennis Morgan played Ranger Jim Harris. Harris rounds up a posse to go after Fox Durkin (Harry Shannon) and his gang of two who robbed a bank and killed a sheriff. Having never seen Durkin before, the Ranger unknowingly recruits him as a member of the posse of three. When the posse closes in on two members of the gang, they open fire. Durkin ends up shooting the two desperadoes, but Harris is suspicious of how easily Durkin got to the gang members without them shooting him and concludes the posse member is really Durkin. ABC expressed some interest in syndicating the series, but by March 1956 the idea had been abandoned.

Two days after "The Fox Hunt" aired, another tale of the Texas Rangers was broadcast as an installment of the Four Star-produced *DuPont Cavalcade Theatre.* Titled simply "Texas Ranger," this story was based on an actual case the Rangers handled involving gunslinger John Wesley Hardin (William Tallman) who is being transported by a Ranger portrayed by Jim Davis from Alabama to Texas.

While Four Star's attempts to bring a Texas Ranger series to fruition in the mid-fifties did not work out, the company did finally, in 1957, succeed with a Western about a Texas Ranger called *Trackdown.*

## DuPont Cavalcade Theatre

This anthology was produced by Four Star in conjunction with ABC beginning with its fourth season in September 1955. Four Star also produced about ten episodes that aired on *DuPont Cavalcade Theatre* during the 1956-57 season.

Johnny Crawford, who later starred as Mark McCain on *The Rifleman,* made an early television appearance on an episode titled "The Boy Nobody Wanted" based on a true story. Billy Brandon (Crawford) lived in a boarding house with his widowed father, a gambler. One day, after being left alone, Billy wants to play with a neighborhood boy who rebuffs him. The boy threatens Billy with a baseball bat. Billy shoves him, and the boy's head hits the concrete killing him. The boy's father, a newspaper editor, has Billy's father investigated and finds that Billy had previously accidentally set a girl's dress on fire resulting in her death. Billy is labeled a "two-time killer," and his dad is incarcerated. No one wants to adopt Billy until his caseworker finds a farming couple willing to take him. Later, Billy's father is released from jail and petitions the court for custody of his now grown son. However, Billy is drafted into the army and is cited for bravery during the war. After being discharged, the father, who has started a new life, invites his son to partner with him in his restaurant business. But Billy, finding that his foster parents are about to give up their farm, decides to stay with them and work the farm.

As noted in the next chapter, *Cavalcade Theatre* also aired episodes that were originally to be part of *The Frank Leahy Show*, a failed anthology that never made it to air.

Don Sharpe and his producing partner Warren Lewis planned to film additional episodes of the *DuPont Cavalcade Theatre* with their own production company. Four Star filed suit against the two producers on September 11, 1956. The suit charged that Sharpe violated his obligations of trust and conspired with Lewis to seize business belonging to Four Star Films. Specifically, the complaint said that Sharpe and Lewis used confidential information obtained while working at Four Star to sell *DuPont Cavalcade Theatre* scripts independently to an advertising agency. Four Star asked $250,000 in general damages and $250,000 in punitive damages.

## *Chevron Hall of Stars* (aka *Stage 7* and *Don Ameche Presents*) and Its Pilots

Before he was deposed as president, Don Sharpe was apparently hard at work making deals for series in late 1955. As *The Billboard* reported, ". . . Sharpe was dealing so fast this week on both Coasts that nobody will know exactly what happened until some of the smoke has cleared. The mystery resulted from the fact that suddenly Sharpe's Four Star Productions became the owner of two separate dramatic series both titled 'Stage 7.'"[12] As previously described, Four Star had launched *Stage 7* on CBS for Bristol-Myers which ended shortly after the start of the 1955-56 season. Apparently, Mr. Sharpe wanted to use the *Stage 7* title for a new syndicated anthology series to be produced by Four Star and Television Programs of America. The program did eventually premiere in January 1956. On the West coast, its title was *Chevron Hall of Stars*; on the East coast, the anthology continued to use *Stage 7* as the title; and in the Midwest, Don Ameche introduced each episode under the title *Don Ameche Presents the Drewry's Play of the Week*.

The initial episode of the anthology, "A Man Named March," featured actors James Whitmore, Peggy Webber, and Johnny Crawford in a story about a hobo who sees a scrawled message on the side of a freight car and decides to reform. He finds how complicated and sometimes dangerous normal living is compared with life on the road. Another installment of *Chevron Hall of Stars*, titled "The Secret Weapon of 117" was writer Gene Roddenberry's first science fiction teleplay. It concerned beings from another planet sent to Earth (planet 117 according to their society) to evaluate Earth's defenses against an interplanetary attack. The beings are transformed, by their technology, into an attractive Earth couple. Ricardo Montalban and Susan Morrow starred in the episode.

Production of the thirty-nine episodes of *Hall of Stars* began around the middle of November 1955. As with other Four Star anthologies, *Chevron Hall of Stars* also aired pilots for potential television series.

### "Double Cross"

Four Star piloted the detective series, *Richard Diamond* in April 1956 with Don Taylor in the lead. Reportedly actor Dennis O'Keefe and actor/singer Johnny Desmond had been considered for the role before it was given to Taylor. The *Diamond* pilot, produced by Dick Powell, aired on *Chevron Hall of Stars* in November 1956. The story, "The Double Cross," had the private eye accused of murdering a woman. Another woman tips off Diamond as to whom the real killer is. *Variety* noted that the pilot was "...run-of-the-mill crime stuff that doesn't whip up much interest at the set."[13]

### "Roommates"

Written by Katherine and Dale Eunson and directed by Harry Keller, "Roommates," about college students, starred Diane DuBois as Gabrielle, a French student, and Sue George as Janet, an American student, whose mom, played by Maureen O'Sullivan, was the house mother of Janet's college sorority. The O'Sullivan character had the idea that all French people were immoral. She changed her mind, however, after becoming acquainted with Gabrielle.

While the pilot never became a series, it did air as an episode of *Chevron Hall of Stars* on October 19, 1956. As *Variety* wrote, "Old pilots never die. They just show up on other series."[14]

Never one to abandon a series concept if it didn't work the first time, in May 1957, Four Star revised the premise of "Roommates" to be about two male friends who shared the same bed. Keeping in mind this was the 1950s and Four Star was rarely cutting edge in its series ideas, the new concept of "Roommates," to star comic Gene Baylos and actor Ray Danton, was that the friends did not actually sleep together – one character worked during the day, while the other character worked all night.

### "The Lone Hand"

Based on the Zane Grey character Arizona Ames, Four Star attempted to make a Western series starring Richard Anderson as the title character. The show was intended for the 1956-57 season but was not picked up. The pilot, produced by Hal Hudson, who made the *Zane Grey Theatre* episodes, was shown as an installment of *Chevron Hall of Stars* titled "The Lone Hand," In the episode, Ames saves a former dance hall girl from the clutches of her dastardly husband played by Raymond Burr.

# Chapter 4:
# Other Four Star Projects and Pilots, 1952-56

During this period, the production company considered several other projects as potential television series.

*Former Notre Dame Football coach, Frank Leahy.*

## The Frank Leahy Show

This never-sold anthology, hosted by ex-Notre Dame Football coach Frank Leahy, was intended as a series for ABC. Produced by Don Sharpe and Warren Lewis for Four Star in 1954, the series would have featured true inspirational stories. Thirty-nine episodes were planned.

The pilot, which aired as an episode titled "Saturday Story" on *Cavalcade of America* on May 4, 1954, starred Dabbs Greer as small-town football coach Mark Wilson who imbues his team with good sportsmanship so that the players will learn how to lose as well as win. Ill health forces the high school coach to resign, but his prize pupil, Otto Graham, goes on to Northwestern University and then joins the Cleveland Browns as a quarterback. Otto Graham played himself in the story. Following the drama, Frank Leahy interviewed the real Mark Wilson and his wife along with Otto Graham.

In addition to the pilot, Four Star made five other episodes of the series which aired as part of *DuPont Cavalcade Theatre*. The episodes included:

- "A Time for Courage' (September 13, 1955) which starred Hugh Beaumont as Jack Cody and Noreen Corcoran as Nancy Merki in a true life story of a swimming coach who helps a young girl afflicted with polio become an Olympic swimmer;
- " Toward Tomorrow" (October 4, 1955) which starred James Edwards as Dr. Ralph Bunche, a person of color, who became an undersecretary of the United Nations;
- "A Life to Live By" (March 20, 1956) about Leon Patterson who suffered from an incurable disease but nevertheless became the world's interscholastic shot-put record holder before passing away in 1954;
- "The Jackie Jensen Story" (April 17, 1956), centering on the famous California fullback and outfielder for the Boston Red Sox; and
- "Leap to Heaven" (January 15, 1957) focusing on Rev. Bob Richards, an Olympic pole-vaulting champion, who later joined the ministry.

A TV film highlighting the career of basketball star, Bob Cousy, was also to have been made.

## Sheena, Queen of the Jungle

While the vast majority of pilots made by Four Star that are described in this book never sold, the company made a pilot in 1954 based on the female Tarzan comic book character "Sheena, Queen of the Jungle" that did become a series. Don Sharpe and Warren Lewis produced the pilot with Frank McDonald directing and Joel Murcott doing the script. The pilot starred Irish McCalla as Sheena who arrives in the jungle in search of a crashed plane that, years before, had carried her and her parents. Her mom and dad were killed in the crash, but she survived being cared for by natives and then returned to England. Sheena's uncle doesn't believe that she is really his niece, thinking instead that she is after his money.

Exteriors were filmed in Mexico and Africa. Nassour Studios did the Mexican scenes. When, in 1955, the series was syndicated to local stations, Four Star did not produce these additional episodes.

Actress Anita Eckberg was to have originally played Sheena, but she never showed up for the filming of the pilot. After a talent search, Irish McCalla won the role.

## Bulldog Drummond

In spring 1955, Four Star was supposed to film a pilot for a mystery series based on the movie hero Bulldog Drummond. The character of Bulldog Drummond was a World War I veteran who became an adventurer after the war. Apparently the departure of Don Sharpe from Four Star led to this project being assigned to Douglas Fairbanks Jr.'s production company in 1956. Directed by David McDonald and scripted by Irving Rubine, the Fairbanks' pilot was titled "The Ludlow Affair." Set in London and filmed there, Harriett Ludlow (Greta Gynt) contacts Drummond about her husband Felix (Michael Anthony) who has been kidnapped. Felix Ludlow is a scientist who has developed a formula for a new antibiotic which the kidnappers want in exchange for his release. The kidnappers warn Mrs. Ludlow not to go to the police so she visits Drummond. He subsequently discovers that Mrs. Ludlow hired the kidnappers to get rid of her husband so that she and

Roger Benning (William Franklyn), the doctor's assistant, could control the formula. After Drummond frees Dr. Ludlow from a house near the Ludlow's own home, Mrs. Ludlow and Benning are arrested.

Fairbanks had a tentative deal with ABC Film Syndication to sell *Bulldog Drummond* to local stations, but the sale never materialized. The pilot did subsequently air as an installment of *Douglas Fairbanks Presents*.

### Hurricane Kelly

For the 1955-56 season, Frank Lovejoy was supposed to star as "Hurricane" Kelly in this proposed adventure series set on the high seas. The teleplay was presumably written by Ricard Von Kleist. An actual pilot was never filmed. In 1957, Von Kleist filed suit against several people including Don Sharpe asking the court to declare him the sole owner of the script.

### Grand Motel

Four Star thought of turning a book by William and Milarde Brent about their experiences running a motel either into a feature film starring George Gobel or making it a television series. The book, *Grand Motel*, described the Brent's adventures in managing a motel focusing on the establishment's clientele. For example, the Brent's detail one customer looking for a room for his wife, his daughter, and himself, ". . . the wife accompanied us down to see the room, which he didn't even glance at – in his haste to make the toilet in time. It must have been a rush job, all right, because he didn't even close the bathroom door behind him, and, talk as loud and fast as I could, I couldn't drown out the sounds from inside."[15] To compound the problem, after coming out of the bathroom, the man argued about the price of the room.

Another experience in the book describes complaints from some motel guests about peculiar odors emanating from a room. The manager found a customer named John in his motel room ". . . sitting placidly on the floor milking a long-eared goat while another browsed, just as placidly, off our grass and flowers, which John had cut, carried in, and placed on a newspaper in the bathroom."[16]

MGM protested that the title was too close to their classic movie *Grand Hotel*, which seemed to put an end to this project.

## Wire Service

Before he left Four Star, Don Sharpe executed a deal in October 1955 for the company to produce twenty-six episodes of a series called *Wire Service* to be filmed in Hollywood, Paris, and London for ABC. During the company's history, it strived to sell a series about newspaper reporters beginning with the pilot for *Nightbeat*. *Wire Service* was a variation on the anthology genre with three different stars appearing on their own episodes. The actors played the same character on each installment in which they appeared. Dane Clark, George Brent, and Mercedes McCambridge were signed for the leads, each appearing in separate stories as reporters working for the Trans-Globe wire service.

The one-hour drama premiered October 4, 1956 and lasted for a season. The program was not produced by Four Star but by the newly-formed production company of Sharpe-Lewis Productions owned by Mr. Sharpe and Warren Lewis.

## I Am Storm Carlson

Four Star considered developing a half-hour drama series about noted events and people in the world of sports. Actor John Hodiak had initially agreed to host and narrate the program but died before any pilot could be made. Barry Nelson was next thought of for the series but ultimately dropped out. "Storm Carlson" was the fictional name of a sports writer who would introduce each episode of the proposed series highlighting a major sports event or sports figure. Apparently, no pilot was ever filmed. Sportswriter Art Cohn was to write the series as well as act as editorial supervisor.

## Claudia

In February 1956, Four Star initially undertook the financing and production of a pilot based on Rose Franken's books about Claudia, a young married woman. But the company dropped its participation in the project in April. Frank Sinatra then indicated a willingness to finance the pilot. However, he also lost interest. Next Screen Gems and then NBC and producer Jess Oppenheimer expressed an intention to develop the project, but they also passed. Finally, George Burns' McCadden Corporation made the pilot in late 1958, but it never became a series. Coming full circle, Four Star, in 1960, wanted to buy the property from Rose Franken, but a deal was never consummated.

## The City

In March 1956, Four Star entered into a financing and co-production deal with actor Mark Stevens concerning the pilot for an anthology series, originally called *Decision*, about those moments in which a person must make a decision that may affect the rest of his or her life. The unsold pilot titled "The Fighter" by Turnley Walker involved a has-been boxer who must win a bout to prove a point to his son. It was produced in April 1956.

## American Masterpieces

In an October 31, 1956 ad in *Variety*, Four Star announced *American Masterpieces* as a potential project for the company. Presumably, this series would have been an anthology, but no further mention of the project could be found.

The same October 1956 ad also mentioned two other Four Star projects – *Outpost* and *He Who Laughs First*. Details about each of these projects are not known, but *Outpost* would appear to be a possible Western series, while *He Who Laughs First* may have been a game show proposal.

# Chapter 5:
# The First Four Star Comedy Series, 1956-60

An early December 1956 meeting of the partners of Four Star Films – David Niven, Charles Boyer, Dick Powell, and William Cruikshank – realigned individual duties. Niven would handle Four Star Films public relations and advertising, Boyer would head the finance committee, Powell would act as liaison with the William Morris Agency, and Cruikshank, the president of the company, would handle the firm's legal matters.

In spring 1957, Four Star Films formed a new corporation – Dayton Productions as the production arm of the company to handle partnerships with outside entities. Powell, Boyer, and Niven were all stockholders in Dayton along with unspecified outside holders. And then in August 1957, an announcement was made that William Cruikshank had stepped down and was replaced by Dick Powell as president of the company. Cruikshank continued to be a member of Four Star's board.

While the company had several successes at selling drama series including Westerns to the networks, it never was as lucky with situation comedies. Four Star seemed unable to cultivate sitcom writers and producers as it did for dramatic series.

## *Hey, Jeannie!* and Its Sequel

Four Star's first sitcom to be picked up as a series featured Jeannie Carson as Jeannie MacLennan, a young woman from Scotland who immigrates to America. Upon her arrival in the States, cab driver Al Murray (Allen Jenkins) gives her a tour of New York City and offers to become her sponsor. She moves in with him and his sister Liz (Jane Dulo) and begins exploring the people and the customs of the United States.

The series was almost a musical comedy with Jeannie Carson, a fine vocalist, singing in virtually every episode.

Created by Charles Isaacs, the CBS show, originally titled *Kathy*, debuted on September 8, 1956 Saturdays at 9:30 pm. Four Star jointly produced the series with Isaacs' Tartan Productions.

On the opening episode, "Jeannie, the Cab Driver," Jeannie takes over driving Al's cab when he decides to attend a baseball game. He will be fired if his boss discovers he took the afternoon off. The problem with Jeannie driving the cab is that she doesn't know her way around New York City.

"Jeannie's Here," episode five, was a flashback installment about how Jeannie arrived in America. She is supposed to have been sponsored by a man named David Forester, but she is not able to locate him. Al Murray offers her a ride in his taxi. She has him stop in the middle of the George Washington Bridge between New York and New Jersey where she departs the cab and sings "I Feel a Song Coming On." Traffic backs up, the police arrive, and Jeannie ends up before the U.S. Immigration Board. After telling the board how much she loves America, charges are dropped, and Al reluctantly volunteers to become her sponsor.

The writers loved to have Jeannie involved in unusual occupations on the CBS episodes. In one, she becomes a golf caddy to persuade members at an exclusive resort to purchase handmade golf clubs crafted by a Scotsman she knows. In another installment, Jeannie takes a job at a donut shop where she enters a contest to sell the most donuts and win a trip to Washington D.C. She accidentally makes "double decker" donuts causing a sensation leading her to win the trip. In still another episode, Jeannie joins the auxiliary police force to identify strangers harassing women in the park. All the situations were mined for maximum comic affect.

*Hey, Jeannie!* was canceled by CBS after one season. Reacting to the demise of the comedy, Dick Powell commented, "They're (CBS) always talking about ratings. Well 'Jeannie' has the highest rating in its time period, and even topped Lawrence Welk in the latest Neilsen survey. Wouldn't you think CBS would try to find another sponsor? But no, they're being piggy again, and want their own show in there instead of an outside package."[17]

### The Jeannie Carson Show

After its cancelation, Four Star attempted to reformat the series with Jeannie Carson playing a flight attendant. In the new series, called *The Jeannie Carson Show*, her character helps others out of their difficulties. Jack Kirkwood played Jeannie's landlord, Charlie O'Connell, on the revamped series with Vera Vague (aka Barbara Jo Allen), as her boss Mabel and fellow tenant in her apartment building. Six episodes of the reformatted series were made and syndicated to local stations in 1958.

The first episode, "The Landlord," had Jeannie on her maiden flight. A group of musicians on the plane ask her to take care of their dog while they work. She has to stay in Mabel's apartment until her place is ready but finds that O'Connell will not allow pets. She sneaks the dog into the apartment, but when a complaining neighbor hears the dog bark, the landlord orders her to remove the pet. Jeannie has the musicians play loud music at midnight enraging the complaining neighbor. She points out that the lease doesn't address the playing of live music after hours, and so the complaining neighbor decides to move.

One episode featured future *The Rifleman* star Chuck Connors as a wealthy cowboy who charters a flight for himself to New York City. Buck Matthews (Connors) asks Jeannie to show him the city. She is irritated when he offers her money to go out with him and when he buys her a mink coat. He bets that she can't go one day without spending money. She takes him up on the wager and proves he is wrong until she is asked to pay her rent. However, Matthews learns that "money isn't everything" – the title of the episode.

The final episode of *The Jeannie Carson Show*, "The Rainmaker," had Jeannie meeting an Indian chief on a return flight from Washington where he had sought drought relief for his tribe. Ever-helpful Jeannie wants to seed the clouds above the chief's reservation to make it rain. After the cloud seeding, Jeannie is arrested because the rain washed newly planted grain out of the ground of a neighboring tribe. The tribes declare war on each other, but things settle down when the previously drought-stricken tribe reimburses the other tribe for its grain loss.

## *Mr. Adams and Eve* and Its Back-Door Pilot

Four Star produced this smart, sophisticated comedy starring Howard Duff as Howard Adams and Ida Lupino as Eve Drake - married motion picture stars, in conjunction with Duff and Lupino's own company Bridget Productions. The series began on CBS on January 4, 1957.

Supporting the married couple in their first and only TV series together were Hayden Rorke as their agent Steve, Olive Carey as Elsie, their housekeeper, and Alan Reed as J. B. Hafter, the boss of the movie studio where the couple worked. Lee Patrick later joined the series as Eve Drake's mother, Connie.

Reminiscing about the series, Ida Lupino noted that her former husband, Collier Young, came up with the concept. "He created the characters, Eve Drake and Howard Adams. Collie was a very sharp boy. I guess he watched Howard and me in action. Within an hour I was sold! I agreed to do a thirty-minute pilot for Four Star Television, written by Collier Young and Charles Lederer. I wanted Howard to play Howard. Four Star handled all of the background production details."[18]

Ida Lupino foreshadowed playing a somewhat over-the-top actress in the *Four Star Playhouse* production of "Award" in 1955. Lupino starred as famous movie star Valerie Banks whose first Broadway show is a flop because of her lack of experience appearing on stage. She visits director Ben Cheney (Franchot Tone) to ask him to help her improve her acting to which he eventually agrees.

As "Award" attempted to do, many episodes of *Mr. Adams and Eve* satirized show business mores. For example, Eve's life is to be featured on the then-popular television show, *This Is Your Life*, but everyone has to keep it a secret from her. When her husband and friends all say they have to be somewhere on a Wednesday afternoon, she becomes suspicious. Her suspicions increase when she bumps into Howard at a bar with a beautiful woman from the program thinking that he is having an affair. When Howard returns home, he finds Eve has left and gone to her mother's. Her mother encourages her to show up that evening at a hotel for a supposedly important business meeting. Arriving at the hotel, Eve realizes she is on the television program, but the emcee soon loses control when all the guests converse with each other and not with him.

In "The Academy Awards" episode, both Howard and Eve are nominated for acting's highest honor. Eve wins her Oscar, but Howard loses to a twelve-year-old boy. Next day on the set, everyone compliments Eve's acting but ignores Howard. Tensions between the couple escalate when they appear on a *Person-to-Person*-type program to illustrate their happy marriage and that Eve's win has not affected their relationship. Eve shows viewers her Oscar; Howard presents an award he had received for winning a potato sack race. The couple continues to trade barbs with Howard ending up sleeping on the couch. The following day, Howard invites the occupants of a tour bus to see Eve thinking it will upset her, but a fan starts flirting with Eve making Howard upset. In the end, Howard and Eve make up despite Eve's award. This installment - the series pilot, was originally to be filmed as an episode of *Four Star Playhouse*

David Niven appeared on one episode, "Taming of the Shrew" as his character Phileas Fogg from *Around the World in 80 Days* when he drops into Howard and Eve's backyard in his balloon.

As he would do on other series with which his production company was involved, Dick Powell also guest starred on one episode of *Mr. Adams and Eve* titled "Backwash." On this February 18, 1958 installment, Howard is offered an opportunity to direct his first motion picture, but he is handed the world's worst script. Dick Powell shows him how to turn the script into a good picture.

*Mr. Adams and Eve* was Four Star's most successful comedy series simply because it lasted for more than a single season. Ida Lupino was nominated for an Emmy for her comedy performance on the series in both of its seasons.

### "Teenage Idol"

This proposed spin-off from *Mr. Adams and Eve* featured a young Patrick Wayne as a shy teenager who wants to become a rock 'n roll star, like his idol, Swivelhips Jackson. Presumably, if the pilot had become a series, its focus would have been on the life of a 1950s teenage rock star.

Written by Louella MacFarlene, who subsequently scripted episodes of *Dennis the Menace* and *Hazel*, the "Teenage Idol" pilot aired on July 8, 1958 as the final episode of *Mr. Adams and Eve*.

As part of publicity for the pilot, Duff and Lupino announced a nationwide search in March 1958 for a young man who could sing, act, and play the guitar – a combination of Elvis Presley and

*Patrick Wayne, Ida Lupino, and Darrell Howe in "Teenage Idol," a back-door pilot from* Mr. Adams and Eve.

Tommy Sands. Auditions were to be submitted in the form of tape recordings and a full-length photograph.[19] Over 1500 auditions were submitted. Darrell Howe, a former tractor-trailer truck driver, won the search and was cast along with Patrick Wayne, the son of John Wayne. Supposedly, three songs from the pilot were to be recorded and released before this episode of *Mr. Adams and Eve* aired.

On the episode, the Adams' approve their housekeeper's hiring of a young man to help with her duties. The teenager turns out to be her nephew from Kansas, Walter Hannigan (Wayne), who is very shy but is a great fan of rock 'n roll star Swivelhips Jackson (Howe) and wants to be just like him. Walter constantly plays Swivelhips' records. The Adams' conspire to mould Walter into a teenage copy of his idol with mixed results.

## Late Fifties Comedy Projects and Pilots

During the late 1950s, Four Star attempted other situation comedy projects without any success.

### Paradise Campus

Advertised as a teenage situation comedy to be filmed on the University of Hawaii campus, this 1956-57 Four Star project never came to fruition.

### The River

This Four Star project was described as a modern family comedy set on the Mississippi River, but no pilot was ever made.

### Cindy

During the 1956-57 television season, the company attempted to develop a series to be called *Cindy*. A script by Leonard Freeman was written dealing with the exploits of a little girl and her widowed father on a dude ranch. Four Star never filmed a pilot. However, Hal Roach Studios may have taken over this project because, in 1957, that studio filmed a pilot for ABC called *Cindy* starring Evelyn Rudie about a young girl, who, after her parents are killed in an auto accident, comes to live with her bachelor uncle.

## The Joker

During fall 1956, Four Star looked at a possible comedy series called *The Joker* about the experiences of two writers trying to make a third-rate comic a success on television. Keenan Wynn was considered for the role of one of the comedy scribes; and Lew Parker was discussed as a possibility for the comedian.

## The Press Agent

In January 1956, George Burns' McCadden Productions pondered producing a comedy pilot written by Fred Shevin about a press agent. Starring Jack Carson as Danny Scott – a press agent who takes young talent and builds them into stars, the vehicle involved Scott setting up a movie outfit, but just when the breaks come his way, he decides to take a bigger commission from his client than he should. *The Press Agent* ended up being produced by Meridian Productions as an installment of *Schlitz Playhouse of Stars* and aired on September 7, 1956. Four Star believed in the project and wanted to turn it into a series even if they had to recast the role of the press agent because of the unavailability of Jack Carson. However, the company was never able to sell the show to an advertiser or network.

## The Stubby Kaye Show (aka Full Speed Ahead)

Rotund comic actor Stubby Kaye starred in this effort subtitled *Full Speed Anywhere*. Kaye played Coast Guard yeoman Stubby Fox who is fed up with always being assigned duties near the shore line. He dreams of the time his small patrol boat will be sent into real action. Conrad Janis was featured as Ensign Jones, in charge of the patrol boat confined to the harbor. Others in the cast included Gonzales Gonzales as Pedro, George Dunn as "Doc" Clemens, Glenn Turnbull as "Slim" Jackson, Jonathan Hole as Commander Welch, and Edwin Bruce as Johnny Burns. Orders finally come through for real action just when one of the crewmen comes down with mumps. At night, Stubby and his crewmates plan to drop off the sick crewman at a hospital ship. Unfortunately, it is very foggy, and the men lose their way. Eventually, they find the hospital ship and attempt to drop the sick man off without being seen so that no one will know which ship the man came from. The doctor discovers their plan and quarantines everyone.

At the end of the pilot, Stubby explains to viewers the types of situations and characters that will be in future episodes. Conrad Janis points out the benefit of a cast that can sing, dance, play instruments, and do comedy.

The trade publication, *Variety*, in reviewing the pilot, wrote "Kaye put all his 265 lbs. behind his role and out of sheer vigor made most of the rest of the cast appear more animated than they were. . . . At one juncture when dullness grew foreboding Kaye sang "Minnie the Mermaid" and the other hands joined in with what looked like amateur night at New London."[20]

Charles Isaacs and Jack Elinson scripted this unsold pilot which was directed by Don Taylor. The pilot was made in spring 1957. While all three networks expressed some interest in this possible series, by January 1958, the project was dead since none of the networks picked it up.

### The Judy Canova Show

Danny Thomas financed this January 1959 pilot starring country and western comedienne Judy Canova presumably after the comedienne had appeared on a funny episode of Thomas' self-titled series in 1958 where she played a woman trying to get a former wrestler a job as a night club singer. Written by Charlie Stewart and Jack Elinson, Four Star produced the pilot which supposedly was somewhat like the hit ABC comedy *The Real McCoys*. Stewart and Elinson had written episodes of the *McCoys*.

*The Judy Canova Show* had the star inheriting a combination diner and gas station that was heavily in debt. Her character is a widow with a young son. A banker from whom she borrows money and a trucker who frequents the business are both romantically interested in Judy. Her attractive blonde sister from Arkansas helps her run the establishment.

Flash forward to August 1, 1972 with *Variety* reporting that Four Star planned a weekly syndicated version of *The Judy Canova Show*. Whether this project was to be a situation comedy or more likely, a talk/variety series is not known, but the show never got off the ground.

# Chapter 6:
# Four Star's First Contemporary Continuing Character Dramas, 1956-60

In October 1957, Dick Powell was formally elected president of Four Star by the stockholders. Charles Boyer was named vice president and treasurer; Niven, vice president and secretary. All were elected to the board of directors with William Cruikshank leaving the board.   Dayton Productions also elected officers with Charles Boyer chosen as president; Powell as vice president and secretary; and David Niven as vice president and treasurer.

Reflecting on his years at Four Star under president Dick Powell, production manager Frank Baur noted that:

> Dick Powell was a very honorable guy. He gave a lot of fellows chances, like myself, Aaron Spelling, and Sam Peckinpah and others. Dick loves that company with a passion, it was his little baby. He was a hardworking son of a gun. We hired crew people that knew what they were doing and we had their interest at heart and took care of them, treated them decently and gave them opportunities.[21]

Writer Christopher Knopf described the chain of command at Four Star after Powell assumed the presidency. "There was Dick at the top, two story editors under him, one of whom was the beloved Nina Laemmie, whose job were mostly to find material and put through contracts. No vice presidents or intermediaries to contend with, no 'Head of Development' who would take your idea 'upstairs' and translate it wrong."[22]

In July, 1958, Dick Powell announced a new venture for the company – making television commercials. The first advertisement Four Star made was an Eastman Kodak spot that aired on *The Ed Sullivan Show*.

During the period 1956 to 1960, Four Star premiered its first continuing character dramas. One starred a young actor named David Janssen; the other featured famous movie star Robert Taylor.

## *Richard Diamond, Private Eye*

On January 25, 1957, Four Star announced that the role of Richard Diamond would be played by David Janssen with production to start in February of that year. As noted earlier, actor/director Don Taylor had played the role in the pilot. Referring to the program, Dick Powell commented, "We start with the character. The *Richard Diamond* series called for a certain specifically defined character, and a young chap named David Janssen seemed to fit the picture."[23]

Based on the radio series on which Dick Powell had played the private detective, *Richard Diamond* first appeared on CBS in July 1957 as a summer replacement for the comedy *December Bride*. The drama returned to CBS as a midseason replacement in January 1958 on Thursday evenings until September of that year. It came back again in February 1959 on Sundays at 10:00 pm. Beginning in October 1959, the series popped up on NBC where it ran for twelve months.

On the premiere, set in New York City, Diamond becomes involved with Mickey Farmer, a man who robbed a payroll with his partner Red Benson. Wounded by the police in a shoot-out, Farmer, before he dies, asks Diamond to protect Sally Kane, a girl he likes, from Benson. When Diamond tracks down Kane and Benson, he discovers that Sally is not being held hostage by Red but is actually in cahoots with him. The police arrest the pair before they flee. Regis Toomey, who later played a detective on Four Star's *Burke's Law*, appeared as Detective Dennis (Mac) McGough on the initial seasons of *Richard Diamond*.

In 1959, with the premiere of its third season, the Richard Diamond character moved to California. Russ Conway as Lt. Pete Kile became Diamond's police contact. The change of locales meant more daytime outdoor scenes and more beautiful women on the show. Diamond became somewhat of a playboy character. He subscribed to an answering service whose operator was named "Sam." Viewers only saw Sam's mouth and legs, never her whole profile.

The character was initially portrayed by Mary Tyler Moore. Also added to the series was a love interest for Diamond named Karen Wells (Barbara Bain), a fashion designer, whom he had met while working on a case involving a dead race car driver, Larry Forsythe. Before the race car driver was killed, his mother had given him $50,000 that he intended to invest in Karen Wells' design business, but he ended up giving it to a friend. The friend used the money to pay off his gambling debts. When Larry found this out, the friend ran Larry's car off the road killing him. The friend tries to kill Diamond as well, but the PI gets the upper hand.

The fourth and final season of the series was on NBC with the Richard Diamond character still in California but with less emphasis on his playboy lifestyle. One fourth season episode, "Seven Swords," was scripted by the mystery writing team of Richard Levinson and William Link, who later created *Columbo* and *Murder, She Wrote*. In the episode, Diamond receives a ticket from Joyce Nugent, a magician's assistant, to a performance of a magic show starring Marvello (Jerome Cowan). The assistant is placed in a box through which Marvello inserts seven swords. When the box is opened, Nugent is dead of strangulation – not of wounds from the swords. Lt. Kile and Diamond investigate. The victim was strangled when she was in the basement underneath the stage before the swords were shoved into the box. Diamond interrogates Nugent's boyfriend and her theatrical agent, Sally Chandler (Carol Ohmart). The police inform Diamond that Nugent deposited $5000 in her bank account before she was murdered. Later, someone shoots Chandler, while Diamond is in her office. Diamond discovers that Marvello was smuggling heroin into the country in magicians' wands and that Nugent found out about this scheme and blackmailed the magician for $5000. Sally Chandler also participated in the smuggling operation. Marvello killed Nugent before the performance that Diamond witnessed and then had Chandler pose as Nugent by wearing a dark wig and makeup. Chandler placed Nugent's body in the box after Marvello removed the swords. When Chandler then wanted out of the operation, Marvello killed her as well.

Roxanne Brooks replaced Mary Tyler Moore as Sam in the final season of the detective series after Moore requested an increase in salary. The producers figured that they could substitute any actress in the role given that only her legs, mouth, and sometimes her back were filmed for the show.

## *The Detectives*

On October 16, 1959, actor Robert Taylor made his television series debut on this detective show. Originally on ABC in a thirty-minute format, the series was expanded to sixty minutes when it moved to NBC in 1961. Several titles were considered for the show before settling on *The Detectives*. *I Am the Enforcer* and *Captain of Detectives* were two considerations.

Taylor's character, Capt. Matt Holbrook, led a team of three detectives – Lt. Jim Conway (Lee Farr) of homicide, Lt. Johnny Russo (Tige Andrews) of burglary, and Lt. Otto Lindstrom (Russell Thorson) of Bunco. Lee Farr and Russell Thorson left the series after the first season. Beginning with the second season, Mark Goddard as Lt. Chris Ballard joined the program. Goddard became a regular on the show after *Johnny Ringo*, a Four Star Western on which he appeared, had been canceled. Dick Powell told Goddard that he could be a regular on either *Michael Shayne* or *The Detectives*. As the actor describes the meeting with Powell about his future career, Goddard told the head of Four Star that "'Either one sounds great.' . . . '*The Detectives* has been on for a year and you would be working with a Motion picture star and real professional,' he (Powell) suggested. 'That's great,' I said again. 'Then it's *The Detectives*,' he calmly stated. 'Great!' I repeated for the fourth time. 'And Mark,' he casually said, 'Things aren't always so great. They are for now, but you should know that things change very quickly in Hollywood.'"[24]

In the third season, Adam West came on board as Sgt. Steve Nelson. Weekly episodes would usually focus on investigations by one or two of the team of detectives.

The deal with Taylor allowed the actor plenty of time off since his character, while in every episode, was not in every scene. The Holbrook character was the central one in six episodes a season. On the other episodes, Taylor appeared in an opening scene to set up the story with one or two of his detectives carrying the rest of the story line and Taylor returning in the climax to solve the crime or confront the criminals.

The shooting schedule called for Taylor to be on the set two days a week to film two back-to-back episodes. With each half-hour episode taking three days to make, Taylor would appear on the third day to film his two scenes for that installment and then, on the next day, film his two scenes for the following episode. The shooting schedule allowed the actor to continue to make movies and still have his own television series. This was the second method used by Four Star to accommodate veteran actors to the rigors of a weekly television series. The first, as noted above, was to hire different lead characters for a show who would usually never appear together in the same episode but only on the installments in which they had the main role.

*The Detectives* was sold without a pilot. As Dick Powell remarked, "we sold it so quickly because of several factors – Taylor's name, the people who are doing the series (Arthur Gardner, Jules Levy, and Arnold Laven and Four Star) and the script."[25] Gardner, Levy, and Laven also produced *The Rifleman*, *The Law of the Plainsman*, and *The Big Valley* in conjunction with Four Star. For *The Detectives*, their production company was called Hastings Productions.

An episode from the first season titled "Karate," written by Gene Roddenbery, dealt with the detectives investigating the murder of a man beaten to death near Holbrook's apartment. Holbrook concludes that the victim may have been killed by a karate expert. The police believe that Holbrook himself was the intended target. At a local karate school, Holbrook runs into a former high school rival. Later, when the former classmate comes by Holbrook's garage, he begins beating the captain, jealous of Matt's accomplishments. Holbrook is able to subdue him with the handle from a shovel.

While Taylor's character appeared throughout the "Karate" episode, his scenes on other episodes were limited, as noted above, to the beginning of the story, perhaps a middle scene, and then one at the end. In a second season episode titled "The Reason," police officers are being killed by a sniper. Holbrook suspects that the culprit may have been a cadet who washed out of the police academy. He assigns detectives John Russo and Chris Ballard to investigate, and

*A scene from the "Karate" episode of* The Detectives. *From left to right: Actors Teru Shimadu, Robert Taylor, and John Anderson.*

they carry most of the episode with Taylor's character having just a few scenes.

Even when the series expanded to one hour during the third season on NBC, Taylor still limited his scenes in most episodes. For example, on the May 4, 1962 installment, "Stranger in the House," Taylor appears in one scene at the beginning telling his team of detectives that he is out of the office testifying at a trial. Detectives Russo and Ballard investigate a case involving four prep school students who steal a car and run over a night watchman. The detectives believe the boys attended Wellington School whose headmaster, Dr. Harvey (David Sheiner), wants to protect the institution's reputation and so offers little co-operation with the police. The headmaster has a good idea that a student named Grant (Chris Robinson) led the other guys into stealing the vehicle. Taylor appears in a second scene arguing with Dr. Harvey about the police interrogating his students.

Later, Harvey confronts Grant but doesn't expel him from the school not wanting to lose the tuition. In a fit of rage, Harvey slaps Grant who vows revenge against the headmaster. To get back at Dr. Harvey, Grant sends him a ransom note for $3000 and then takes another member of the gang named Frankie (John Karlen) hostage holding him in an abandoned mine. Harvey delivers the ransom money, and finally informs the police about the kidnapping. In the meantime, Peter (Claude Johnson), one of the other gang members, confesses to the detectives about the car theft. Dr. Harvey suspects that Frankie may be held in the abandoned mine. The police arrive at the location just as Grant tries to create a cave-in to trap Frankie forever, but Grant is the one injured in the rock slide as Robert Taylor's character in his third brief scene in the episode rescues him.

This episode was written by Peter Stephens and directed by Tom Gries.

Moving to NBC, *The Detectives* was scheduled against *Route 66* on CBS and *The Flintstones* on ABC. It did not do well in that time slot. After the series was canceled in its third season by the network, Taylor received Four Star stock in exchange for his ownership interest in the series. In May 1963, he was named a vice president of the company.

The character Robert Taylor played on this series was one of the few leads in a Four Star non-anthology drama who was a typical "hero" in the sense of always abiding by the "straight and narrow" and having a very "vanilla" persona. Most of the continuing character leads in Four Star dramas either had a somewhat checkered past or else some other characteristic that made them unique.

# Late Fifties Continuing Character Drama Projects and Pilots

### Salvage Master

This project involved stories of ocean salvage operations based on the files of Merritt, Chapman and Scott, a large salvage corporation. Evidently, no pilot was ever made for this project.

### Old Man Coffee

Written by Alan Le May, this proposed series was to star Chill Wills in the lead role as a mountain man who hunts predators in cattle country for a bounty and raises dogs for hunting. His acute sense of perception makes him an informal crime solver for the town of Tarnation, Nevada. Set before World War II, the Le May script, titled "The Bean," dealt with the murder of a man who had just completed a poker game and was killed for his winnings. Old Man Coffee and his dog Sam, a bloodhound, attempt to solve the crime.

### Harbor Inn

M. Bernard "Ben" Fox, the creator of the syndicated series *Waterfront* with Preston Foster as a tugboat captain in Los Angeles harbor, decided to update that series with a new cast. In October 1955, Hal Roach Studios was set to make a pilot for the new series but, for whatever reason, it was never made. By fall 1956, Four Star sought to finalize a deal for the show. However, by January 1957, the idea was abandoned. The series was intended to be distributed by ABC Film Distribution.

### U. S. Information Service

Another idea by Four Star was to develop a series about the U.S. Information Service. This federal agency existed from 1953 to 1999 and spread information about the U.S. government and peoples to foreign countries through various forms of media. The Voice of America and Radio Free Europe were probably its most recognized components. The proposal for a television series about the agency was floated in October 1956. No pilot was ever filmed. However, the State Department did grant approval for the project.

### Flight Line

A proposed series called *Flight Line* would highlight stories about the different air branches of the armed forces as well as tales of civilian flying. The action would take place around an air field operated by Tom Hudson, an ex-Marine pilot who had flown missions during the Korean conflict. Four of every six episodes would deal with civilian flying. Supposedly, Four Star had made a deal with an air field and would also receive cooperation from the U.S. armed forces and aircraft manufacturers. Jack Robinson wrote a script for this endeavor. The pilot was to have been made in spring 1957 but was never produced.

In the pilot script titled "Flight from Fear," a young man learning to fly named Robert Avila crashes his plane, a Cessna 182, with his father and Tom Hudson as passengers. Robert then helps with their rescue.

### Night Court

To be produced by Vincent M. Fennelly, this project was a drama dealing with police work in New York City. No evidence of a pilot being made for the series could be found.

### If You Knew Tomorrow

Another pilot produced by Vincent M. Fennelly for Four Star, this drama focused on newscaster Ned Carver (Bruce Gordon) who possessed a unique teletype machine that forecast future events. In the pilot, Carver learns that a just-married couple will meet a tragic fate on their honeymoon. Carver goes after the newlyweds to warn them that their car will be hit by a train. Carver pulls up beside the car as the train rolls by. Just when it appears that the couple has been saved from certain death, a train smashes into a car at the crossing and the victims are identified as newlyweds. The off-screen narrator intones, "Did we change tomorrow or didn't we?"

*If You Knew Tomorrow* was based on a 1944 movie starring Dick Powell called *It Happened Tomorrow* about a turn-of-the century newspaper reporter who finds he can get a copy of the next day's paper.

## MacCreedy's Woman

For a possible 1957-58 series, Four Star Films made a pilot for Jane Russell called *MacCreedy's Woman*, which was a little like a female version of *Dante*. Directed by Allen H. Miner, the show was written by Gloria Saunders and Dick Carr. As with most lead actors in Four Star productions, Ms. Russell had a participation interest in this effort if it had become a series. In the pilot, the actress appears as Brandy MacCreedy, the singing hostess/owner of a night club her late husband had left her. Helping her run the establishment are Aristotle (Sean McClory), the bartender, and Felix (Jonathan Harris), the maitre d'.

Nicky Weston (Don Durant) comes to MacCreedy's establishment to claim that the late Mr. MacCreedy owes him $500 for a gambling debt and produces an IOU to that affect. Mrs. MacCreedy refuses to pay but offers the man a job in the club playing piano. Nicky, wanting the money to continue his gambling habit, asks a friend to rob MacCreedy's for the funds owed him, but the friend refuses and informs Brandy. Eventually, she does pay Weston what is owed. She explains that she had kept the $500 originally because she knew he needed a job more than the money and that her late husband always would have given a person another chance.

Discussing *MacCreedy's Woman*, Russell indicated that "A lot of people liked it, but none of them would buy it. They were just looking for westerns last fall and weren't in the mood for anything else."[26]

## Stewart Granger Projects

*Variety* reported in 1959 that Stewart Granger had signed a deal with Four Star for his own one-hour adventure series to be filmed in Africa and titled *Safari*. The show was to be produced in association with his production company, Tracy Productions, named after his daughter with then wife, actress Jean Simmons. However, later that year, the actor apparently changed his mind about filming a series in Africa since he didn't want to be away from his own animals on a ranch he owned in Arizona.

In late 1959, Granger contemplated starring in an action-adventure yarn created by David Karp called *The House of 4 Keys*. His character was to operate an art gallery in upper midtown Manhattan. The pilot was scheduled to be made in February 1960, but a movie deal prevented Granger from making the pilot. By October 1960, the idea for the series without Granger centered on a character named David Dulane, the junior partner of Dulane Galleries that specialized in art treasures. With a sidekick, David finds adventure all over the world. By December 1960, the project had been abandoned.

## The Searchers

The concept of this Four Star project, similar to other ones pursued by the company, was that of an adventure series with a cast of four leads each starring on their own episodes tied together with a central theme. *The Searchers* were private investigators headquartered in different cities around the world. New York City, San Francisco, and Chicago as well as a city in Europe were considered for the locales. Lead actors discussed for the show ranged from Rossano Brazzi and Charles Boyer to David Niven and Robert Ryan. Talk also centered on perhaps Edward G. Robinson and Curt Jurgens for the leads. By November 1960, the proposal was dead.

# Chapter 7:
## *Dick Powell's Zane Grey Theatre* and Its Pilots, 1956-61

Premiering on October 5, 1956 on CBS, Dick Powell hosted this Western anthology series during its five season run. Hal Hudson, a former producer for CBS, had a partnership with Romer Grey, son of Zane Grey, for the rights to his Western stories. While stories written by Zane Grey were adapted for the initial episodes, later seasons featured stories of other writers.

Four Star had hoped to get a Joel McCrea or Gary Cooper-type to host the series, but the sponsor, Maxwell House Coffee, insisted on Powell. According to Powell, "They (the sponsor) said it was no sale unless I played the host. I tried to talk them out of it, but they insisted, so I was outvoted."[27]

The first episode of *Zane Grey Theatre* titled "You Only Run Once" starred Robert Ryan as Matt Jessup, a man falsely accused of horse stealing and murder who faces a lynch mob. Two men, Scott and Ramsey, staying at Jessup's ranch, are found to be horse thieves. After a teenager is killed in the course of a horse theft, vigilantes arrest Scott and Ramsey and also seek Jessup presuming he conspired with them in their criminal activities. Jessup's wife encourages him to run from the vigilantes, but he decides to face them. He says that he is innocent, but the head of the vigilance committee wants to hang him anyway since Jessup was against the formation of the committee. Jessup convinces the members of the committee to vote on whether or not he should be hanged. The majority vote against hanging him.

"You Only Run Once" was not the pilot for the series. The pilot, originally called "Man on the Dodge," was not aired until June 21, 1957 – the final episode of the first season. When it was broadcast, the title changed to "Man on the Run" purportedly because Ford

Motor Company was a sponsor of the Dick Powell anthology and didn't like a reference to another carmaker in an episode title.

Starring Scott Brady as gunslinger Jeff Duane, "Man on the Run" concerned the character, trying to evade the law, arriving at a ranch in the middle of nowhere in Texas. The ranch has been taken over by a man named Lee Bland (Hugh Sanders) seeking dominion over the area and planning to marry Kate Longstreth (Eve Miller) who, along with her sister Ray (Nancy Hale), owns the ranch, inheriting it from their father. Ray is desperate to leave the place and wants Jeff's help. Ray and Jeff attempt to flee but are stopped by Kate. After a ranch hand intervenes, Jeff and Ray finally depart. The gunslinger decides to turn himself in to authorities hoping that Ray will wait for him until he is freed from jail.

Dick Powell first appeared as an actor on the third episode of the series, "The Long Road Home," playing a lawyer, Sam Gracie, who returns to his hometown three years after the end of the Civil War to seek justice for the death of his brother. Sam, who doesn't carry a gun, fought on the Union side in the war much to the dismay of his father and most of the townspeople. His brother had been killed by men from the neighboring Hatton ranch, but Sam's sister-in-law admits that her husband started the feud with the neighbors. At the town's saloon, Kimbal Hatton (Ainslie Pryor) attempts to goad Sam into a gunfight, but Sam resists. When Sam's brother Ben (Conrad Janis) seeks to challenge Kimbal, he is wounded in the shoulder for his efforts. Sam finally agrees to face Kimbal provided whoever wins, the feud between the Hatton's and the Gracie's will be called off. Sam's father gives him his gun. Kimbal shoots first but misses Sam who then shoots and kills Kimbal.

Two of Powell's colleagues from *Four Star Playhouse* also appeared in episodes from the first season of *Zane Grey Theatre*. Ida Lupino starred in an October 1956 installment, "Fearful Courage," as a witness to murder who is hunted by the gunman who wants to kill her for fear she'll testify against him. A March 1, 1957 episode, "Village of Fear" starred David Niven as a meek book salesman venturing into a Western town to find its citizens held at gunpoint by outlaws. He outwits the gang to free the townspeople. Niven also starred in an October 1958 installment of the series, "The Accuser," as a rancher who discovers that his neighbor has been murdered and then is accused of the crime by the man's mentally disturbed son and by a nasty deputy.

Writer/producer Aaron Spelling started working for Four Star scripting the introductions for Dick Powell to *Zane Grey* episodes. Powell didn't want the traditional openings most hosts of anthologies did by describing what each episode was about, and so, instead, Spelling composed little stories about Western lore for Powell to recite. Spelling went on to write and produce episodes of the series as well as produce several other Four Star series.

One episode Spelling wrote featured Sammy Davis Jr. as a member of the all-black 10th Cavalry assigned the mission of escorting a Comanche chief to the fort in order to sign a peace treaty. The Apaches attack the 10th Cavalry because they want to prevent the chief from executing the agreement. The Indians wound the cavalry's sergeant who subsequently dies leaving Harper (Davis) in charge of the unit. Because the Indians continue to attack his group, Harper considers turning over the chief to them in return for safe passage back to the fort. In the end, Harper decides to dress as the Comanche chief and give himself up to the Apaches so his men and the real chief can return to the fort.

This episode of *Zane Grey Theatre* represented Davis' first dramatic role on television.

According to Aaron Spelling, "He (Powell) taught me everything I know about television. He always said, 'If it ain't broke, don't fix it.' . . . He taught me that the secret to good television is attention to detail. He taught me to spend as much time as possible in the editing room, because that's where good film is made."[28]

In the final season of *Zane Grey*, in response to claims of too much violence on television, Dick Powell began a policy of doing human-interest stories on the anthology. "The critics raved, but the ratings dropped. Then, just to convince himself, he reverted to the old-style shoot-'em-ups. The ratings rose again to their previous satisfactory level. The sponsors smiled and said 'O.K., Dick, you've had your little fling, but now that you're back on the beam, let's keep it that way.' 'No thanks,' said Powell, and he folded the show at the season's end."[29] *Zane Grey Theatre* ran until 1961 with 156 episodes

*Sammy Davis, Jr. with actor Abraham Sofair who played the Comanche chief in "Mission" on* Zane Grey Theatre.

Dick Powell's *Zane Grey Theatre* aired many pilots for potential series during its run. As detailed below, some like "Badge of Honor," "Threat of Violence," "The Sharpshooter," "Man Alone," and "Trouble at Tres Cruces" each resulted in their own series. Many others did not. Known for having famous stars on each *Zane Grey* episode, Four Star would often give established stars top billing in a pilot with an actor, who would be the regular lead if the pilot became a series, billed after the more well-known actors.

## "Badge of Honor"

The Hoby Gilman character from the Western *Trackdown* was introduced in a March 5, 1957 episode titled "Badge of Honor." Gilman, a former soldier for the Confederacy, is visiting his sister in Crawford, Texas. He finds that the town has been taken over by a Colonel Nelson (Gary Merrill) and his gang. Nelson doesn't recognize the end of the Civil War and wants the South to rise again. After Hoby disagrees with Nelson's political views, the Colonel demands that Hoby leave town. When a Texas Ranger comes to Crawford to take Nelson to Austin for questioning, the Colonel has him killed. Hoby, a member of the Rangers before he became a rebel soldier, confronts Nelson, and, with backing from the townspeople, fights the Colonel and has him jailed.

## "Fugitive"

Eddie Albert starred in a projected series to be called *Adventures of Mike Scott* in which he would appear as a freelance journalist and author who imagines himself to be the central character of each of his stories. Aaron Spelling created the concept and co-wrote the pilot with Fred Fox. The proposed anthology would have involved the Eddie Albert character in drama, comedy, suspense, and action shows.

The pilot aired March 22, 1957 as an episode of *Zane Grey Theatre* called "Fugitive" with Albert appearing as Sam Barlow, a Civil War veteran who is accused of blowing up a bridge after the war had ended. Sarah Kimball (Celeste Holm), a lonely woman with a young son, discovers an injured Barlow in her barn and nurses him back to health. When the marshal comes looking for Barlow, Sarah says that she never saw him and introduces Barlow as her husband who has just returned from fighting on the Union side in the Civil War. Barlow tells her that he was with her husband when he was killed and further confesses that he is the Confederate soldier who shot him while he was guarding a bridge Barlow blew up. Neither Sarah's husband nor Barlow had known at the time that the war had ended. Sarah's son overhears the confession and asks a neighbor to turn Barlow in. The neighbor wants to torture Barlow before giving him to authorities and begins firing at him. In self-defense, Barlow shoots back killing the neighbor. He then turns himself into the marshal hoping that files from the Confederacy will show that he destroyed the bridge as an act of war and not as an act of terror.

While the pilot never became a series, the same concept was later used by Four Star for *The Lloyd Bridges Show* which ran for a season on CBS in the early sixties.

### "Decision at Wilson's Creek"

For the upcoming 1957-58 season, Four Star conceived of a new Western anthology series about the Civil War based on the writings of Civil War historian Bruce Catton to be called *Battle Flag*. A pilot was shot with John Forsythe as a lieutenant named David Marr drummed out of the Confederate Army for cowardice who returns to his wife and child in Springfield, Missouri. He takes a job assisting the town's doctor in helping wounded soldiers. When Marr sees the doctor remove a dispatch from an injured rebel soldier and not inform the battlefield hospital's Union commander, he confides to the doctor that he is really a Confederate spy and that his discharge was all a ruse. With the doctor's help, Marr obtains secret plans about the Union's next attack. He leaves his wife to report back to the Confederates information about the pending attack and is promoted to Captain for his service.

"Decision at Wilson's Creek" aired on May 17, 1957 on *Zane Grey Theatre*. When the pilot failed to become a series, Four Star thought of broadening the concept of the proposed series, as described in Chapter 9, to include stories from all wars – not just the Civil War.

### "A Gun Is for Killing"

This October 18, 1957 installment of *Zane Grey Theatre* was the pilot for another anthology series to be titled *Action*. The program would have included adventure stories – some set in the present, some in the past – taking place in various locales as well as in the air and on the sea. Four Star was seeking Van Johnson as the host with Edmund O'Brien starring in the pilot as Russ Andrews, a farmer whose nineteen-year-old son is killed in a gunfight by Billy

Jack (Robert Vaughn). Male TV viewers were to be the primary audience for the series.

Andrews seeks to avenge his son's death even though the gunfighter killed in self-defense. His wife Claire (Marsha Hunt) wants no guns in the house. Russ hides one in the barn where his younger son finds it, plays with the gun, and then stashes it elsewhere in the barn. When Russ ventures into town, Billy Jack attempts to goad him into a fight. Andrews beats him up. Billy Jack challenges him to a gun duel which Russ ignores. At night, Billy Jack comes to the Andrews' farm to once again entice Russ into facing him. Making it to the barn, Andrews tries to find the gun he hid there. He finally locates it and shoots Billy Jack.

### "The Freighter"

Barbara Stanwyck made a pilot for a series to be called *Lady Law* which aired as the January 17, 1958 installment of *Dick Powell's Zane Grey Theater*. In the episode titled "The Freighter," Stanwyck had the role of Belle Garrison, a tough woman who was an expert at using a bull whip. She took over her grandfather's (James Bell) freight line which was being terrorized by Rufus Murdock and his three sons. Murdock wanted to merge his freight line with the Garrison line, but Belle would have no part of the deal. The Murdock's attempt to steal Belle's customers. Disguising her wagon to look like Murdock's, she is able to evade him. He mistakenly blows up his own wagon being driven by two of his sons which dissuades him from pursuing his takeover of Belle's freight line. John Archer played Ad Masters, Belle's assistant in the pilot which was written by Fred Freiberger and directed by Christian Nyby.

While *Lady Law* never resulted in a series, Stanwyck would later star on another Four Star Western – *The Big Valley*.

### "The Sharpshooter"

The pilot for Four Star's most popular Western, *The Rifleman*, aired as part of *Dick Powell's Zane Grey Theater* on March 7, 1958 with an episode titled "The Sharpshooter." Starring Chuck Connors as Lucas McCain who always carried a modified Winchester rifle with a large ring which cocked the weapon as he drew, the pilot featured widower McCain and his young son Mark (Johnny

Crawford) arriving in North Fork, New Mexico to buy a ranch to settle down. The town is having a turkey shoot which McCain enters hoping to win the $500 grand prize for a down payment on the ranch. Also in town are sharpshooter Vernon Tippert (Dennis Hopper) and his uncle. The town's boss Jim Lewis is betting for Tippert to win. Tippert and McCain shoot to a tie. Lewis then privately threatens Mark's life if Lucas wins the tie-breaker. McCain purposely misses a shot allowing Tippert to win. However, when Tippert's uncle demands his share of the winning bets from Lewis, Lewis shoots him. McCain then takes on the Lewis gang with the help of Vernon Tippert, killing the bad guys.

The original script for "The Sharpshooter," written by Sam Peckinpah, did not include the Mark McCain character. It simply told the story of a marksman entering a shooting contest for the money, but, when his life is threatened by a saloon keeper who wants his own man to win, the marksman misses the target on purpose and leaves town.[30] To make the pilot more appealing to advertisers, the idea of the main character having a young son whose life is threatened if the marksman wins the shooting contest was included as the new story line.

### "Man of Fear"

Another unsold pilot for a series, *Doc Holliday*, written by Aaron Spelling, had Dewey Martin as the lead character. In a March 14, 1958 installment, "Man of Fear," Doc visits Lee Brand, a friend, and his wife. Brand is suffering from hysterical paralysis in his right arm because he is being extorted by the town's new sheriff for protection money. He pays the extortion, but Doc retrieves the money angering the sheriff and his gang who come to Brand's ranch to kill Lee. Lee's wife and Doc return fire when the gang starts shooting. After his wife is shot, Lee regains the use of his right arm and starts firing a rifle. Doc and he subdue the gang.

One issue that appeared to have doomed this pilot being picked up as a series was that actor Dewey Martin was deemed too young for the role of Doc Holliday.

## "The Doctor Keeps a Promise"

Cameron Mitchell portrayed Dr. Allan McMurdo in this pilot for a show, *McMurdo's Town*, broadcast on March 21, 1958. "The Doctor Keeps a Promise" had McMurdo caring for a man who had robbed another man at gun point. The robber is wounded, while his victim is thrown from his horse and knocked unconscious. The robber's wife (Carolyn Kearny) asks the doctor to promise not to divulge her husband's whereabouts because she is concerned he will be lynched. Dr. McMurdo is not held in high esteem by the town's wealthiest resident, Hod Strosnider (Ken Lynch), because he treats the poor. Strosnider, for whom the stolen money was intended, suspects McMurdo knows where the robber is, and so he beats him up. After the robber dies from his gunshot wound, his wife gives the money to McMurdo to return to Strosnider. She says her husband only took the money as compensation for Strosnider running his cattle over the robber's farm, ruining his crops, and leaving him and his wife destitute.

Hal Hudson produced the pilot based on a story by Luke Short. If the pilot had resulted in a series, Carolyn Kearny would have been a regular on the show along with Cameron Mitchell.

## "Threat of Violence"

The pilot for the Western, *Black Saddle*, aired as the May 23, 1958 episode of *Zane Grey Theatre* with Chris Alcaide playing Clay Culhane. The installment concerned Culhane thinking he had been hired by the Topaz Mining Corporation to represent them in a case, only to be told that the company wanted a more experienced attorney. Culhane then defends a man he met on the trail named Carlos (Cesar Romero) who has been accused of murdering a man who had confiscated his family's ranch. During the preliminary hearing, Culhane shows that Carlos was in a different place at the time of the murder. Carlos is released from custody. But later, Culhane finds that Carlos actually did kill the man committing the act earlier than everyone had thought.

The pilot was later reshot with Peter Breck as Clay Culhane.

## "Utopia, Wyoming"

The premise of this pilot starring Gary Merrill, as the leader of the town of Utopia, Wyoming, was to show how and why a Western town came to be and its prospects for the future. Written by Aaron Spelling and airing June 6, 1958, two mapmakers – Blake Scott (Robert Gothe) and Jet Mason (Pernell Roberts) happen upon a small town whose residents don't like outsiders. The populace came from Georgia after the Civil War to create their own town and do not want anyone else to know about it. The leader, Luke Cannon (Merrill) disarms Scott and Mason and contemplates killing them. After Cannon's young son falls into a pit in the livery stable and Mason helps rescue him, Cannon has second thoughts. But then gold is discovered near the town, and the town's leaders insist that Scott and Mason be killed so they do not divulge the gold find to outsiders if they are set free. Two of the residents become greedy over the gold and plot to steal it. Cannon decides to let Scott and Mason go as the townspeople surround the barn where the two thieves are. The two mapmakers help the town take care of the thieves before they leave.

"Utopia, Wyoming" was the first of several pilots Four Star made focusing on a specific town and its inhabitants. More such projects are described in Chapters 12 and 13.

## "Trail Incident"

Somewhat similar to *The Rifleman* in the pairing of an older man and a younger boy, "Trail Incident" (January 2, 1959) for a series to be called *The Trailsman,* focused on Andy McCall (John Ericson, who later co-starred on *Honey West*), a cattle driver taking his herd to Wichita. Along the way, he comes upon Pete Owens (Tim Considine), the spoiled son of a Chicago banker, who missed his stagecoach and became stranded in the desert. Peter joins the cattle drive where he meets the cook, Charlie Patch (Cameron Mitchell), a friend of Andy's who, because of an injury to his foot, cannot command his own herd. Peter eventually volunteers to help herd the cattle and finds that he likes the work. Meanwhile, Charlie conspires with other men to take the herd from Andy. Charlie tries to send Peter away, but Peter learns what Charlie is up to and warns

McCall who returns to the campsite. A shoot out ensues. With Pete's help, Andy takes care of Charlie as well as the men Charlie hired to steal the herd and, in the process, Charlie is wounded.

## "Man Alone"

Don Durant appeared as gunslinger Johnny Ringo in this March 5, 1959 pilot written by Aaron Spelling. Dick Powell had requested Spelling develop a new Western as a potential series for CBS.

Tired of being a gunfighter, Ringo accepts the job of sheriff in the town of Velardi where the acting sheriff, Case (Thomas Mitchell), the town drunk, was appointed after the death of the most recent incumbent in that job. The town is being run by Moss Evans (Scott Forbes), the owner of the saloon. Evans tries to co-opt Ringo by offering him a share of his profits, but Johnny refuses the offer. After a man is killed in the saloon, Ringo closes the establishment and orders Evans and his men to leave town the next day. When they don't, Johnny faces them alone and is able to take them down with last minute help from Case, who is killed in the process. Ringo decides to leave town. However, when he is challenged again by another gunfighter seeking to make a name for himself, Ringo decides to stay.

## "Trouble at Tres Cruces"

The pilot for *The Westerner*, titled "Trouble at Tres Cruces," aired on March 26, 1959. Another Sam Peckinpah project, the story dealt with Dave Blassingame's uncle, who lives in Mexico, testing a new Winchester rifle. A Greek man, Nick Karafus (Neville Brand) to whom the Mexican government has granted land rights, takes the rifle and kills the uncle. Blassingame receives a three-month old letter from his uncle asking him to visit. Arriving in Tres Cruces, he encounters Karafus and sees that he has his uncle's Winchester. Dave challenges Karafus to a fight which Dave loses. Blassingame goes after Karafus with his uncle's rifle, which the Greek had left behind, and shoots him.

As *Variety* wrote in reviewing this episode, "Television producers haven't yet come up with beebee guns as the basis of a series, but Four Star Films, in "Trouble at Tres Cruces," has pegged a pilot film on the talents of the Winchester rifle . . ."[31]

## "Checkmate"

This pilot for the unsold series, *The Man from Denver*, aired on April 30, 1959. It is an example of Four Star top billing special guests in a project where a lesser-name actor was the central character of the proposed series. James Whitmore starred as bank employee Joel Begley who had to take a position at the local bank after being injured in a mining accident causing him to limp. Marsha Hunt played Dr. Sarah Martin, who was in love with Begley. The central character, the man from Denver, was Ward Cameron (Mark Miller), a private detective for a chain of banks.

While having breakfast at the local hotel, Cameron and Begley witness a bank payroll robbery. Cameron helps the sheriff with the investigation. He finds that Begley along with a new salesman in town named Keller are responsible for the robbery. After Keller asks Begley for his share of the stolen loot, Begley knocks him out with his cane and throws the body out of his hotel room window. Cameron finds where Begley hid the payroll money and, as Begley tries to kill him, Cameron shoots Begley.

## "Sunday Man"

Dean Jones starred as a full-time, tough deputy sheriff in this pilot for a series, *Hardcase*, which aired on the February 25, 1960 edition of *Zane Grey Theatre*. Bill Devlin's (Jones) brother Walt (Ross Elliott) had been elected sheriff but spends most of his time running the local general store, and so he makes Bill the seven-day-a week deputy. Bill arrests the son of Cash Wilson for murder. Local bad guy Wilson (Leif Ericson) makes it known that he will free his son from jail. When Wilson and his men arrive in town, the local banker, Fred Childress (Brian Donlevy) disarms Bill and Walt and frees Wilson's son hoping that the father will leave the town alone. He doesn't. After beating up Bill, he robs the local bank. After Bill Devlin recovers, he resigns as deputy to go after Wilson and his son. Bill ends up shooting the son, and the townspeople rally to support Bill's arrest of the elder Wilson.

"Sunday Man" represents another example of Four Star billing more famous actors like Leif Ericson and Brian Donlevy above the name of Dean Jones, the actor who would have been the regular star if the pilot had become a series. Dean Jones seemed to have been a favorite of Four Star. In addition to the *Hardcase* pilot, Jones also appeared on the premiere episode of *The Dick Powell Show* as well as in an episode of *Target: The Corrupters*. In addition, the company produced *Ensign O'Toole* starring Jones, and, after that series was canceled, Four Star made more comedy pilots with the actor.

### "Seed of Evil"

Mostly known for his bad-guy roles, actor Myron Healey starred as former Union Secret Service Agent Sam Brady in this pilot for a Western broadcast April 4, 1960. Brady is opening an office as a private detective in Kansas City after the end of the Civil War. Upon arriving, he is forcibly taken to meet Malachi West (Raymond Massey), a wheelchair-bound old man, who lives with his brain-damaged son Paul (Charlie Briggs) and his daughter-in-law Irene (Cara Williams). West blames Brady for the hanging death of his other son Simon, to whom Irene had been married before West forced her to marry Paul so he could have a grandson. Simon West, using the name Peter Stowe, had been executed by the Union for being a Confederate spy. Malachi West wants to kill Brady, but before he can, Sam, using a gun he has hidden under his coat, tries to escape. In the scuffle, Irene retrieves the gun and decides to take her anger out on Malachi for forcing her marriage to Paul. She shoots and kills Malachi. Sam returns to his office and hires the West's cook as his secretary.

### "The Man from Everywhere"

Burt Reynolds starred in this April 13, 1961 pilot as Branch Taylor, a former Cavalry guide who, with his partner Moose (Peter Whitney), takes on various jobs escorting people throughout the West. Branch comes to Carson City and is asked by the sheriff to take gambler Tom Bowdry (Caesar Romero), in jail for robbery and murder, to another town for his trial. The people of Carson City want to try Bowdry in a kangaroo court, but Taylor and Moose free him. On the way to the other town, the group encounters Jenny Aldrich (Ruta Lee) who had fallen in love with Bowdry and wants to free him. Bowdry attempts to shoot Taylor, but Taylor knocks him unconscious and delivers him for trial.

### "The Release"

Starring Cesare Danova as Lee DuVal, an unusual combination of gunfighter and artist, this pilot for *The Adventurer* aired April 27, 1961. Produced by Laven, Levy, and Gardner, DuVal is released from prison five years early by the Governor of Texas on condition that he discourages violence along the Texas/Louisiana border. The Governor wants DuVal to be the thorn in the side of the lawbreakers by creating mischief among them to reduce their tendency to ignore the law. DuVal is befriended by Dee Pritcher (Lee Kinsolving), a young man he knew as a boy. Pritcher works for a crime boss named Ken Kenyon (Gary Merrill) who is suspicious of the circumstances under which DuVal was released from prison. Kenyon challenges Pritcher to face DuVal in a gun fight. Naturally, DuVal shoots first injuring Pritcher. He then shoots Kenyon when challenged by him.

The title, *The Adventurer*, was later re-used by Four Star for another project in 1964.

### "A Rope for a Lady"

Guy Madison (*Wild Bill Hickok*) made an attempt to return to series television in a show, *Jericho*, where the actor appeared as Mr. Jericho, an agent for the Attorney General's office in Washington D.C., who seeks to undo any apparent injustice the legal system may have done to individuals. In the pilot, airing May 18, 1961, Jericho reviews the case of Amy Schroeder (Beverly Garland), sentenced to die for shooting her husband after he beat her. She doesn't deny shooting him but says she shot him in the arm and not the head as the autopsy revealed. Jericho believes that Amy's husband, known for his practical jokes and for having an affair with another woman in town, may have shot a saddle tramp and then burned down his house making it look as though his wife had killed him. Thinking he has been found out, Schroeder, who has been hiding in his mistress's attic in town, opens fire on Jericho and a deputy. Jericho shoots and kills him.

As described later, Powell's next anthology series – *The Dick Powell Show*, would also air several episodes as pilots for potential series.

# Chapter 8:
# Four Star Westerns, 1957– 61

Four Star rode the wave of the era of prime-time Westerns from 1957 to 1961. During the 1956-57 television season, the networks aired a total of eleven Westerns. But that number almost doubled to twenty in 1957-58, thirty-one during the 1958-59 TV season, thirty in 1959-60, and twenty-six in 1960-61 before the number tailed off during the remainder of the early sixties.

Commenting on the number of Western series on television, Dick Powell remarked,

> Success depends on the series, how it's handled, who is in it. On television we haven't come close to the percentage of western stories done by the movies. Actually, the western has been the backbone of the movie industry ever since 1903, when they made "The Great Train Robbery," and I can see no reason why it shouldn't be the backbone of the television industry. It's the best possible escape material – and it's American right down to its boots.[32]

Referring to the several young actors that had main roles on Four Star Westerns, Powell stated in an October 1959 press release:

> There's plenty of good young actors, writers, producers and directors if you take the time to look for them. Then you've got to give them plenty of independence and incentive.
>
> We've been able to do that because Four Star is a partnership . . . People like to work for us because there are no bosses. I handle the business on the telephone; the people on the shows know there won't be anyone breathing down their necks.
>
> We've always had the policy of not taking our money out of the company. In that way, we're able to give our people incentive via a share of the profits. All of our stars and

producers have a percentage of the shows, even those who weren't top names before. That's the way they stay happy.

In late 1959, Dick Powell hired Tom McDermott from Benton and Bowles advertising agency, where he had served as vice president in charge of radio and TV, to take over from him certain of his duties as president of Four Star Films. McDermott was brought on to be the creative head of the company sitting in on scripts, casting, editing, etc. His arrival at the production firm was seen as an opportunity for expansion.

One area of expansion that Powell contemplated included making pilots expressly to sell to local stations as well as syndicating Four Star's own series internationally. Concerning the former endeavor, Powell was looking at making pilots for $30,000 or less such as a series based on the Malibu Beach Patrol and another ". . . a less-expensive western."[33]

The addition of McDermott to Four Star was not without controversy among the writers and other staff. As writer Christopher Knopf put it:

> . . . he was everything Powell was not. The first thing he did was bring in a platoon of executives whose functions were hard to define. . . . I found him aloof and competitive, and I wasn't alone. Tell him an idea you had for a new series, he'd more often than not answer with, "Yeah, I had that idea myself last week." But he had the job and in the beginning delivered, selling a collection of new series, most of which were short-lived.[34]

In April 1960, Four Star announced its entry into the motion picture field. Plans called for making one or two films per year. Two properties already owned by Four Star for feature-length films were *Somewhere They Die* and *No Riders*. The films were never made.

Four Star underwent another corporate restructuring on July 28, 1960, becoming Four Star Television with Four Star Films, Dayton Productions, BNP Music Publishing, and Trend Music Publishing all to be merged into it. At that time, Powell owned 42.5% of the stock, Boyer and Niven, 21.25% each, and Tom McDermott,

15%. In addition, the reorganization led to the issuance of 120,000 shares of common stock to be sold to the public.

All Four Star Westerns during this period had certain elements in common. As noted above, they all starred young male actors with one exception – *Wichita Town* which featured veteran Joel McCrea in the lead but with his son, Jody co-starring with his father. However, Four Star only filmed that series which was produced by the Mirisch Corporation. The lead characters on Four Star Westerns were all either loners with atypical back stories such as being former gunslingers or, in the case of *The Law of the Plainsman*, a Native American with a Harvard degree, or else they were widowers raising young sons. And many of the heroes of Four Star Westerns had unusual firearms that were used as "hooks" to promote the different series to young male viewers.

## *Trackdown* and Its Back-Door Pilot

Premiering October 4, 1957, the first of Four Star's continuing character Westerns dealt with the adventures of Texas Ranger Hoby Gilman (Robert Culp). *Trackdown* was produced in cooperation with the Texas Rangers. Writer John Robinson, who had done scripts for *Dragnet*, created the series, and several episodes included off-screen narration and plotting similar to that police series.

On the series opener, the Marple Brothers have killed Gilman's partner, Sam Talbot, and head to Stockton, Texas where they take a Sunday school class hostage in order to seek treatment for one of the brothers who had been wounded by Gilman. They demand a doctor and a fresh set of horses in exchange for releasing the captives. The wounded brother is taken to the doctor's office where he subsequently passes away. Gilman and some of the townspeople kill and/or capture the other brothers.

On the early episodes, Gilman alone traveled to several Texas towns to track down wanted men. For example, on a December 13, 1957 installment, "The Town," written by Sam Peckinpah, Hoby is on the trail of two bank robbers. One of the thieves, Ben Fraser (Lee Van Cleef) kills his partner and then heads to a town where his brother Cal (Stuart Whitman) runs the saloon. Gillman follows, but, once in town, his gun and horse are taken from him. No one in town wants to help him either because they support the Fraser brothers, or they are intimidated by them. Hoby does receive some assistance from the local blacksmith who allows the Ranger to hide out in his stable. Gilman is able to wrest a gun from one of Fraser's men and kills Cal Fraser. He then calls out Ben Fraser, but Ben's dance hall girlfriend shoots him first.

By March of its first season, Hoby Gilman locates to Porter, Texas to help out after the town's regular sheriff dies. The citizens of Porter wanted him to stay as acting sheriff in addition to performing his Ranger duties, and some new characters were added to the show – Aaron Adams (James Griffith), the town's barber, Henry (Norman Leavitt), who helps out at the sheriff's office, and Henrietta Porter (Ellen Corby), the editor of *The Porter Enterprise* newspaper and one of the town's founders.

These characters first appear in "The Judge" – a story about Judge Henry's son Malcolm (Steve Terrell) whom Hoby arrests for shooting a man that the Judge's son claims was cheating at cards. A saloon girl helps Malcolm escape from jail. He goes to the newspaper office to hide. Hoby, the Judge (John Litel), and Adams search the town for him. When they arrive at the newspaper office, Henrietta runs off a special copy of the latest edition of the paper for Hoby which states that Malcolm is hiding there. After the three depart the office, the Judge returns alone to warn his son to leave, but, when Malcolm tries to shoot Henrietta, the Judge kills his son.

While many of the series remaining episodes were set in Porter, Hoby would still, from time to time, travel outside the town in pursuit of bad guys. Later in the series run, Peter Leeds was added to the cast as Temme Smith, a saloon owner, and Addison Richards appeared as the town's doctor, Jay Calhoun. Seventy episodes of *Trackdown* were filmed. The series ran until September 1959.

As with virtually every Four Star Western, certain episodes were pilots for spin-off series. For example, *Trackdown* aired a pilot for Steve McQueen's *Wanted: Dead or Alive*.

## "The Bounty Hunter"

Josh Randall (Steve McQueen) shows up in Big Ben, Texas where he meets Hoby Gilman. Randall is seeking Nate Phillips because a man named Mr. Black is offering $500 for locating him. Randall quizzes a saloon girl and Phillips' wife attempting to find the man. Gilman and Randall end up in Franklin, Texas where they learn that Phillips was supposedly murdered by the man with whom he was rooming. However, the body is actually that of the roommate – not Phillips. The two track Phillips to Houston where they capture him. Randall then goes to see Mr. Black for his reward. Black is in jail and is upset that Phillips is now also incarcerated. He had wanted to kill Phillips after he was found because Phillips had run away with Black's wife.

## *Wanted: Dead or Alive* and Its Back-Door Pilots

Future movie star Steve McQueen had the lead in this Western concerning the exploits of a bounty hunter searching for wanted criminals. Like many other Four Star Westerns, Randall carried a unique gun – a .30-.40 sawed-off carbine. As *Variety* pointed out in its review of the premiere episode, "'Wanted,' was different only because the hero did not carry a .45 or a buntline or any known brand of sidearm – not even the true cynic's sawed-off shotgun. He had instead a sawed-off carbine. The worthiness of this weapon – except as a promotional point for CBS flacks – is not made clear."[35]

*Variety* also critiqued McQueen's minimalist style of acting noting, "Steve McQueen, a young actor who proved himself worthy as the lead in Broadway's 'Hatful of Rain,' could, in this latest instance, do little else than preserve a wax-like countenance and say the few words (like carbonated water gone flat) he had to say."[36]

Despite *Variety's* criticism of the show, *Wanted: Dead or Alive* was different from other Westerns in that it dealt with the exploits of a bounty hunter – almost an anti-hero in the West competing with law men to capture desperadoes for his own financial gain. As McQueen once described his role, "There's a certain honesty and realism in this series . . . The hero isn't always a nice guy – you don't stay alive in the Old West being nice."[37]

Evidently actor James Best, who guest starred on several Four Star Westerns, was first offered the lead role in *Wanted: Dead or Alive*. But he was under contract with producer Jack Chertok to do another series. As Best wrote in his autobiography, "He would not let me out of the contract, even though I could have done *Wanted* without even testing for the part. I later asked who got the part, and my agent said, 'Some New York actor named Steve McQueen.'"[38]

Producers at Four Star were initially doubtful that McQueen had the screen presence to be the lead in a Western. "... McQueen was short and wiry, not brawny and handsome the way a Western hero was supposed to be. But in the end, this worked to his advantage, because the bounty hunter was a heavy, and the producers decided it would be smart to put a guy in the role who was tough yet boyish, maybe even a hint of vulnerability."[39]

The Western premiered on CBS September 6, 1958 and ran for three seasons (ninety-eight episodes). It was produced by Malcolm Productions, co-owned by producer Vincent M. Fennelly, and by Four Star Films. During its first season, the show ranked number sixteen in the ratings.

The first installment, "The Martin Poster," featured two actors who would go on to star on their own Westerns – Nick Adams and Michael Landon. They played the murderous Martin brothers. Josh Randall arrives in Las Tunas to see the marshal about the reward offered for Andy Martin (Adams). He finds that Andy is holding the marshal hostage while freeing his brother Carl (Landon) from jail. Andy kills the marshal; Josh is knocked out but comes to and manages to wound Carl as the brothers flee. Some of the townspeople think that Josh really wanted to free Carl from jail to collect the bounty on him and killed the law man in the process. Randall quickly departs the town and goes after the Martin boys. He locates their campsite, but Andy gets the drop on him. Randall escapes and eventually finds the Martin homestead where the brother's sister Louise (Jennifer Lea) has no idea that her brothers have committed murder. She prevents Carl from murdering Randall. When Andy returns to the farm, Randall shoots him as Andy tries to throw a pitchfork at him. Josh collects the bounty on both brothers but gives the reward to the marshal's widow.

At midseason during 1958-59, producer Fennelly instituted a practice of having guest stars on each episode. Stars included Mona Freeman, Jay C. Flippen, and Everett Sloane. For example, a March 1959 episode titled "The Legend" guest starred Victor Jory as Sam McGarrett who hires Randall to help in finding a treasure of gold hidden in the desert. Randall, McGarrett, and McGarrett's son Clay (Michael Landon making another appearance on the series) eventually locate the cave in which the gold is supposedly hidden but when they enter the cave, they find only empty strong boxes. Exiting the cave, Randall is pinned down by gunfire from two men who followed him there and want the gold. Clay McGarrett acts as a decoy to draw the men's fire so that Randall can shoot them boosting Clay's image in the eyes of his dad.

Sherry Alberoni, who had a role on Four Star's *The Tom Ewell Show*, remembers that Steve McQueen was filming *Wanted: Dead or Alive* at the same time as her show. He ". . . would come by our set, pick me up on his motorcycle and drive me to make-up/hair dressing. I was just a kid, but I had such a crush on him and he was so kind and nice to me. Finally, as he became a bigger star, the studio wouldn't let him ride his motorcycle any longer."[40]

*Wanted: Dead or Alive* initially did well in the ratings when it was on Saturdays at 8:30 after *Perry Mason*, however, when CBS moved the Western to Wednesday nights in September 1960, the series ratings declined leading to its cancelation by spring 1961. The show was replaced by the British series *Danger Man* starring Patrick McCoohan which later expanded to one hour as *Secret Agent*.

*Wanted: Dead or Alive* aired three pilots as potential spin-off series.

### "Six-up to Bannach"

This pilot for the Western, *Stagecoach West*, starred James Best as Luke Perry and Sam Buffington as his partner Abb Crawford. The January 10, 1959 installment of *Wanted: Dead or Alive* had the Steve McQueen character taking the stagecoach on a three-day trip to Bannach to save a friend named Murdock from hanging for a crime he didn't commit. Murdock was convicted of murdering his partner John Gillette (Stacy Harris), but Gillette is actually alive and murdered another man making it look like Murdock killed him. Randall is taking Gillette to Bannach to prove he is still alive. He has to arrive there in three days before the execution occurs. Perry initially doesn't want Randall and Gillette on the trip because the coach is carrying a large shipment of dynamite. However, he begins to appreciate Randall when Josh uses some dynamite to dam a river to create a temporary road when a bridge is out. With all the problems Randall and the stagecoach drivers experience getting to Bannach, when they arrive, they find the town almost empty because of a gold rush with Murdock's hanging postponed until the sheriff can round up enough witnesses for the execution.

## "The Kovack Affair"

This pilot for a series to be called *The Outrider*, written by D.D. and Mary Beauchamp, dealt with the exploits of a young man and woman who run an Outrider hotel in Kansas. Jean Willes appeared as Meghan Francis, the owner of the hotel, a stopping off place for people en-route to the West. James Coburn played Jesse Holloway, the hotel manager.

In the episode titled "The Kovack Affair," airing March 28, 1959, Josh Randall is invited by his friend Jesse Holloway to the Outrider to take care of Peter Kovack (Jacques Aubuchon) who wants to purchase the hotel after having the gambling concession at that establishment for a year. Because Meghan Francis does not want to sell the place, Kovack has his henchmen vandalize the bar and casino forcing the hotel to close. When Jesse confronts Kovack, he is beaten by Kovack's men. Josh forces Kovack to sign papers giving up the gambling concession under threat of bringing in gunslingers if he doesn't sign. Sufficiently recovered from his beating, Jesse takes on Kovack and his men killing Kovack in the process.

## "Barney's Bounty"

The final episode of *Wanted: Dead or Alive*, "Barney's Bounty," broadcast March 29, 1961 was a pilot for a series to be called *Durant* starring Noah Beery, Jr. Barney Durant and his son, David (Jonathan Bolt), own a horse farm. Josh Randall visits to rent some horses in order to take two desperadoes to Nevada. Always trying to make an extra buck, Barney wants to sell Josh the horses and not rent them. The two guys in Randall's custody escape with two of Durant's horses. Josh and Barney go after them. Randall captures one of the felons, but one of Durant's horses is killed in the process. Both Barney and Josh then catch the other guy. Durant returns to his horse farm where his son resides. Barney, who had insisted that his son go to San Francisco so he could avoid the gun violence in the area, decides that Davey can stay in El Dorado.

Of the three pilots that aired on *Wanted: Dead or Alive*, the only one that resulted in a series was "Six-up to Bannach," which, after recasting, became *Stagecoach West*.

## *The Rifleman* and Its Back-Door Pilots

Four Star's most successful series, ratings-wise, was created by writer/director Sam Peckinpah and produced by the team of Jules Levy, Arthur Gardner, and Arnold Laven in association with Four Star. "Jules Levy was the wheeler-dealer in the group; he'd make the deals with agents for properties, etc. Arthur Gardner was a very, very good close-to-the-vest administrator, and Arnold Laven was the creative force."[41]

ABC's *The Rifleman* starred Chuck Connors as Lucas McCain and Johnny Crawford as his son, Mark. The first episode was a repeat of "The Sharpshooter" pilot that had aired on CBS's *Zane Grey Theatre*. The only difference was that Dick Powell's introduction was deleted and a new one made with Connors introducing viewers to the show.

On the second episode of the Western, Lucas and Mark prepare to fix up the house on the ranch McCain purchased. However, two men – Sam Montgomery (Lee Farr) and Billy Lehi (Steven Randel), who work for a cattle corporation owned by Jackford (Harold J. Stone), insist that their cattle graze on McCain land. They burn down the ranch house and take McCain's rifle. Lucas goes after them, retrieves his rifle, ties them up, and confronts Jackford resulting in a fist fight with McCain knocking Jackford unconscious. Upon regaining consciousness, Jackford agrees to rebuild McCain's house and stay off his ranch.

The fourth episode introduced Micah Torrence (Paul Fix), a lawman who is now a drunkard, having lost the use of his right arm in a gun battle. McCain hires Micah to build a corral for him. Meanwhile, Flory and Andrew Sheltin (Robert Wilke and Warren Oates) arrive in North Fork with Lloyd Carpenter (James Drury) to seek vengeance on Micah for perceived past wrongs. McCain forces the two brothers to leave his ranch when they threaten Micah. Arriving back in North Fork, they proceed to trash the saloon. The current town marshal (R.G. Armstrong) wants to throw them in jail, but Carpenter comes to their defense and kills the marshal. Carpenter then lies to Lucas that the Sheltin brothers murdered the lawman. McCain goes to North Fork to face the brothers. Micah, fearing trouble, goes after him. McCain shoots Flory Sheltin but is wounded by the other brother. With a shot gun, Micah takes care of Andrew Sheltin and Lloyd Carpenter and is made the new town marshal.

This was the first episode to be directed by Sam Peckinpah based on a script that he co-wrote.

*The Rifleman* premiered September 30, 1958 and was ranked number four in the ratings for its first season. In 1959, creator of the series, Sam Peckinpah quit *The Rifleman*. He was quoted as saying: "I walked away from the series because Jules Levy and that group had taken over my initial concept and perverted it into pap. They wouldn't let Johnny (Crawford) grow up. They refused to let it be the story of a boy who grows to manhood learning what it's all about."[42]

During the 1960-61 season, producers introduced a female character on the Western – Mildred Scott (Joan Taylor) as a potential love interest for Lucas McCain. After Milly takes over the general store in North Fork, she refuses to grant customers credit until their past due bills are paid. Two men new in town, Jack Adams (Richard Devon) and Marty Ryan (Warren Oates), volunteer their services as bill collectors hoping to make money out of the arrangement by intimidating the town's citizens into paying up. When McCain's friend is almost beaten to death by Ryan, Lucas and the marshal confront the two men. The marshal tries to arrest them, but they open fire and are killed by McCain and the marshal. Scott witnesses the event and resumes offering credit to her customers.

The Milly Scott character appeared sporadically on the series until the end of the 1961-62 season. By then, *The Rifleman* had fallen to number twenty-seven in the ratings and finished its final season (1962-63) out of the top thirty shows.

In its final season, the Western introduced another female character after Joan Taylor left the series. On an October 1962 episode, Lou Mallory (Patricia Blair) arrives in North Fork buying up a lot of land and other properties including Milly Scott's general store. Among her land purchases is property owned by the Jackman family. Neb Jackman (Peter Whitney) has three sons - Moss (Thom Carney), the bright one of the group, Haslim (Conlan Carter), the dumbest one, and Bo (Mel Carter), the strong one. Initially the Jackman's think they made out well with the land sale but then find out that the railroad is coming to town and want to get their land back. They kidnap Lou to try to entice her into marrying Haslim. When Lucas and Micah can't find her, they suspect that she is with the Jackman's and go to their farm. After Lucas rescues her, she decides not to press charges against the Jackman's.

As described below, the Jackman family would appear again on *The Rifleman* in an episode designed as a back-door pilot for their own series.

Four Star in conjunction with Sussex Productions owned by Gardner, Levy, and Laven, made a total of 168 episodes of the Western.

In 2011, CBS thought about remaking *The Rifleman* in association with Carol Mendelsohn Productions, but the reboot never went forward.

*The Rifleman* also had several episodes as spinoff pilots for potential Westerns.

### "The Indian"

The *Law of the Plainsman* pilot aired as an episode of *The Rifleman* in early 1959. The installment titled "The Indian" had Sam Buckhart (Michael Ansara), a Native American, seeking an Indian suspected of being an arsonist who killed a husband and wife. He learns that the real culprit is a white man living in North Fork. Lucas McCain is concerned that some people in North Fork will not accept an Indian arresting a white man. When a mob tries to intimidate Buckhart while he is arresting the suspect, McCain pretends to side with the mob saying that they should take the law into their own hands. The members of the mob then disburse allowing Buckhart to proceed with the arrest.

## "The Lariat"

This March 29, 1960 episode introduced the character of Lariat Jones played by Richard Anderson, a well-dressed gambler and sharpshooter who was an acquaintance of Lucas McCain. Jones once dated Lucas' late wife before she married the rifleman. Matt Wymerman (George Macready) proposes to Lariat that they open a casino in North Fork. Wymerman has a reputation for running crooked gambling operations, but Lariat wants everything on the up and up. Micah is suspicious that the new saloon called the Silver Dice may be cheating customers. When a wheeler-dealer starts winning big at the establishment, Wymerman forces Jones to cheat on cards to get the money back. Jones purposely loses and shoots Wymerman when the latter tries to kill him. Lariat decides to leave town and presumably engage in other adventures if *Lariat Jones* had become a series.

## "Death Trap"

Four Star had success with Westerns about a gunslinger turned lawyer (*Black Saddle*) and a gunfighter turned sheriff (*Johnny Ringo*) and so why not try a gunslinger who became a doctor? Such was the premise of *Simon Battle* starring Phil Carey which aired May 9, 1961 as an episode of *The Rifleman* called "Death Trap."

Battle had promised his dying wife, who had nursed him back to health after a gunfight, that he would become a doctor. He is on his way to Lone Pine, Arizona with his teenage daughter, Vicki[43] (Gigi Perreau) when he stops in North Fork. A man named Stark was shot in a gunfight with a man named Spicer (James Drury) and is presumed dead. But Lucas McCain finds him still alive and brings him to North Fork's doctor. Since the doctor happens to be out of town, Dr. Battle volunteers to care for the wounded man. Lucas had encountered Battle ten years earlier and knows him only as a gunslinger. Reluctant to let him treat Stark, McCain has no other choice. When Spicer learns that the man he shot is not dead, he threatens to take care of McCain, Battle, and Stark. Stark survives. McCain and Battle face down Spicer and his men with Battle knocking Spicer unconscious.

## "Which Way'd They Go?"

This back-door comedy pilot focused on Neb Jackman (Peter Whitney) and his three sons – Moss (Mickey Manners), Haslim (Conlan Carter), and Bo (John Craig). Manners and Craig replaced Thom Carney and Mel Carter who had originally appeared as these characters in the "Lou Mallory" episode.

"Which Way'd They Go?" aired on April 1, 1963 as the next-to-the last episode of *The Rifleman*. Arthur Browne Jr. wrote the back-door pilot which was directed by Arnold Laven.

The Jackman's are being evicted from their farm for failure to pay taxes, and so they abandon their property and head to Pair-O--Dice, a town currently without a sheriff because no one in the town wanted the job. When the Jackman's enter the saloon and hear the word "job," Neb becomes the sheriff and his boys the deputies. Beatrice King played Miss Goldie Drain, a dance hall girl; Dallas McKennon appeared as Judge Maze; and Vitto Scotti portrayed Marcello Carbini, the banker – all residents of Pair-O-Dice.

Meanwhile, Lucas McCain receives a note from Micah that a gang of bank robbers headed by Wade Stack (Leo Gordon) has broken out of prison and may be headed to Pair-O-Dice to rob the bank because the town is without a sheriff. Lucas is asked to ride to the town to warn them. On his way, he is knocked unconscious by Stack's gang who steals his note. When the gang arrives in the town, the head of the bank recognizes them and has Neb and his sons arrest them.However, the gang says they were sent by Micah to warn the town of the bank robbers and show the note to the Jackman's. Wade Stack tells Neb that he and his sons can watch the bank at night and his gang will relieve them in the morning. The next morning, after the Jackman's return to the sheriff's office, Haslam sees a wanted poster for Wade Stack. Bo and Moss are able to knock out most of the gang except for Wade whom Haslam collides with and the money from the bank lands in Neb's arms. The townsfolk throw a party for their heroes – Neb and his sons.

This proposed spin-off has been termed "the worst *Rifleman* episode ever."

The only spinoff from *The Rifleman* that actually became a series was the one starring Michael Ansara as Sam Buckhart.

## *Black Saddle*

Another thirty-minute Western from Four Star, this one, originally titled *Law Gun*, had a central character who was a former gunfighter turned lawyer. Clay Culhane (Peter Breck) traveled throughout the New Mexico territory with his law books in his saddle bags. Sherriff Gib Scott (Russell Johnson) shadowed Culhane in his exploits. The series premiered on NBC on January 10, 1959, Saturdays at 9:00 pm as a midseason replacement for *Steve Canyon*.

Created by Hal Hudson, who produced *Zane Grey Theatre*, and by John McGreevey, the producers ignored the pilot for *Black Saddle* that had aired as an installment of *Zane Grey Theatre* with Chris Alcaide and made a new pilot with Breck in the lead role. Culhane heads to Latigo, New Mexico to represent Nora Travers (Anna Lisa), the town's hotel owner, in his first case. He meets Marshal Gib Scott who, knowing Culhane's background as a gunslinger, wants him to leave. Hannibal Pardee (Onslow Stevens), a local rancher whose son was killed in a gunfight in town, now wants to destroy the place. Travers wants Culhane to defend her against Pardee's attempt to take over her business establishment and land she owns. Pardee plots to kill Culhane and the marshal for arresting two of his men for trespassing on Travers' property. Culhane is able to get the drop on one of Pardee's snipers and ends up shooting Pardee when he fires at him. Gib Scott takes care of another of Pardee's men. Culhane ultimately decides to set up his law practice in Latigo.

The first episode of *Black Saddle* was titled "Client: Travers." Most of the episodes had the word "client" in the title followed by the name of the person Culhane was representing. On the second episode, "Client: Meade," the lawyer represents Billy Meade (Clu Glauger), a gunslinger who has killed members of the Tibbet family in different gunfights. After Meade is arrested for his most recent killing, Culhane defends him. The lawyer finds a witness to the gun battle who says that Meade fired in self-defense, but, at the preliminary hearing, after being intimidated by the Tibbet's, the witness changes his story. Culhane and the marshal subsequently convince the witness to admit that he lied, but Meade, after breaking out of jail, is shot in the back by one of the Tibbet brothers.

After its run on NBC ended in September 1959, *Black Saddle* was picked up by ABC for the 1959-60 TV season. Both networks were interested in the series, but its sponsor, Liggett & Myers, didn't like the fact that NBC wanted to schedule the Western on Thursdays at 7:30 since that network wished to place Henry Fonda's Western, *The Deputy* on Saturdays at 9:00. ABC had Fridays at 10:30 open following *Robert Taylor's The Detectives* and so *Black Saddle* was placed in that time slot.

The final episode of the series, coincidentally titled "End of the Line" had Culhane and Nora arriving in a town called Chloride to meet with a mining supervisor about a freight line contract. They run into Cole and Luke Castleberry, wanted for robbery, who are causing trouble in the town. The Castleberry's want to eliminate the mine foreman with whom they do not get along. When they hold one of the miner's hostage hoping to engage the foreman, who is not a gunfighter, in a dual, the miners confront them. Scott and his deputies come to Chloride looking for the Castleberry brothers. A gun battle ensues, and the Castleberry's are vanquished.

A total of forty-four episodes of *Black Saddle* were produced. Treatments for some never-made episodes were prepared including one about an attorney friend of Clay's who turns out to be a conman and gunslinger. Another treatment concerned two families feuding over a bridge that one clan claimed was built with lumber that it owned; and a third treatment dealt with the town's barkeeper who advertises for a female companion for an older woman but really intends the companion to be his wife.

After *Black Saddle*, Peter Breck became a regular on another Four Star Western – *The Big Valley*. *Black Saddle* was the rare Four Star Western that did not air any back-door pilots during its run.

## *Wichita Town* and Its Back-Door Pilots

Although Joel McCrea did not become one the hosts of *Four Star Playhouse*, the actor did enter into a deal between his own company and Mirisch Enterprises to produce this Western series for NBC which debuted September 30, 1959. Four Star filmed the series.

The program was sold to the network without a pilot based simply on the name recognition of Joel McCrea.

Commenting on his company's first TV project, producer Walter Mirisch remarked about the series:

> It will be a pure historical western with a tear and a laugh, a sort of profile of a town growing up. To be sure there'll be horses and gunplay but I think we have a different approach in the way of presenting McCrea as the marshal and his son Jody, in a featured role. We won't be copying any of the current westerns and will strike off in many directions. Character and mood will be uppermost in our design to be different, with lesser emphasis on gunning down the bad-man or shooting up a town.[44]

On the show, McCrea appeared as Marshal Mike Dunbar of Wichita assisted by Deputy Ben Matheson (Jody McCrea) and by Deputy Rico Rodriguez (Carlos Romero, Cesar Romero's real-life brother). Other characters included Dr. Nat Wyndham (George Neise), Aeneas MacLinahan (Bob Anderson), Wichita's blacksmith, and Joe Kingston (Robert Foulk), the bartender at the local saloon.

The opener told how Dunbar came to be the town's marshal. He came to Wichita as the trail boss of a cattle drive with his men and other cowboys celebrating the end of their drives. The town's marshal orders Dunbar to better control his men, but he responds that he is no longer their boss. The marshal vacates the town after being harassed by the trail gangs leaving his deputy to take care of things. After a little boy is killed by a ricocheted bullet fired by one of the cowboys, Dunbar becomes involved in law enforcement. He works with the deputy to bring order back to Wichita and is made the marshal.

As with other stars from motion pictures who played a continuing character on a television series, Joel McCrea sought to reduce his acting schedule on *Wichita Town* by having his son carry the story on several episodes. For instance, in the episode "Death Watch," the elder McCrea appears at the beginning and at the end of this story about Charlie Wilks who robs Luke Connors and leaves Connors for dead. Charlie likes a saloon girl who will only run away with him if he is rich. He ends up shooting the girl when she is about to reveal to the deputy that he shot Connors. Charlie flees unrecognized. But when Connors dies from his wounds, Charlie reveals himself as the killer and is shot by Deputy Matheson.

Another way Joel McCrea reduced his screen time on the series was by having the story play out with the supporting characters of the episode in most of the scenes. In "Brothers of the Knife," two men arrive in Wichita from Italy representing the Mafia. They shake down a local watchmaker to initiate a protection racket and collect $10 a month from other Italian-Americans. In a brief scene with Dunbar, the watchmaker's son informs him of what is happening and is subsequently murdered by one of the Mafioso. Most of the episode concerns how the characters react to the "brothers of the knife." In the conclusion, Dunbar finds out about the son's murder and prevents the group of Italian-Americans from carrying out revenge on the Mafioso.

Sponsored by Proctor & Gamble, NBC slotted *Wichita Town* on Wednesday nights at 10:30. After its contract for the series ended, Procter & Gamble did not renew *Wichita Town*, and so the Western ended but not before airing a few back-door pilot episodes.

### "The Ordeal of Otis Stockett"

One back-door pilot on *Wichita Town*, called "The Ordeal of Otis Stockett," starred character actor Gene Evans. Written by Bob Schaffer and Eric Freiwald and airing March 2, 1960, the pilot for the potential series, *The Frontiersman*, featured Evans in the role of a former commandant at a military prison who is now a teacher. To the town council, he proposes being hired for one year to help the current female teacher. The council challenges him to teach a young criminal to read in three days and also balance the town's books to see if there is enough money to pay him. He figures out the town's bookkeeping system, wins over the current school students, and succeeds in teaching the young man to read. The accused criminal divulges where he hid some of the town's money he stole that will help to cover Stockett's salary.

At the conclusion of the pilot, Evans addresses the camera directly explaining that, in dealing with situations, his character first uses knowledge, then his fists, and only as a last resort, a gun. He also describes some future episodes if the pilot had become a series. They included story lines where an empire builder donates his wealth to learn to read and write and where a criminal wants to make sure his money goes to his son's education.

### "The Hanging Judge"

Frank Lovejoy starred as Judge Parker with Suzi Crandall as his wife, Mary, in this March 9, 1960 installment of *Wichita Town*. Set in Fort Smith, Kansas in the 1870s, Judge Parker sought to maintain law and order in this town.

In the pilot, Marshal Dunbar escorts murder suspect Jim Kling (Yale Wexler) to Fort Smith to stand trial. When he arrives, he sees six men hanging from the trees. Judge Parker's only answer for criminals is hanging. The judge's reputation as "the hanging judge" prompts a visit from a U.S. Senator to investigate him.

Neither of these pilots became a series.

## *Johnny Ringo* and Its Back-Door Pilots

Created by Aaron Spelling, this Western, based loosely on the 1950 Gregory Peck film, *The Gunfighter*, portrayed the exploits of a gunslinger-turned-sheriff Johnny Ringo (Don Durant). Ringo's deputy was Cully (Mark Goddard). Ringo's love interest, Laura Thomas (Karen Sharpe) had a father named Case (Terence de Marney) who initially was Ringo's deputy but then became the owner of the general store in Velardi, Arizona.

The series debuted October 1, 1959 on CBS. Ringo had a unique weapon – a seven-shooter gun which surprised those who challenged him. They thought that every gun in the West was a six-shooter, and, after Ringo had fired six shots, his antagonist would think he was out of bullets.

The first show, "The Arrival", was a reworking of the original pilot, "Man Alone" that had aired on *Zane Grey Theatre*. Ringo rides into Velardi wanting to be the new sheriff and give up gun fighting. The town's boss named Taylor (James Coburn), not "Evans" as in the pilot, owns the saloon and several other properties and installed the acting sheriff Case Thomas, a drunkard, after the permanent

*The cast of* Johnny Ringo: *Mark Goddard on the left, Don Durant on the right, and Karen Sharpe in the center.*

sheriff had been killed. When Ringo appoints Case as a regular deputy, Case gives up alcohol and makes Ringo a seven-shooter with a separate barrel for a shotgun shell. The "seven-shooter" was not featured in the *Zane Grey* pilot. Ringo establishes a curfew in town. After a local rancher is killed by one of Taylor's men, Ringo decides to close the saloon and order Taylor and his gang to leave town. When they don't leave, Ringo stands up to them with his new seven-shooter. He fires off six shots. Taylor thinks Johnny is out of bullets, but with the seventh shot, Ringo kills Taylor.

The second episode brought changes to the regular cast. Kid Adonis (Mark Goddard) arrives in town with a traveling carnival show. Billed as the fastest gun in the West, Max (Bruce Gordon), the show's owner, wants a shoot-out between the Kid and Ringo to garner publicity for his show. He has been telling the Kid that Ringo shot the Kid's father. In case the Kid, whose real name is William "Cully" Charles, Jr., fails at beating Ringo to the draw, Max hides a gun in a camera he will use to take photos of the showdown. When Cully learns of this, he draws his gun to shoot the camera. Ringo, thinking Cully is going to shoot him, wounds Cully in the arm. Meanwhile, Case is buying the town's general store thinking he is too old to be a deputy. He resigns and advises Ringo to hire Cully as his new deputy.

For his audition for the role of Cully, Mark Goddard thought he would perform an over the shoulder gun trick he once saw in a movie. As he describes the scene, "The dialogue was going along well when I stood up to do the gun trick. I pulled the gun from the holster, flipping the pistol up over my shoulder. I smugly caught the other actors watching the scene when I suddenly fumbled the catch. Don (Durant) was drinking during the scene and the white, pearl-handled Colt 45 landed on the table, spilling coffee all over the place."[45] Aaron Spelling's then wife Carolyn Jones was watching the audition and pointed out to the producers that Goddard was an actor who would take risks and that they should cast him as Cully.

The writing team of Richard Levinson and William Link did their first teleplay for a Four Star production for an episode of *Johnny Ringo* called "Ghost Coach." The November 12, 1959 installment had Ringo and Cully finding an Army coach with a skeleton in the back in an abandoned mine. Later, Fletcher, a shopkeeper, is murdered and suspicions fall on a man named Nelson. An Army colonel arrives in Valardi to investigate the circumstances behind the "ghost" coach. Subsequently, another man is killed in the town. Ringo questions Nelson about Fletcher's killing. Nelson says that he will be murdered next. He admits that he and the other murdered men were Army deserters who abandoned the coach on their way to deliver a message to an Army company, the members of which were then killed. If the message had been delivered, the company would have avoided its massacre. The three deserters killed the fourth member of their team who didn't want to desert – hence the skeleton found by the coach. Ringo discovers an old photo of the colonel with the deserters. The colonel killed the two men seeking revenge for the murder of his son who was part of the company to which the deserters were to deliver the message. In a shoot-out, Nelson wounds the colonel who returns fire and kills Nelson.

In 1959, Four Star offered Levinson and Link a term contract to write for the company. "We accepted, and for the next two years we had the advantage of working, in our early twenties, at one of the busiest film studios in Hollywood. Our function was to serve as troubleshooters, moving from show to show, sometimes as writers, sometimes as script doctors; and the sound stages, editing rooms, carpenter shops, special effects departments, and scoring stages were open to us."[46] In addition to developing scripts for *Johnny Ringo*, the team also worked on *Black Saddle*, *Richard Diamond*, *Michael Shayne*, and *The June Allyson Show*, and later on other Four Star series like *Burke's Law* and *Honey West*.

Two potential series pilots aired as episodes of *Johnny Ringo*.

### "Border Town"

Ed Nelson played a man simply known as "Kirk" in this pilot from *Johnny Ringo*. Kirk owned the Garden of Eden gambling establishment located on the border of Arizona and New Mexico with the borderline running through the casino. Produced by Aaron Spelling, Joyce Meadows appeared as Julie, a singer at the Garden of Eden, and Matt Dennis was Gabe, the piano player.

The pilot, also written by William Link and Richard Levinson, focused on Al Parker (Paul Carr) who, while robbing Case's general store, shoots and kills him. Ringo and Cully think that Parker is hiding out at the Garden of Eden. Parker's father had loaned Kirk the money to build the bar and casino, and Al is hiding in the back room of the establishment. Kirk doesn't believe that Parker was involved with the crimes. He eventually turns Parker over, but

Ringo can't arrest him since Parker is on the New Mexico side of the saloon. Cully is watching Parker when Kirk distracts him and Parker escapes. Julie, knowing where Parker is, goes to see him with Ringo following her. Seeing Ringo, Parker takes Julie hostage. Kirk arrives and faces down Parker. When Parker tries to shoot Ringo, Ringo returns fire killing him.

### "The Reno Brothers"

Another potential Western created by Aaron Spelling centered on the Reno Brothers, Mike (Ben Cooper) and Chris (James Beck), who are attempting to make up for the misdeeds of their older, train-robbing brothers. Airing March 23, 1960, the brothers arrive in Velardi looking for Carter Scarborough (Jacques Aubuchon), a notorious robber who was in cahoots with the older Reno's and was responsible for the death of the brothers' father. Mike Reno, with black hair, wore a white hat; Chris, with blonde hair, wore a black hat. Scarborough is posing as a writer in Velardi. The two brothers help Ringo track him down, and, in a blazing gunfight, all three kill Scarborough and his men. In the end, Ringo suggests and the brothers agree to become lawmen in southern Arizona. But, since the pilot never became a series, viewers didn't get to see them in that position.

## *Law of the Plainsman* and Its Back-Door Pilot

Harvard-educated, Deputy U. S. Marshal Sam Buckhart (Michael Ansara) served under Marshal Andy Morrison (Dayton Lummis) in the New Mexico territory. He was also Native American, making this spinoff from *The Rifleman* one of the few 1950s Western series with such a lead character.

Although not a Native American himself, Michael Ansara, who was born in Syria, had previously played the role of Cochise in the 1950s Western, *Broken Arrow* on ABC.

Produced by Four Star and Cardiff Productions, *Law of the Plainsman* lasted one season (thirty episodes) on NBC debuting Thursday, October 1, 1959 at 7:30.

Before the title *Law of the Plainsman* was selected, producers bandied about other titles like *Tales of the Plainsman* or simply *The*

*Plainsman.* Laven, Gardner, and Levy, who produced *The Rifleman,* also made this series. In addition to the pilot for the series airing as an episode of *The Rifleman,* the character of Sam Buckhart made a second appearance on that series in June 1959 in an episode, "The Raid," helping Lucas McCain free his son Mark who had been taken hostage by a renegade Apache.

On the first regular episode of the *Law of the Plainsman* called "Prairie Incident," Buckhart comes upon a covered wagon whose driver is dead and whose daughter is cowering in the back of the wagon. The girl named Tess says that a man robbed her father and then shot him. Buckhart takes Tess to Santa Fe where she sees her father's killer and his partner. The Deputy Marshal goes after them, but, in the meantime, the duo visit the boarding house where Tess is staying. She runs back to her father's ranch where the two men follow her as does Buckhart. He engages in a shoot-out, killing the man who murdered her father.

About the series, *Variety* noted that, "When the pilot was done as a 'Rifleman' segment, it stressed the natural theme of prejudice of the white man against an Indian in authority. It was sold to NBC largely on that premise. So what happened? NBC preferred to duck the racial angle and play it deadpan. So the outcome is a wishy-washy, sometimes unbelievable show where the basic premise is studiously ignored."[47]

After being canceled by NBC, ABC brought the series back in reruns during 1962 as a summer replacement for *The Rifleman.*

*Law of the Plainsman* aired one episode as a possible series of its own.

### "Trojan Horse"

The final episode of *Law of the Plainsman* was a pilot starring Gene Nelson and James Westerfield for a comedy-western called *Rambling Man* produced by Levy, Gardner, and Laven. Bob Barbash wrote the pilot script.

A traveling show troupe consisting of Hardy O'Hara (Nelson), a quick draw artist, and his pitchman named Joshua (Westefield) arrive in Santa Fe. Buckhart wants to capture outlaw Frank Seed and his men, who have committed various crimes, but doesn't want to risk the lives of innocent people. He decides to use the show wagon as a "Trojan horse" to capture the outlaws. Hardy O'Hara has Buckhart dress as an Indian chief pretending he is a member of the troupe. They arrive in Del Rio where Seed and his men hang out. However, Seed decides to use the wagon as his own "Trojan horse" to rob a bank while Hardy, Joshua, and Buckhart put on a show. Buckart is able to subdue the man guarding them and goes after Seed with the help of Hardy. They interrupt the robbery with Hardy beating up Seed.

In addition to his acting career, Gene Nelson directed several episodes of various television series including *The Rifleman* and *Burke's Law*.

## *The Westerner*

Brian Keith starred in this half-hour Western that debuted September 30, 1960 on NBC. The series was the most realistic Western ever made by Four Star. Keith played Dave Blassingame, a drifter wandering the Old West. Created by Sam Peckinpah, who by this time, freed from the constraints of working on *The Rifleman*, had been given his own office at Four Star to develop TV projects, this Western was initially called *Winchester*, but Four Star could not get permission from the Winchester Gun Company to use that name. Blassingame's faithful sidekicks on the series were his dog, Brown and his Winchester 405 rifle.

David Levy, head of programming at NBC at the time, and Dick Powell gave Peckinpah creative freedom to develop *The Westerner* as he saw fit. Peckinpah's father's first name was "David," and, as a youth, the director/writer knew a family whose last name was "Blassingame," hence, the name of Brian Keith's character on the series.

*The Westerner* was Four Star's shortest-lived series lasting for only thirteen episodes. NBC had agreed to air the program for thirteen weeks prior to Westinghouse sponsoring a half-hour series at 8:30 pm on Fridays. The idea was that *The Westerner* would have time to develop an audience and maybe by midseason Westinghouse would sponsor it. If not, and the series was a ratings success, the Western could be a replacement for a less successful show. Neither happened, and *The Westerner* disappeared after half a season.

*Brian Keith as Dave Blassingame in* The Westerner.

The initial episode had Blassingame arriving in a Western town to see a woman named Jeff (Diana Millay) whom he has known since her childhood. She is working in a dirty saloon for a gambler/pimp named Denny Lipp (Geoffrey Toone). Dave wants to take her away from this dump, but Lipp has other ideas. Lipp wants to box Blassingame. Dave eventually knocks Lipp unconscious. When he revives, Lipp informs Dave that he can leave with Jeff. However, Jeff decides to stay. The episode was written by Robert Heverly and Sam Peckinpah and directed by Peckinpah.

"Hand on the Gun" was another episode in the series that portrayed a somber picture of the Old West. Written by Bruce Geller and directed by Peckinpah, the installment has Blassingame rounding up wild horses along with Oresquote (Michael Ansara), a Mexican friend. Cal Davis (Ben Cooper), a man from the East, shows up at their campsite demonstrating his twirling skills with a handgun. He tells Dave that he will teach him how to read in exchange for a job with the team of horse wranglers. Blassingame continues to be upset with Cal for constantly playing with his firearm. Davis is looking for a gunfight and begins calling Oresquote a "pepper gut." The Mexican challenges Davis to a showdown. Davis knew how to draw his gun quickly but evidently never took target practice because when he draws his weapon against Oresquote and fires several shots, he misses him entirely. Oresquote doesn't miss, killing Davis.

Some episodes of the series had a lighter tone with the introduction of conman Burgundy Smith played by John Dehner. The Smith character first appears in the third episode where Blassingame meets the conman in a town celebrating the Fourth of July. Dave would like to win the horse race the town is having as part of its celebration; Burgundy wants to buy Dave's dog Brown to use as a lead sled dog. Smith arranges for Dave to lose the horse race so he will need money and have to sell him Brown. Still Blassingame will not part with the dog. Both men get drunk, and Smith has Dave put in jail. The conman attempts to leave town with Brown, but Blassingame retrieves his dog but not before engaging in fisticuffs with Smith. This episode, directed by Sam Peckinpah, was also written by Bruce Geller. Peckinpah and Geller would later resurrect the characters of Dave Blassingame and Burgundy Smith for a pilot episode of *The Dick Powell Show* called "The Losers."

As one of Peckinpah's biographer's points out, "In each episode Blassingame is confronted with a difficult, ambiguous situation that calls for tough decisions without the presence of God or a set of tangible social laws or values to guide him. He must chose who he is, what he stands for, what he can live with and what he can't, and through the decisions he makes he defines himself."[48] This characterization of Blassingame could describe many characters in other Peckinpah projects – both movies and TV shows. See, for instance, the profile of *The Dusters* in Chapter 21.

According to Brian Keith, CBS considered airing *The Westerner* after NBC canceled it. "So much fuss was raised when we went off the air that CBS came running with an offer to put 'The Westerner' back on. We found out they wanted us to stretch it to an hour and put it on at 7:00 at night. That meant that we'd have to cut the realism and make it for kids – in other words, cut everything out of it that made it good."[49] Keith and Peckinpah rejected the offer.

## *Stagecoach West* and Its Back-Door Pilot

Four Star's first one-hour Western series concerned two stagecoach drivers – Luke Perry (Wayne Rogers) and Simon Kane (Robert Bray) who drive a stagecoach for the Timberland Stage Coach Line from Outpost, Missouri to San Francisco, California. Also featured on the series was Richard Eyer as David Kane, Simon's son. The series combined a character (Perry), a loner who had fought for the Confederacy, with a character (Bray), a widower and his young son who had fought on the Union side during the Civil War.

Produced by Four Star and Hilgarde Productions, the Western began on ABC on October 4, 1960 and lasted one season (thirty-eight episodes). The series was up against another Four Star production, *The Tom Ewell Show* on CBS and *Thriller* on NBC. Commenting on the show, star Wayne Rogers said, "We're a Western in name only. Our stories are about people and we build character instead of shooting it out for the sake of violent action. . . . For our classified format we have less violence than the so-called pure westerns. We're getting good stories and have good people to project them under the knowing eye of producer Vincent Fennelly . . ."[50]

When the thirty-minute pilot that aired on *Wanted: Dead or Alive* didn't sell, Four Star recast the lead roles with Wayne Rogers replacing James Best and Robert Bray instead of Sam Buffington as his partner. The premiere of the series related how Kane and Perry got together and how Kane became a widower.

In the "High Lonesome," Kane withdraws $2000 from his bank account in order to repay a debt to Thomas Osgood (Robert F. Simon). Kane had used the money to try to track down his wife who had left him and his son. Osgood hires Les Hardeen (James Best), a gunslinger, to kill Kane and retrieve the paid-in-full promissory note he reluctantly gave him. Kane and his son board the stagecoach driven by Luke Perry to travel west. Hardeen follows the coach and is waiting for the stage when it arrives at a stopover for the night. He tells a woman staying there that he is going to kill someone. The woman turns out to be Kathleen Kane, Simon's estranged wife. She warns Simon of Hardeen's plan. Hardeen challenges Simon to a gunfight, but Kathleen shoots the gunfighter at the same time that he shoots her. Kathleen dies, but Hardeen is just wounded. Luke takes care of him before he has a chance to kill Simon. When Luke informs Simon that he needs a new driver, Kane decides to take the job.

The final episode of the series featured Ruta Lee as Jenny Forbes, a dance hall girl who is trying to escape a gambler named Mingo (Mort Mills) who had hired her as a singer for his saloon but wanted more than just her vocal talents. When she left him, she took money for the back pay she was owed. Because Mingo thinks that Luke took Jenny from him, he orders a grave marker showing the date he plans to kill Luke. Luke finds Jenny a job as a cook at a remote stagecoach stop run by the elderly Zeke (James Burke). Mingo finds where Jenny is and shows up with two gunslingers. He challenges Luke to a duel with knives. Meanwhile, Jenny knocks out one of Mingo's accomplices, and Simon fights with the third man. Luke is able to defeat Mingo in the knife fight.

*Stagecoach West* did air one pilot for a potential series to be titled *Wyoming Mustang*.

## "The Remounts"

Two guys – Clete Henry (James Beck) and Hutch Barnett (Don Burnett) wrangle wild horses to sell to the Army as remounts and to stagecoach lines to pull their coaches. Four scoundrels plot to steal not only a herd of horses intended for the Army but also the money the Army is sending to buy the herd. The four kill the soldiers transporting the money for the purchase and take over a stagecoach depot. When Luke, Simon, and Davey arrive at the depot, the four take them hostage. They need Luke and Simon to help them steal the horses since two of the gang already attempted this and would be recognized by Clete and Hutch. Two of the thieves and murderers hold Davey hostage so that Luke and Simon will cooperate. Arriving at Clete and Hutch's campsite, Luke and Simon start brawling with Clete and Hutch to distract the two gang members who accompanied them. They end up shooting the two bad guys. Luke, Simon, Clete, and Hutch then plot to free Davey. Returning to the stagecoach depot at night, Hutch and Clete act as decoys as Simon and Luke shoot the remaining two horse thieves and free Davey.

In reviewing this unsold, back-door pilot, *Variety* observed: "Burnett is a close cut to James Stewart, easy-going with a faint drawl; Beck is on the serious side and the more dominant of the two. They play off each other well and are easy to take visually. Their acting met all the requirements of script and direction and they don't bruise easily after being belted, buffeted and bounced around with fists and gun butts."[51]

## Other Western Pilots 1957-61

Besides airing several pilots as episodes of its Western series, Four Star developed same stand-alone pilots between 1957 and 1961.

### Indian Scout

Produced in spring 1957, this pilot dealt with the adventures of a scout played by Casey Tibbs and a young boy. Casey Tibbs, a prominent and successful rodeo rider, was probably better at that profession than as an actor. Unlike its many adult Western series, this project was designed for a kids' audience

### The Tall Texan (aka The Tall Man)

Aaron Spelling created a Western series, initially called *The Tall Texan*, about a special investigator for the railroad starring Michael Rennie. In the pilot, that aired July 27, 1958, Rennie as Col. T.J. Allan and his assistant are sent to a small town to capture the notorious Dawson brothers after a train robbery and the murder of an express man.

## The Horse Detective

Set in Denver of the 1890's, this proposed series was to feature three continuing characters. Details of the concept of the project could not be found. At one point, there was discussion of making this an episode of *Dick Powell's Zane Grey Theatre,* but that idea was nixed.

# Chapter 9: More Star Playhouses, 1957-60

## *Alcoa/Goodyear AWARD Theatre* and Its Pilots

In January 1957, David Niven was thinking of starring on his own television show. However, with Niven's feature film commitments, the concept changed to having three rotating hosts for a new Four Star anthology series. In addition to Niven, Charles Boyer and an unnamed female star would host and act on different episodes. The working title for the series was *The Man from Cook's* dealing with international trouble shooters.  By February, Jane Powell was to be the third host with episodes to be filmed in Hollywood, Paris, London, and other locales. The following month the number of stars for the series, now titled *Gulliver's Travels*, went from three to four with the addition of Jack Lemmon. Subsequently, actor Robert Ryan was added as the fifth star, and the idea of filming abroad was abandoned because of the cost.

*Gulliver's Travels* morphed into an anthology called *Alcoa-Goodyear Theatre* produced by Four Star which had been in competition with Screen Gems to make a series to be sponsored on alternating weeks by Alcoa Aluminum and by Goodyear Rubber and Tires. The show premiered September 30, 1957 at 9:30 pm Mondays on NBC with David Niven, Robert Ryan, Jack Lemmon, Jane Powell, and Charles Boyer. Each host would also have an ownership interest in the series to be produced by Dayton Productions, Four Star's subsidiary.

As David Niven stated,

> . . . this sale to Alcoa and Goodyear was about the easiest we've ever made. We didn't have a pilot or even a formal presentation. We just said we were going to make an anthology series, something like the old Four Star Playhouse, with some faces that will be new on TV – Jane Powell, Jack Lemmon and Robert Ryan – as well as a couple of old timers like Charles (Boyer) and me, and they said, "We'll take it," just like that.[52]

Thirty-nine episodes were produced with Robert Ryan and David Niven each starring on nine of the installments. Jack Lemmon was the lead on eight episodes and Jane Powell starred in seven. Charles Boyer was featured in only three episodes with the remaining installments starring Franchot Tone, Barbara Stanwyck, and Lew Ayres.

The first episode featured Robert Ryan in "Silhouette of a Killer." The review in *Variety* stated in part, "Opener was a fairly dull, obvious little so-called suspenser with Ryan as an amnesiac who thinks he's a fugitive killer instead of the prosecuting attorney he really is and Beverly Garland as the girl in whose home he seeks shelter and who falls for him right quick. There was nothing to separate this one from the multitude of 'old look' film dramas inundating television."[53]

After a single season, Four Star stopped producing the series because the sponsors wanted to reduce the amount of money they were paying the production company for each episode. The sponsors also wanted to have Four Star make only half of the number of installments they had done during the 1957-58 season with Screen Gems producing the other half. All of the hosts Four Star had lined up for *The Alcoa-Goodyear Theatre* initially rejected other series commitments hoping that the anthology would be revived by the production company, but that never happened.

Dick Powell did try to sell the series to CBS under the title *Six Star Playhouse* by considering Joan Crawford and then Barbara Stanwyck as part of the roster of hosts, but that network rejected the idea.

The *Alcoa-Goodyear Theatre* continued for another two seasons but without Four Star making any of the episodes. Two Four Star pilots for potential series did air as part of the anthology.

## "Adventures of Johnny Risk"

This episode featured Michael Landon in an early role as Johnny – a young gambling-boat entrepreneur on the frontier of Alaska in 1896. Alan Hale Jr. played his sidekick Sven Swenson. Lew Ayres guest starred as Risk's crooked brother, Jed. Risk's brother conspires with the town's judge, Judge McAfee (Robert Green) and the marshal

(DeForest Kelley) to appropriate mines owned by immigrants because they are not American citizens. Risk is partnered in one of the mines with Sven and sides with the immigrants against his brother. Johnny and Sven steal a claim book as proof of ownership of the mines. The claim jumpers want the book back which leads to a gunfight between them and Johnny's allies. Jed Risk tries to persuade his brother to return the claim ledger which leads Johnny to call into question his brother's lack of moral character. Jed, having a change of heart, decides to defend Johnny. The marshal shoots Jed. Mortally wounded, he reconciles with Johnny before he dies.

Bonnie Bolding appeared as Johnny's girlfriend, Jan Wilson. The unsold pilot was written by Fred Frieberger, directed by Donald McDougall, and produced by Vincent M. Fennelly.

### "Days of November"

In spring 1958, Four Star filmed another pilot for *Battle Flag* expanding its concept beyond solely Civil War stories. The original pilot for the proposed series had aired as an installment of *Zane Grey Theatre* as described in Chapter 7. The new pilot aired as an episode of *Alcoa/Goodyear Playhouse* with Jack Lemmon as a lieutenant, newly arrived from America, leading his men into battle during the Korean War. His men wager that their new lieutenant will be killed in action. From a pool, the men draw numbers indicating the day in November the lieutenant's life will end. If he is killed on that day, the winning serviceman will receive $30. The lieutenant saves the lives of his battalion by shooting what appears to be a woman but turns out to be a sacrificial North Korean loaded to the teeth. The lieutenant survives the thirty days and is given the $30. He buys beer for all his men. The men were somewhat ashamed that they had bet on his fate that had claimed three former lieutenants.

## *The David Niven Show* and Its Pilots

David Niven got his own anthology beginning April 7, 1959 on NBC. The series had an animated opening showing white gloves, a top hat, cane, and pocket watch with Niven then appearing to introduce the episode dressed in a tuxedo and bow tie.

The first installment guest starred Cameron Mitchell as a compulsive gambler whose wife has left him and moved to Reno for a divorce. He visits his wife and asks for a second chance. While she is sleeping, he goes out for cigarettes and predictably begins gambling but winning this time. He wins enough to pay off his gambling debts, leaves the money under his wife's pillow, and departs.

Niven himself acted in only one episode, "The Last Room," airing June 2, 1959. Wearing a beard, the actor played an inquisitor for a totalitarian state interrogating a teacher, Anton Helg (Eduard Franz) who has been arrested for being a member of a church that has been outlawed by the state. Helg is asked to reveal the two church organizers which he refuses to do despite being tortured. The inquisitor is given a Bible that belongs to a mute girl, Ilsa (Susan Oliver), who lives in the same boarding house as he does and whom he befriended. Since torture is not working on Helg, the state begins executing two men each day from Helg's village until he divulges the organizers' names. However, Helg still does not reveal the information. The inquisitor is perplexed as to why the man has not broken. When told that Helg is dying, the inquisitor visits him in his jail cell, apologizes for how he has been treated, asks for forgiveness, and gives him the Bible. The inquisitor then goes to the church, prays, and is arrested.

Before *The David Niven Show* aired, Singer, its sponsor, guaranteed twenty-six weeks of episodes. However, NBC took its time slot away leaving only thirteen episodes to air.

As with other Four Star anthologies, *The David Niven Show* aired pilots for potential series.

### "Maggie Malone"

In this re-working of the Jane Russell pilot, *MacCreedy's Woman*, singer Julie London played the title character, part-owner of a nightclub in Los Angeles with Steve Brodie as Pete Murdock, her partner. Regis Toomey appeared as Andy Cullen, a police sergeant who is friends with Maggie and Pete, in this June 9, 1959 *David Niven Show* episode. The story line concerned a Frank Dennison wanting to purchase Maggie's place to set up a gambling operation. Maggie doesn't want to sell, but Dennison creates problems for her by having a young man, who is underage, unknowingly served drinks at the bar and by having Pete beaten up. Pete goes away for awhile hoping to get information on Dennison that could be used against him. However, Dennison turns up dead obviously ending his efforts to buy the club. Produced by Vincent M. Fennelly, "Maggie Malone" was one of Four Stars more expensive pilots to make because of the music involved. Julie London sang a couple of songs as the story played out.

### "The Vengeance"

Mark Johnson (Dan Duryea), the justice of the peace for a small California town called Aston, deals with crime and other problems in this pilot. Johnson is married to Ruth and has a young son, Skipper. Harry Nichols (Wright King) is his assistant. Johnson learns that a man, George Hilton (Adam Williams), whom he had sentenced to a mental hospital for murdering a family, has escaped and is headed to Aston to kill him. Johnson has his wife and son leave town, and the police are stationed outside his home. However, Hilton is still able to gain entry to the home and finds Johnson's shotgun. A neighbor pounding on Johnson's front door unnerves Hilton causing him to discharge the rifle through the door. This gives Johnson enough time to fight with Hilton, and the police to subdue him.

Written by John Robinson and directed by Donald McDougall, the *Justice of the Peace* pilot aired on June 30, 1959. Commenting on the show, *Variety* wrote, "Whether Dan Duryea as a small-town justice of the peace in a contemporary setting could go well as a series is open to debate . . ."[54]

Apparently, the pilot did not have time to be considered by advertising agencies as a possible series, and so, in 1965, Four Star made another pilot starring Mark Stevens in the lead role for a second try. This pilot also took place in the town of Aston where an attempted bank robbery has taken place with a bank guard killed and one of the would-be robbers wounded. The robbers take over a house in the town whose residents are away. They hold a boy delivering the local paper hostage and want to exchange him for medical supplies for the wounded perpetrator. When the location of the criminals is found, Justice of the Peace Johnson attempts to negotiate with them without success. After they demand a doctor, Johnson decides to pretend to be a physician. He is able to remove the bullet from the injured robber and then uses a smoke grenade hidden in his satchel to allow the police to capture the suspects.

As with the first pilot, this pilot was written by John Robinson and directed by Donald McDougall. This second pilot didn't sell either.

### "Good Deed"

Four Star made another attempt at a television series, *Gentry's People*, about a newspaper reporter working the night beat. Keefe Brasselle starred as Gentry, a reporter and TV show host who wrote a column called "Gentry's People." Jay C. Flippen appeared as Sgt. Charley Nelson, Gentry's confidant on the police force. In this episode, "Good Deed," airing July 7, 1959, Gentry receives a call from ex-con Frank Simms (James Best) asking to meet with him. Simms is wanted for killing a cop. The police say they have arrested Simms, but, as Gentry was leaving his office with Nelson to speak to him, Simms calls Gentry advising him where to meet him and saying he wants to turn himself in. When Gentry goes to the designated meeting place, he finds Simms' wife who had turned him into the authorities before. Simms shows up threatening to kill his wife before surrendering. Gentry subdues Simms as Simms tries to shoot his spouse.

Prior to the Keefe Brasselle pilot, Dick Powell and producer Vincent M. Fennelly planned to star David Janssen as newspaper reporter Gentry in a series to be titled *District 7*. A script, "The Man Who Made No Defense," was written in late 1958 but apparently never filmed. It involved Gentry becoming interested in the trial of George Strand accused of robbery. Gentry finds that Strand's brother-in-law and his lover conspired to frame George for the crime. In the end, the lover throws George's wife through a window; she dies, and George's brother-in-law dies. The lover, the mastermind behind the crime, is jailed.

## *The DuPont Show with June Allyson* and Its Pilots

This anthology, hosted by Dick Powell's wife, premiered on CBS September 21, 1959. The show lasted for two seasons and featured guest appearances by stars such as Ginger Rogers, Harpo Marx, Bette Davis, and David Niven. Four Star produced the anthology in association with Pamric Productions, a company Powell formed with June Allyson.

The premiere outing, "Those We Love" (aka "Ruth and Naomi'), related the story of a wife, whose husband had died, and the wife's mother-in-law. Ruth's mother-in-law Naomi (Ann Harding) invites Ruth to move in with her. After a period of time, Ruth begins dating David (Peter Mark Richman), an attorney, but doesn't want the relationship to become serious. Naomi encourages the relationship. Subsequently, David asks Ruth to marry him. She initially refuses saying she owes a debt to Naomi. David speaks with Naomi about the marriage proposal. Naomi resists his assertion that Ruth is too dependent on her. After he leaves, Naomi says that her deceased son must be allowed to die meaning that both Ruth and she should get on with their lives. Naomi tells Ruth that she needs to love someone who is living. Ruth calls David to resume their relationship.

The fourth installment of the first season featured a joint appearance by June Allyson and Dick Powell as two married people who meet by chance. In "A Summer's Ending," Allyson plays Sharon Foster on vacation at her summer home in Northern California and wanting her husband to spend Labor Day weekend with her, but he is too busy with work. While using a phone booth (what people had to do before cell phones), Sharon runs into lawyer Paul Martin (Powell). Martin invites her to a picnic on the beach. They talk about their lives and, later, he asks her to dinner where they continue to bond. Martin is leaving the next day to fly back to his home in Seattle and wants Sharon to accompany him. He confides that she is the woman that he should have married. She flies with him to Seattle but, on arrival, Paul's son shows up to drive him home, and Sharon's husband phones saying that he misses her. Paul and Sharon end their brief encounter and go back to their respective spouses.

*June Allyson and her husband Dick Powell in a scene from "A Summer's Ending."*

Reflecting on the first season of her series, Allyson said "The show had gotten off to a rocky start, to say the least. We had been doing soap operas, and not very good ones." She pointed out, "I had been promised good clothes and good scripts and, in my opinion, I hadn't been getting either one."[55] One day she walked off the set.

After that, the series got a new producer, a new clothes designer, and better scripts.

The second season brought an episode starring Harpo Marx in a rare dramatic story set at Christmas time. In "Silent Panic" (December 22, 1960), Marx, without his usual wig, horn, and overcoat, played Benson, a deaf mute, who works in a department store window as a mime. While in the window with a crowd facing him, Benson observes a man behind the crowd who is shot and killed. He can't verbally describe to the police the perpetrators but attempts to do so through mime to no avail. After he is released by the police, he sees the killers and runs to hide in a warehouse where he is found by Daniel (Ernest Truex), the night watchman who befriends him. The killers zero in on where they think Benson is hiding. When Benson sees the men, he tries to warn the watchman. Unsuccessful, the murderers hold Daniel hostage while looking for Benson. Benson eventually comes upon a police cruiser and leads the officers to the warehouse where they capture the killers.

In a second season episode, June Allyson teamed with Van Johnson, her co-star in several MGM movies in the 1940s like *Two Girls and a Sailor* and *The Bride Goes Wild.* They played husband and wife, Joe and Louise Robertson. Joe is running for Senate, and Louise likes to speak her own mind despite counseling from Joe's campaign manager. When Joe is asked to support a slum clearance project sponsored by a corrupt mayor in return for the mayor's endorsement, Louise advises him not to do it. Later, thinking her husband will take her advice, she says to a newspaper reporter that Joe will not be supporting the project only to find out later that he did support it. Joe is told to muzzle his wife before Election Day. She takes their son and moves to a cabin. On the day of the election, Joe concedes and informs TV viewers that he would rather maintain his integrity than win an election. He and Louise make up.

A year later in 1961 after her anthology series ended, June Allyson and Van Johnson reportedly considered starring in a half-hour situation comedy together. That project never got off the ground. In 1963, another Four Star comedy, *Byrd's Nest,* written by Harvey Bullock and Ray Allen, was under consideration by Ms. Allyson, but this idea was abandoned without a pilot being made.

*The DuPont Show* also aired pilots in its final season.

## "The Secret Life of James Thurber"

The life and works of writer/cartoonist James Thurber served as the basis for at least two unsold pilots. The first was produced by Screen Gems in 1959 starring Arthur O'Connell in the lead role with Georgann Johnson as his wife. Four Star subsequently made a pilot that aired on March 20, 1961 as an installment of June Allyson's anthology series. This version starred Orson Bean as John Monroe, a magazine cartoonist, who is surrounded by females at home. His wife Ellen played by Sue Randall, his eight-year-old daughter Lydia (Patty McDonald), his dog Josephine, and a temporary maid named Della (Louise Beavers) comprise the females. After repeated interruptions at home by the women in his life, including his sister-in-law (Joan Tompkins), John's boss, Mr. Fitch (Adolphe Menjou) says that John is dominated by women. Monroe decides he can't work at home and so rents a New York office but can't work there either because of interruptions from too many men such as the maintenance man, his sister-in-law's husband Steve (Charles Cooper) who works in the building, and Steve's coworkers. Monroe has lunch with Steve and his buddies, drinks too much, and falls asleep on his office couch. When he returns home, and his family says that they will no longer disturb him while he is busy, John decides to resume working there. Some of Thurber's cartoons were used as bridges between scenes in the unsold pilot.

Eight years later in 1969 producer Sheldon Leonard was successful in selling a pilot to NBC for a comedy based on James Thurber. In *My World and Welcome to It*, William Windom appeared as cartoonist John Monroe. The series lasted for twenty-six episodes.

## "Our Man in Rome"

Another pilot that aired in the final season of *The June Allyson DuPont Show* featured Rossano Brazzi in "Our Man in Rome." Airing March 27, 1961, Brazzi played Count Vittorio, a lawyer in Rome working for an American firm. Philip Roberts (Jack Mullaney), the son of one of the partners in the firm, is sent to Rome to work with Vittorio for one year. Roberts arrives in Rome to handle a $3 million merger. However, the stock certificates he is carrying are stolen. Meanwhile, Vittorio is involved in the case of a man killed by a protection racket for lack of payment. Pepe, a shoe shine boy, witnessed the murder but refuses to divulge the identity of the killer. The other shoe shine boys call him a coward for not revealing the murderer. Pepe finally informs Vittorio who the killer is. Also, with the help of Vittorio, Philips retrieves the missing stock certificates.

The initial title of the potential series was *Gentleman from Rome* and was to be set in New York City. But Four Star ultimately decided to change the location to Rome with the main character making occasional trips to the United States in future episodes. Also, if Brazzi had not been available for the pilot, Fernando Lamas was under consideration for the main role in which case the title would have been *Gentleman from Argentina*.

### "Death of the Temple Bay"

As a precursor to his own anthology series, Lloyd Bridges starred on an installment of June Allyson's anthology on April 3, 1961. Bridges, in a solo performance, played Captain Anderson in an episode titled "The Death of the Temple Bay," written by Christopher Knopf. Anderson is alone on a cargo ship after the crew abandoned the Temple Bay in life boats during a hurricane. While hoping for a rescue, Anderson starts drinking and remembering his version of the events leading up to his current situation. He blames his troubles on the ship's engineer, Mr. Yorty, whom he says turned the crew against him. Fearing for his own life, Anderson admits he slugged Yorty, and Yorty went overboard. Anderson hears on the radio that he is being described as a hero. However, on the ship's radio he attempts to broadcast a message that Yorty was the real hero who tried to save the ship.

## Late Fifties Anthology Projects and Pilots

### *Albert Payson Terhune Anthology (aka Dogs Courageous!)*

In spring 1957, Four Star became interested in developing an anthology series based on the works of Albert Payson Terhune, author of books like *Lad: A Dog* and *Buff: A Collie*. Produced by Michael Kraike, actor Denver Pyle was signed to host the series portraying Terhune. The pilot opened showing a closed book standing upright and then swiveling to show on its flyleaf a photo of Terhune. The figure in the photo made up to look like Terhune comes alive and introduces the story.

Pyle as Terhune intones: "Hello, dog lovers. Tonight's story – JOCK – is about the death-defying devotion of a boy and a dog for each other. . . and how this feeling opens the eyes of their elders to their own shortcomings. Anyone who has ever owned a dog – or wanted to – will, I'm sure, respond to the high emotion and exciting action of this tale. In a moment, then the story of JOCK."[56]

Based on the revised draft script for the pilot by John McGreevey from the story by Albert Payson Terhune, Jock is a dog owned by nine-year-old Ken Welton whose father Don has been away working in Bolivia for the past three and a half years. Ken's mother Amy got the dog for her son to make him less lonely while his father was in South America. The father and son are in the process of becoming reacquainted with each other. One thing Don dislikes about his son is Ken's tendency to tell tall tales especially about what his dad did in Bolivia.

Ken likes to visit the local zoo, particularly the wolf cage, with Jock and knows Monohan, the zookeeper. On a field trip to the zoo with his classmates including his friends Jerry and Spike, Monohan lets Ken unlock the wolf cage. Distracted by the roaring of grizzly bears, Monohan momentarily leaves the cage with Ken still holding the key. Ken's friends relate stories of how their fathers saved their lives. Ken responds by making up a story that Jock saved him from being attacked by a wolf at the zoo. His father had told him previously that, if he made up one more story, his dad would send Jock back to the pound.

Afraid that his father will find out about the tall tale he told Spike and Jerry, Ken decides to go that night to the zoo to unlock the wolf cage and have Jock save him from the wolf so that the story he told becomes true. After unlocking the cage, the wolf escapes, and Jock and the animal fight each other. Zookeepers stop the fight and subdue the wolf. Ken's dad helps bind up the wounds Jock suffered in the fight and says he will never give Jock away. Dad and son begin to reconcile.

### I Love a Mystery

In 1955, ZIV Television made a pilot for an anthology series to be called *I Love a Mystery*, directed by Ida Lupino and starring her husband Howard Duff along with Maria Riva. The pilot never sold reportedly because Screen Gems already had a mystery series in production. However, in December 1957, Dick Powell expressed interest in purchasing the rights to the series, but no Four Star pilot was made.

# Chapter 10:
# Four Star's Male-Centered
# Contemporary Dramas, 1960- 62

The 1960-61 television season was the highpoint for Four Star with twelve series on the networks – *Dante, The Rifleman, Stagecoach West, The Tom Ewell Show, Wanted: Dead or Alive, Peter Loves Mary, The DuPont Show with June Allyson, Zane Grey Theatre, The Detectives, The Law and Mr. Jones, The Westerner,* and *Michael Shayne.* By the end of the season, all of these series had been canceled except for *The Rifleman, The Detectives,* and *The Law and Mr. Jones* which actually had been canceled by ABC but then brought back by the network in April 1962 for a few months.

Production chief Tom McDermott commented that "Sponsors and agencies have lost their guts. They won't gamble on anything but a sure thing, which is no gamble at all." He went on to say, "Nothing changes. You take an old idea and just try to make it better."[57]

In May 1961, Tom McDermott had to announce to the press that things were not as dire at Four Star as they appeared after the demise of so many shows. "Too many people whose interests touch on this industry have been taking our numerical drop at face value without any investigation as to what's been added." Referring to the upcoming 1961-62 TV season, he said further, "We've almost balanced the scale with new or extended series to supplant the loss."[58] "Almost" was the key word in this quote since Four Star premiered only three new series in 1961-62 and had two holdover shows – *The Rifleman* and *The Detectives.*

By the end of the 1960-61 season, Four Star announced that it had bought all the stock in Danny Thomas' production company, Marterto Productions, from Thomas and his wife, Rosemary. This meant that Four Star now had the syndication rights to ninety half hours of *The Danny Thomas Show* (*Make Room for Daddy*) as well as to 146 half-hour episodes of *The Real McCoys* starring Walter Brennan.

The company also purchased an ownership interest in Astrojet which made educational and training films for the military and academe.

The new Four Star dramas that premiered at the beginning of the 1960-61 season included one based on an iconic private eye, one featuring a character Dick Powell had portrayed on *Four Star Playhouse*, one about a lawyer named after the sixteenth President of the United States, and one about a crusading newspaper reporter.

## Michael Shayne

Starring Richard Denning as the main character, this one-hour detective drama premiered on NBC September 30, 1960. Shayne was a sophisticated private detective living in Miami who solved murder cases. Tim Rourke (Jerry Paris) was Shayne's friend, a newspaper reporter, who assisted him with his investigations. Patricia Donahue and then Margie Regan played Shayne's secretary, Lucy Hamilton. Gary Clarke was featured as Lucy's younger brother, Dick. Herb Rudley appeared as Will Gentry, Chief of the Miami Police Department.

Writer Brett Halliday (real name Davis Dresser) created the Michael Shayne character in a series of novels starting in the late 1930s. Lloyd Nolan and then Hugh Beaumont starred as Shayne in a dozen motion pictures made by Twentieth Century Fox and by Producers Releasing Corporation. *The Adventures of Michael Shayne* also aired on radio in the late 1940's produced by Don Sharpe.

Actor Mark Stevens produced and starred in a 1958 TV pilot as Michael Shayne. Titled "Three Men on a Raft," Shayne is hired by Ann Conway, the widow of a man who had died at sea as he was about to come into a large inheritance. Two seamen survived the ordeal, but one, who kept a diary of the days at sea, subsequently dies in the hospital. The diary could prove exactly when Conway died. If he died before his thirtieth birthday, he would inherit nothing. But if he died on or after his birthday, the inheritance would be his or his widow's. Mrs. Conway wants to prove that her husband died after his birthday. Shayne finds that she had the diary stolen from the journalist who was using it for his news articles. He discovers that Conway died before his thirtieth birthday and that his wife conspired with one of the seamen to send her husband on a rickety schooner that ended up sinking before they thought it would.

When Tom McDermott was with Benton and Bowles, he selected Stevens' pilot for airing as part of a series of unsold pilots as a summer replacement for Loretta Young's show. After McDermott came on board at Four Star, he green lighted production of the *Michael Shayne* series.

The premiere of *Michael Shayne*, an episode titled "Dolls Are Deadly," involved several people receiving voodoo dolls warning them of death with one of the recipients being murdered. Shayne becomes involved in the case and unearths a smuggling ring passing diamonds from Cuba to Miami.

Reacting to the premiere, Brett Halliday, the creator of the Michael Shayne character, told reporters: "I don't know why they chose to open with 'Dolls Are Deadly.' I had no say in the matter. I think the opener was dull, drab and uninteresting! I think Richard Denning is a fine Michael Shayne and given half a chance he and the rest of the cast could be terrific. In the opener, they did the best they could considering ..."[59]

The team of William Link and Richard Levinson wrote five scripts for the *Michael Shayne* series. Their first was "Shoot the Works" adapted from the novel by Brett Halliday. Shayne is asked by Lucy to investigate the murder of Harry Wheeler, part owner of Medallion Books along with his partners Ken Russell (Kent Smith) and Brad Harper (Phil Carey). Harry's wife had arrived home early from a trip and found her husband dead. Two airline tickets to France along with packed suitcases were found by the body. Shayne discovers a note indicating that Harry may have been planning to run off with another woman – a book-cover model named Lois Fuller who worked for the publishing firm. Harry's partners reveal that Wheeler had set up a meeting the next day to discuss the merger of the publishing outfit and that a large amount of negotiable bonds being held in the company's safe in preparation for the meeting has disappeared. Shayne tracks down the book-cover model and finds her dead. After learning that Wheeler had an expired passport, Shayne believes that the airline tickets and the note may have been planted to frame Brad Harper for Wheeler's death since Harper was having an affair with the model. The PI finds that Ken Russell, the other partner in the publishing firm, killed Wheeler and took the bonds because he didn't want the company's merger to go through. He also killed Lois Fuller and framed Harper for Wheeler's murder since he sought sole control of the publishing company.

Link and Levinson also scripted the final episode of the series, "Dead Air," about a female ventriloquist, Ginger Dennis (Merry Anders) who hosts a morning kid's show on local television and has a young son. Her production assistant, Pat Marshall (Audrey Dalton), a friend of Lucy's, is in love with Ginger's husband Tom (John Gabriel). Pat brings Lucy to a party Ginger is having for the cast of her show. Away from the guests, Tom informs Ginger that he wants a divorce. Ginger fires Pat, and, as Pat is leaving, she discovers a gun in Ginger's closet. The next day, Pat meets with Michael Shayne about the gun claiming that Ginger is going to use it to kill Tom. Tom informs his wife that he will be moving out of their apartment. When Ginger returns to the apartment, she finds her husband has fallen down their stairs. The coroner says the cause of death is blunt force trauma to the head. Ginger's lawyer advises Shayne and Gentry that Ginger was meeting with him about the divorce at the time of her husband's death. Shayne determines, however, that Ginger is indeed the murderer. She hit her husband on the head after she came home to the apartment and found him unconscious as a result of falling down the stairs. Ginger, upon discussing her pending divorce with her lawyer, was afraid that she would lose custody of her son in the divorce proceedings and so killed her husband.

Reportedly, in the final season of Four Star's *Wanted: Dead or Alive*, Steve McQueen decided that he wanted a first-floor dressing room like Gary Clarke had for *Michael Shayne* instead of one on the second floor that he had been given. According to Clarke, McQueen ". . . mentioned to the studio head that 'Gary's would be perfect.' And he got it. I argued and got nowhere. I talked to McQueen. He said 'No.' I called him something scatological and told him he'd never make it in the business. Wonder if that's why I never worked with him."[60]

Four Star had the misfortune of having NBC schedule *Michael Shayne* against two of its other productions on ABC – *The Detectives* and *The Law and Mr. Jones*. This was really a no-win situation for the company. *Michael Shayne* disappeared after one season.

## *Dante*

San Francisco nightclub owner Willie Dante (Howard Duff) was the focus of this half-hour NBC series that debuted October 3, 1960 on Mondays at 9:30 pm. Stewart Styles (Alan Mowbray) was the maitre d' at the club, and Biff (Tom D'Andrea) was the bartender. While Michael Shayne's relations with the police were typical for a private detective, Dante was more of an anti-hero having problematic relations with the authorities who were always suspicious of him, given his prior reputation operating a gambling casino.

*Dante* was up against comedies on CBS. The star of the show, Howard Duff remarked, "We'll keep hitting hard and dress up our sets with glamor to give the series an attractive look." He went on to say that "we'll have no kids or dogs on the show."[61]

On the premiere, Dante is in the process of opening his club, Dante's Inferno, in San Francisco making it clear that the club will not have a gambling casino. Meanwhile, Stewart Styles is being blackmailed by someone who knows about his past as a conman. Dante gives Styles the money for the blackmailer hoping to learn his/her identity. However, the money has to be delivered by a homing pigeon. Dante tracks down the suspected blackmailer through the license plate of a car that tried to run him over but finds that the female owner is a blackmail victim herself. Through a process of elimination, Dante learns that the woman and Styles recently visited the same dentist. The dentist's nurse, who administered sodium pentothal to patients, was gathering the patients' secrets to use for blackmail.

The second episode of the series, directed by Duff's wife at the time, Ida Lupino, and written by Aaron Spelling, concerned opening night at Dante's Inferno. The police, the press, and the District Attorney are all suspicious that Dante will have gambling on the premises. The syndicate wants to pressure Dante into partnering with them on a gambling concession. They offer him $100,000, but he refuses the money. The syndicate boss threatens to cause problems at the club by, for example, killing one of Dante's important customers. Dante discovers the suspected killer and beats him up as the police arrive to arrest the suspect.

*Dante* was one of the lowest rated shows on NBC up against *Adventures in Paradise* on ABC and CBS' hit *The Andy Griffith Show*.

In November 1961, after *Dante* had been canceled by NBC and Dick Powell premiered his one-hour anthology series, Powell indicated that he would be reviving the Dante character on his new show stating the episode would ". . . also star Peggy Lee, Alan Mowbray and others in the original Dante cast."[62] However, such an episode never came to be.

## *The Law and Mr. Jones*

Abraham Lincoln Jones (James Whitmore), an attorney, fought for the "little man" in cases involving fraud, embezzlement, property crimes, and criminal matters. Conlan Carter appeared as his law clerk C.E. Carruthers, and Marsha Spear (Janet De Gore) played Jones' secretary. Premiering October 7, 1960 on ABC, the half-hour show lasted for a season and a half.

The series was created by Sy Gomberg. Bing Crosby Productions had made a pilot for the drama in 1959 titled *Lincoln Jones* in which the James Whitmore character becomes involved with a man suspected of setting a bomb. When a freight car is blown up, suspicions fall on Timmy Welsh, a professional bomb maker, who is afraid to go to the police. He explains to Jones that he turned down a bomb-making job and then did not know what to do. Welsh's girlfriend, Molly Ferguson, provides Welsh with an alibi for the time of the explosion and also describes a suspicious truck for a produce company that she saw. Based on the name on the side of the truck, Jones goes to a produce warehouse where one of the workers eventually admits to the bombing. Lincoln Jones offers to defend him.

Peggy McKay played Jones' secretary Marsha Spear in the Crosby pilot. When Crosby's rights to the potential series ran out, Tom McDermott bought the property for Four Star to do a revamped version for ABC.

Sy Gomberg described the series as an "adult eastern." By that, he meant that the show "runs the gamut from drama to tragedy to out-and-out comedy. It's about this contemporary New York lawyer named Abraham Lincoln Jones who takes his name seriously. He won't win all his cases (a la Perry Mason), but he'll have a pretty good batting average. He's a composite of the great lawyers in history, and has an innate sense of humor."[63]

On the opener, Jones defends a retired architect whose name and reputation are being used to represent a shoddily-constructed housing project.

Jones often became involved in unusual criminal cases such as in an April 28, 1961 installment, "The Enemy" where he defends Harry Walker (Harry Dean Stanton) accused of killing a man. Jones thinks Walker is mentally disturbed and should be confined to an institution. Due to the DA using inadmissible evidence, Jones' client is acquitted. Jones wants him to be institutionalized, but Walker disappears and ends up shooting another man. Jones tracks Walker down to a cabin he owns. Walker surrenders to him on the condition that the lawyer will defend him on the more recent incident which Jones reluctantly agrees to do. Jones challenges the District Attorney to prove beyond a reasonable doubt that Walker is guilty. The defendant is found guilty this time and confined to a mental facility for life. However, in most episodes of *The Law and Mr. Jones*, violent incidents were downplayed.

Jones also got involved in civil cases like defending a doctor accused of malpractice. Dr. Thomas Bigelow (Vic Morrow) had stopped to help a young man who had injured his arm while changing a tire. Bigelow advised the boy (Joey Walsh) to seek medical attention for his arm after he put it in a sling. The teenager, a future baseball star, didn't see a doctor right away and now his arm has stiffened making it useless for baseball. The boy's father is suing for $100,000, and the doctor has no malpractice insurance. During the trial, the teenager testifies that Bigelow informed him that his arm would be all right and never said to seek medical attention. The jury awards the plaintiff $7000 for medical expenses. However, Bigelow wants to appeal the verdict. The teenager shows up at Jones' office to say that he didn't want to testify that Bigelow had indeed told him to see a doctor after the accident because he had been driving his dad's car without permission and didn't want his father to find out how he hurt his arm.

On a March 17, 1961 installment, "Everybody Versus Timmy Drayton," Dick Powell made a rare dramatic appearance outside of his anthology series playing an austere Marine colonel who wants to take his son Timmy (Billy Hughes) to Japan with him. Colonel Drayton's ex-wife has just died, and the colonel has no admiration for his son's stepfather. He asks Jones to start legal proceedings for custody of Timmy even though the boy wants to stay with his stepdad.

After the series first season, NBC thought about making a new one-hour pilot for the show, but ABC brought *The Law and Mr. Jones* back in April 1962 due to viewer demand. A Long Island newsman began a letter-writing campaign aimed at resurrecting the series that was picked up by press all across the country. According to reports in *Variety*, "One petition from Tarrytown, N.Y., on adding machine tape, was 150 feet long, and had the names of everybody in town on it. There were letters from law schools, a petition gotten together by the mayor of Indianapolis, protests from Bar Associations in Washington, Ohio, N.Y.; from the Police Detective League, the Prosecutors Association of America, ad infinitum."[64] *The Law and Mr. Jones* was apparently the first filmed series canceled by a network to be revived. The series return was scheduled on Thursdays at 9:30 right before ABC's hit *The Untouchables*. It lasted about another six months before disappearing for good.

## *Target: The Corrupters*

Premiering September 29, 1961 on ABC, this sixty-minute drama dealt with investigative reporter and nationally syndicated columnist, Paul Marino (Stephen McNally) and his undercover agent, Jack Flood (Robert Harland) delving into corruption ranging from bookmaking to protection rackets to government wrong doing. Marino wrote a column titled "The Corrupters." Stories were based on the findings of a Senate Committee investigating underworld activities in the United States and the files of Lester Velie, editor of *Reader's Digest*, who had uncovered serious scandals in public

*Peter Falk (center) and Stephen McNally (right) in "The Million Dollar Dump."*

areas. The goal of the series was to show corruption on every level of society and how it affects the average citizen.

The character of Paul Marino was not that active in investigating potential corruption letting most of the foot work up to Flood or simply allowing the other characters in each episode to carry the story line.

On the opener, "The Million Dollar Dump," which guest starred Peter Falk and Walter Matthau, Marino looks into corruption in Yonkers, New York involving trash haulers. His source, a garbage collector named Gallardo, is killed and his body burned by associates of Nick Long (Falk). Gallardo had left Long's "association" which provided protection for a fee to all garbage collectors in the area and defined their routes. Martin Kramer (Matthau) is the intermediary between Long's association and Frank Guido (Robert Middleton), the head of the syndicate. To observe the operations of Long's association, Marino sends in his undercover agent. Nick Long proceeds to increase the garbage collection fees for his customers and increase the assessments to the trash haulers. Nick puts a contract out on Gallardo's son-in-law, also a garbage collector, after he questions Nick about the disappearance of his father-in-law in a public meeting and is suspected of informing Marino. After the son-in-law is badly injured by the attempt on his life, he tells police what happened. When Martin Kramer informs Guido that Long has been acting capriciously, Guido orders Kramer to get rid of him. The contract killer that Nick Long had hired to kill Gallardo's son-in-law is arrested and informs police about Long. As the police go to arrest Nick, a sniper shoots and kills him.

Other episodes dealt with charity rackets, highway construction graft, crooked lobbyists, college basketball scandals, drug trafficking, and judicial bribery. One story that ABC refused to let the producers film was titled "Weed of Destruction," dealing with illicit narcotics traffic in the Far East. Miyoshi Umeki and Andy Williams were scheduled to star in that two-part story.

"To Wear a Badge," the tenth episode in the series was based on a story by Gene Roddenberry who later created *Star Trek*. Marino is invited by Chief Sweeney (Michael Constantine) to do a story on the negative impact of legalized gambling in his city of Verdun after a reporter is killed by Pete Nicholls (Garry Walberg), a casino operator, while investigating gambling in the city. The murder has prompted the formation of a citizens' reform committee and the appointment of Chief Sweeny who does not support the continuation of legalized gambling. Jesse (Royal Dano), the head of the casino operators, asks his lieutenant Jerry Lace (Robert Vaughn) to attempt to corrupt Captain Richard Meeker (Robert Culp), next in line for the chief's position. Meeker is in need of additional money to pay for his brain-damaged son's institutionalization in a private facility. He and his wife currently run a cabinet making business on the side. Unknown to Meeker, Lace gives the cabinet company a large contract and then withholds payment on delivery of the products. Meeker learns from Marino that Lace is behind the contract. He then goes to see him. Lace says that he will resolve the problem with the contract.

Meanwhile, Jack Flood goes undercover to investigate how the casino operators cheat gamblers. Flood is caught in a police raid of Nicholls' establishment and is jailed with Nicholls. Marino advises Chief Sweeney to personally transport Nicholls to a separate holding facility to keep him out of reach of Lace and Jesse. Having co-opted Meeker, Lace succeeds in murdering both Chief Sweeney and Nicholls, making it look like an accident. Marino informs Meeker that Chief of Detectives, Harry Bell (John Kellogg), tipped off Lace about the move of Nicholls. But Bell was not aware that Lace was going to kill the Chief. Meeker meets with Lace who threatens him with the bankruptcy of his cabinet business. Bell shows up. Lace shoots him with Meeker subsequently shooting Lace. Meeker is suspended from the police force. Jesse is indicted over his unlawful manipulation of casino operations.

## Other Four Star Continuing Character Drama Projects and Pilots 1960-62

### The River

Created by Martin Berkeley, this proposed series chronicled the adventures of Hal Hannegan and Mark Latham, a writer-photographer team working for a magazine called *Judgement*. Their assignment was to travel across the United States to document stories about the rivers of the nation and the people who live along them. Hannegan, a writer, had flown for the Air Force in the Korean War; Latham had been a combat Marine photographer in Korea. Sam Whitlock, editor of the *Judgement*, brought the two together. As Berkeley wrote in a presentation for the series: "'The River.' Is it a travelogue, a documentary, a human interest story, an action adventure series? It is all these and much more."[65]

Two scripts were written for the proposed series. One script, "The Night Buyer," finds the photo-journalists in the Cajun bayou for a story involving the fur trade in that area. Hal and Mark observe a conflict between fur trappers and Jules Paray, a foreman who works for the Bayou Fur and Land Company. To work there, the fur trappers must pay half of their catch to the company. Paray is responsible for grading the furs himself and setting the price. However, night buyers will offer to purchase furs at a much better price. Fur traders are harshly punished if they are discovered to have been trading with night buyers. A fur trader has been forced by Paray to provide information which leads to a family of fur traders being caught dealing with a night buyer. A showdown occurs between Paray and members of the family resulting in the death of the family's grandfather. Paray is indicted for murder.

In the second script, Hal and Mark are sent to the central valley area of California near Yuba City to report on flooding of the Feather River. A flood control project has been initiated for the area, but its implementation has been delayed because of a young woman with a severe heart condition who cannot be moved for risk of a fatal heart attack. The woman lives in a release area for a spillway designed to safeguard the locality from annual flood dangers. Some men in the area represent business interests who want the woman to be relocated so that the dam can become operational and investors can consummate a deal to construct a factory in the area. The men, representing the business interests, confront the young woman's family precipitating the woman's fatal heart attack. The script closes with scenes of water being released into the spillway.

Evidently, the scripts never resulted in Four Star making a pilot for this proposed series.

### Sea Rover

As early as October 1960, Four Star was developing a series that took place on a schooner called the "Sea Rover" along the Pacific coast. The schooner was owned by a marine biologist who carries out assignments for the U.S. Navy. Other characters in the planned series initially included the biologist's wife, ten-year-old son, and an assistant. A year passes. The pilot script is redone by Art and Jo Napoleon. The mother character is written out; the characters now are Jim March, the scientist, his son, Tommy, and Jim's assistant Stash. A pilot was shot in late 1961 starring jazz musician Med Flory in the lead role.

Jim and Stash are working on a SONAR project training dolphins for the Navy. Meanwhile, an old salt named Frank Rafferty is looking to find a lost island off the coast of Baja California. Rafferty claims the island has silver and rivers of pearls. Tom helps the old man build a raft to find the island. Jim forces Rafferty to tell Tom that he can't go with him in search of the island. After Rafferty and Tom make a trial run with the raft to see how well it is made, Rafferty sails off alone. At the end, a package arrives for Tom – a shirt he had left on the raft and a pair of pearls.

### Fabulous Stranger

Based on a script by Terry Maples, CBS expressed interest in a thirty-minute religious series about Joseph, son of Jacob. The purported series would have had adventure, intrigue, romance and suspense. By October 1960, Four Star thought of producing this as a special presentation for DuPont. That never came to pass.

### Joe Falco

Writer/producers Leonard Ackerman, John Burrows, and Palmer Thompson proposed a half-hour private eye show called *Joe Falco*. Who would have played the lead role was not determined, but those privy to the details of the pilot script expressed that it was like a hundred other mystery shows.

### Amusement Park

Another project that Tom McDermott thought of developing as a possible series was called *Amusement Park*, an adventure show centering on people and events in a place like Palisades Amusement Park or Disneyland. Discussions about the idea took place in late 1960 with Michael Ansara, the star of *Law of the Plainsman*, considered for the lead as the operator of the park. However, no pilot was produced.

### Caribbean

This 1961 one-hour project starred Rory Calhoun as Tony Dumont, who runs a hotel in the Caribbean and is the proverbial man of mystery, possibly an American secret agent. Written by Richard Alan Simmons, the title of the pilot was "The Astorga Affair." Tony's former girlfriend, Chris Martine, is hiding her boyfriend Ramon Astorga from gangsters in a Caribbean island republic. Dumont agrees to help them escape. Chris and Ramon are supporting some sort of revolution in Puerto Rico. In the process of escaping, Ramon is killed. Chris escapes with Tony who takes her to Puerto Rico.

The series, if it had been made, was to be produced by Four Star in association with Calvic Productions headed by Calhoun and Vic Orsatti.

### Tigrero

Goodson-Todman, known for producing game shows, considered making this Los Angeles-based crime drama about the activities of a bodyguard for hire in 1960. Harry Julian Fink was to produce the pilot with Robert Culp starring as Tigrero —supposedly the name comes from a South American tiger that does not run when chased but stops and attacks its pursuer. Goodson-Todman postponed the project and, in September 1961, Four Star briefly considered filming it as a proposed spinoff from *The Dick Powell Show* but then abandoned the idea.

### Headquarters

In fall 1961, Four Star envisioned developing a series based on a book by Quentin Reynolds titled *Headquarters*. CBS expressed interest in the proposed series if actor Ralph Bellamy had the lead role of a Manhattan police official. By October 1961, the company decided not to pursue this project.

The 1955 book *Headquarters* chronicled the career and responsibilities of Francis D. J. Phillips in charge of the Central Office Bureaus and Squads that worked out of New York City Police Headquarters. Phillips was responsible for the Automobile, Forgery and Pickpocket Squad; the Safe, Loft and Truck Squad; the

Bureau of Criminal Information; the District Attorney's Office Squad; the Narcotic Squad and the Bureau of Special Services and Investigations. Phillips had worked his way up from a cop on the beat to the head of the Central Office. If Four Star had pursued this project, no doubt the series would have dealt with cases handled by each of the entities under Phillips' command.

### International Lawyer

Producer Sheldon Reynolds proposed a one-hour pilot deal with Four Star in November 1961 focusing on the exploits of an international lawyer. Not much is known about the details of this proposal. Presumably, it would have dealt with criminal cases handled by a barrister around the world and not with legal issues of multinational corporations.

### The Adventures of Sam Spade

NBC showed some interest in Four Star producing a series based on the iconic detective Sam Spade. Thought was given to making the pilot, starring Peter Falk, an installment of *The Dick Powell Show*, but by January 1962, the project had been abandoned.

### Patrick Stone

Jeff Davis starred as New York private eye Patrick Stone in this comedy-adventure pilot, written by Sheldon Reynolds and made in January 1962 which eventually aired on July 10, 1965. The story featured Joanna Barnes as Janine D'Arcy who seeks Stone's help to guard her for a week while her ex-husband is scheduled to testify before a grand jury. She fears that what he will reveal may prompt "Big Bill" Tanner (Keenan Wynn) to seek revenge. From the moment Stone agrees to the assignment, danger haunts his and Janine's movements.

### Van Heflin Project

Very late in the 1961-62 TV season, Tom McDermott attempted to persuade actor Van Heflin to star on a one-hour adventure series for the production company. Heflin had made a rare television acting appearance on the second episode of *The Dick Powell Show* on October 3, 1961. In the installment called "Ricochet," the actor played Sergeant Paul Maxon who acquires a guilt complex after one of his recruits is killed by a land mine. Two of the victim's friends take advantage of Maxon's feelings by asking for special privileges and passes. Heflin's appearance on the Powell anthology no doubt prompted discussions with the actor about his own series, but nothing came of this initiative.

### Ivy Towers

In July 1962, Jerry Briskin along with Buzz Kulik and Don Ingalls worked up the idea of a dramatic series about a privately-owned high school. The title, *Ivy Towers*, was the name of the wife of the school's headmaster. Former Mrs. Dick Powell, Joan Blondell, agreed to play the part of one of the principal characters – the school dietician. The pilot, a co-production between Four Star and Kulik's Jeni Productions was to be filmed in September 1962 but was never made.

### Metropolis

This August 1962 Harry Julian Fink proposal for Four Star was a straight one-hour drama about a large city with an all-star cast. Six to eight recurring characters were to be in the series.

As Fink described the project, "I got to thinking about putting all the best things together from 'Naked City,' 'The Defenders,' and 'Eleventh Hour' and other hit shows. I'll call it 'Metropolis,' and in it will be an attorney, a psychiatrist, three social workers and a judge."[66]

Apparently no script was written or cast hired. By March 1963 the project had died.

### Hall of Justice

This Harry Julian Fink/Four Star project dealt with the legal profession. However, evidently this project ended up with Goodson-Todman Productions in 1963 after Harris Katleman, former Four Star executive, became a vice president for Goodson-Todman. That production company thought of making this a two-hour weekly modern-day legal drama for the 1964-65 season. The company contemplated the series would have six or seven major roles, but the plans never came to fruition.

# Chapter 11:
# Four Star's Early Sixties Comedies, 1960-63

Four Star announced an expansion effort into the music field in October 1961 to produce recordings of themes from its TV series as well as to recruit recording artists and issue singles and albums. The company already had two music publishing firms – ASCAP licensee BNP (Boyer, Niven, and Powell) and BMI licensee Trend Music Inc. The plans even included having Dick Powell resume his career as a crooner to make some records.

In the early sixties, the company once more attempted to launch a successful comedy series. But the sitcoms described below lasted for one season only.

### *The Tom Ewell Show*

Tom Potter (Tom Ewell), a real estate agent, had a personal life dominated by women. Originally titled *David's Harem* and then *Women in His Life*, the comedy was created by Madelyn Pugh Martin Davis and Bob Carroll, Jr. – two veteran writers from *I Love Lucy*. The concept for the sitcom was based on Madelyn Davis' father's life living with a family of females. The two comedy writers had tried to launch this comedy before. On August 10, 1951, "Father's Harem" had aired as an episode of *Hollywood Theatre Time*.

In addition to his wife, Fran (Marilyn Erskine), Tom Potter had three daughters – Carol (Cindy Robbins) age fifteen, Debbie (Sherry Alberoni), age eleven, and Sissie (Eileen Chesis), age seven, and his mother-in-law Irene Brady (Mabel Albertson) living with him. Even his dog and parrot were females. The series debuted September 27, 1960 on CBS and was produced by Four Star in conjunction with Ewell-Carroll-Martin Productions.

On the premiere, Tom has to deal with the over-spending habits of the women in his life as he attempts to bring financial stability to the family.

However, several other episodes departed from the central premise of Tom being the only male in a female-dominated household and focused on his work. For instance, in one, Potter goes to night school to learn how to sell insurance on the side. His first client is an elderly couple, the Steckel's, who invite sales people to their home so they have someone with whom to talk. Tom convinces the couple to take out a homeowners' policy. When the Steckel's old house suffers storm damage, he has the repairs done quickly impressing his bosses who want to use him and the Steckel's in a television commercial. But the couple keeps bombarding Potter with claims of their own making against their homeowner's policy. When Tom is told by his bosses to put an end to the claims, he offers to buy the Steckel's house.

In another episode titled "Storm over Shangrala," the Potter family made no appearances. Tom is asked by a developer to purchase a home owned by three elderly ladies to make way for a shopping center. He is so charmed by the women that he finds it difficult to close the deal. But, when the town threatens to condemn the property, Tom works out an arrangement for the house to be moved to a location that the women love.

To promote Four Star series, Dick Powell would occasionally make cameo appearances on certain shows. In a December 6, 1960 installment of *The Tom Ewell Show* titled "Site Unseen," at the request of the mayor, Tom decides to run for city council but first has to come up with a campaign issue. He decides to bring revenue to his town by leasing city-owned land called Bixby Acres to a production company for location shooting. He meets with Dick Powell to have Four Star use the site for filming Westerns. But Four Star decides to film a TV series about the War of 1812 called *The Boys in Blue* which will have plenty of battle scenes and explosions. When Tom learns of the plan, he rejects the idea thinking that it will disrupt the activities of people who use the area for camping, hiking, fishing, and picnicking, and thus his dreams of becoming a politician are ended.

Ratings for *The Tom Ewell Show* were respectable at the beginning of the season but declined over time. In March 1961, Proctor
& Gamble and Quaker Oats, sponsors of the comedy, indicated
that they would be withdrawing their advertising from the show at
the end of the season signaling the demise of the series.

Sherry Alberoni, who played the middle daughter Debbie on the
series, recalls Tom Ewell as being very funny and outgoing on the
set. She went on to remark:

> He was kind and friendly and there were a lot of laughs.
> I had been on *I Love Lucy* and Madelyn Martin Davis &
> Bob Carroll knew me from that and recommended me for
> the part of the middle daughter on *The Tom Ewell Show*.
> They were such great writers and I loved them both ... not
> everyone on a show goes out of their way to be kind and
> interested in others, but they certainly did. They were very
> "hands-on" with the show and were constantly on the set.[67]

Four Star considered another sitcom for Tom Ewell after the
cancelation of his initial comedy. Originally, the new format would
have featured Mr. Ewell as a Southern farmer, but subsequently the
premise changed to Ewell as the owner of a country store. ABC
was interested in the project for awhile, but no pilot was made.

## Peter Loves Mary

Husband and wife entertainers, Peter Lind Hayes and Mary
Healy, played Peter and Mary Lindsey in this situation comedy that
began airing on NBC October 12, 1960 at 10:00 pm, Wednesdays.
Bea Benaderet appeared as Wilma, their maid. The concept of the
comedy was that Peter and Mary, a show-business couple, moved
their family from New York City to a New York suburb called Oak-
dale where the couple and their kids had to adapt to suburban life.
Dick Powell and Walter Mirisch were the driving forces behind
getting the comedy on the air.

About the show's title, Mary Healy declared that "We wanted
to call it 'Peter and Mary,' but there was some feeling that might
cause confusion with another series called 'Pete and Gladys.' Peter

suggested they call it 'Peter Hates Desi." alluding to *I Love Lucy* to which some critics compared *Peter Loves Mary*.[68]

On the premiere, Peter and Mary Lindsey (in an early draft script, their last name was Windgraves), their children – Leslie (Merry Martin) and Steve (Gil Smith), and housekeeper Wilma move to the suburbs. Mary wants to raise their kids outside the city, but Peter isn't excited about the idea. After moving into their new home, the entertainers are offered a job of substituting for the star of a live television show. Mary turns down the idea wanting to have time to put the kids in school. Peter decides to take the job on his own. Peter and Mary also meet their handsome next-door neighbor, a bachelor, who, unlike Peter, knows how to fix things around the house. Peter becomes increasingly jealous of the neighbor spending time with his wife and children. On the live television show, when Peter tenses up thinking about the handsome neighbor, his back goes out. He has to leave the live broadcast in pain. Mary believes that she and the kids will have to move back to the city to please Peter, but, in the end, he decides to remain in the suburbs.

On several episodes, the Peter Lind Hayes' character was apt to become involved in situations not to his liking. For example, he chaired a committee to replace the commuter railroad with a new freeway only to find that the new highway would cut through his property, and then there was the time he erroneously reported that the town's doctor was retiring prompting civic leaders to plan an elaborate celebration before everyone learns that the doctor has no plans to give up his practice.

Some episodes focused on the show business careers of Peter and Mary. For example, on one installment, Peter is asked to appear in a dramatic role in a movie called *The Racket Man*, playing a mobster named Charles Norman. He is reluctant to take the part without Mary also appearing in the film. He requests that Mary be in his screen test to make him feel more comfortable. At the screening of the test, Peter is seen as overacting, but Mary is excellent and receives a part in the motion picture. But, like Peter, she finds that she cannot work without her husband, and so he has a small role as a butler in the movie.

Danny Simon, brother of playwright Neil Simon, wrote the pilot of *Peter Loves Mary* which was produced by Tom McDermott. William Friedberg produced and wrote other episodes. Originally offered to CBS, which turned it down, NBC picked the series up but, for essentially a family comedy, scheduled it at 10:00 pm – an atypical time for a sitcom. When the show didn't do well in the ratings, the network thought of slotting it on Fridays at 8:30 in place of Four Star's *The Westerner*, and then discussed switching *Peter Loves Mary's* time slot with that of *The Tab Hunter Show* on Sundays but neither action ever took place. The series was scheduled to run for thirty-two episodes.

## *Mrs. G Goes to College* (aka *The Gertrude Berg Show*)

After starring as Molly Goldberg in the iconic comedy, *The Goldbergs*, Gertrude Berg returned to television in this weekly series, premiering October 4, 1961. Ms. Berg appeared as Sarah Green, a widow who desires to receive a college degree. Mrs. Green lived in a boarding house with other college students, run by a single lady named Maxfield (Mary Wickes) – "Maxie" for short. Green's adviser at the college was Professor Crayton (Sir Cedric Hardwicke). Berg and Hardwicke had previously starred together in the play, *Majority of One*. The sitcom, a co-production of Four Star and Berg's Jahfa Productions, was initially titled *Mother Is a Freshman* and then *The Freshman*.

Referring to her new role, the actress remarked, "I go under a different name, but Sarah is still Molly Goldberg, I guess. Perhaps a little more worldly, a little better educated, but still Molly."[69]

On the premiere, Sarah Green arrives at college being dropped off by her daughter Susie (Marion Ross). She meets Joe Caldwell (Skip Ward), a freshman student like herself, who is only in college because his parents want him there. Sarah also encounters stuffy Professor Crayton, her faculty adviser, and moves into a boarding house with other students including Caldwell. Her sister phones from Florida wanting her to leave college and remarry; the grad student and his wife who live upstairs in the boarding house mistake Sarah for a nanny. Furthermore, some of the students make fun of her grandmotherly appearance. She lectures Joe about taking

*Gertrude Berg as Sarah Green in* Mrs. G Goes to College.

only easy courses and the value of a real education. Professor Crayton overhears her speech and her desire to leave school because she feels she doesn't fit in. He advises her that she doesn't need to dress like a college student and that all she requires is a thirst for learning. Sarah decides to remain in school, while Joe informs her that he has changed some of his courses.

Some treatments and scripts were written for the series that were never produced. For example, in "The Big Thirst" written by Jim

Frtizell and Everett Greenbaum, the Gertrude Berg character puts together her course schedule and decides to sign up for five elective courses on top of her required ones. She feels she can handle the ambitious schedule but Professor Crayton has his doubts. Inevitably, Mrs. Green is diagnosed with nervous exhaustion and has to remain in bed for three days. Another treatment – "Excelsior!" by Cherney Berg (Gertrude Berg's son) and Howard Merrill involved the school's engineer-custodian asking for advice from Mrs. Green about his college-age son. The custodian, a very practical man, sees his son as an idealist who wants to join the Peace Corps. Mrs. Green and Professor Crayton informally counsel the father and son by pointing out to the son that an idealist has to sometimes think practically while mentioning to the father that he should think of his son as an "engineer of the mind" and that before physical structures can be built someone has to teach people how to build them.

An unproduced script for the series, "The Conference" by Richard Baer was essentially a dialogue between Sarah and the Professor discussing her schedule for the second semester of her freshman year. In the course of the discussion, the two reminisce about their parents. Crayton's father was a tobacconist named Charles Augustus Crayton from Liverpool, England and his mother Portia became involved in charitable organizations. Mrs. G's parents, Abraham and Lena Mitnoff, were born in Russia and immigrated to the United States where Sarah was born. In addition to her sister Dora, Sarah had a brother Leon who was killed in World War I. Her father died when she was four. In Russia he was regarded as a scholar, but in America the only job he could get was as a laborer.

In the middle of the TV season, *Mrs. G Goes to College* moved from Wednesday's to Thursday nights in the hope that ratings would improve. The title of the program changed to *The Gertrude Berg Show* with the character of Sarah Green buying a partnership in the boarding house from Maxie and with Professor Crayton moving into the house. The slight change in format didn't help the ratings, and the series ended after its first season.

If the series hadn't been canceled, Four Star had big plans for special guest stars on future episodes including Dick Powell and his wife June Allyson as well as Charles Boyer playing a French professor. There were also thoughts of having episodes of the comedy as spin-offs for other series such as *The Milton Berle Show*, where Berle would star in a sitcom based on his life as well as *The Esther Williams Show* starring the actress and Olympic swimmer.

In the planned series, Williams would have portrayed Ellen Barnes, a physical education instructor at Porter College.[70] Her responsibilities included training a swimming team. Ellen lived with her brother Bert, who owned a profitable real estate and insurance business, and his wife Sally who frequently arranged dates for Ellen. The Barnes had three kids, eight-year-old Ronnie, fourteen-year-old Penny, and eighteen-year-old Tommy who was in the Air Force.

Ellen's friends included Dr. Frank Cole, a dedicated orthopedic physician; Barry Longstreet, a professor at Porter College who taught Ancient History; and Harriet Wallace, an Associate Home Economics professor and Ellen's best friend.

For her performance on *The Gertrude Berg Show*, Berg was nominated for an Emmy for outstanding performance by a lead actress, and Mary Wickes was nominated for best supporting actress.

## *McKeever and the Colonel* and Its Back-Door Pilots

Gary McKeever (Scott Lane) and his cohorts were seemingly always getting into trouble at the military school he attended. Col. Harvey Blackwell (Allyn Joslyn) ran the school. He was "Mr. Wilson" to McKeever's "Dennis the Menace" character. Others in the cast included Keith Taylor as Tubby and Johnny Eimen as Monk – McKeever's two friends; Jackie Coogan as Sgt. Barnes, the colonel's aide; and Elisabeth Fraser as Mrs. Warner, the head of the school cafeteria.

John Eimen, who played Monk, recalls meeting one of the owners of Four Star – David Niven. "It was sort of awkward for him, I'm sure. I thought he was someone else! He maintained his composure, though, and was quite nice."[71]

Eimen also reflected on his co-stars, remarking that "Scott and I were good friends. I stayed over at his home in Beverly Hills a few times and he stayed at my family's little place in the San Fernando Valley.... Keith ('Tubby') was very talented and very intelligent. We didn't really hang out together but he was a very nice kid. Of the three of us, Keith got the most work following the series." Eimen went on to say, "I really enjoyed working on the Four Star lot – we had a nice little commissary where actors and others from the other shows filmed there would stop for lunch or a little snack. Dean Jones ('Ensign O'Toole'), Johnny Crawford and Chuck Connors ('The Rifleman') and some guest stars (Mickey Rooney, Sammy Davis Jr.) would show up there, among others."[72]

*McKeever and the Colonel* premiered September 23, 1962 on NBC at 6:30 pm. William Friedberg developed the series, but he left Four Star to form a partnership with Nat Hiken to produce *Car 54, Where Are You?* Tom McKnight took over production duties. In talking about the series, McKnight said of *McKeever* that "It has all the elements of a warmly human show with a fresh idea, that of the humorous adventures of a 10-year-old (Scott Lane) at a boys' school commanded by Allyn Joslyn. . . . We have everything going for us except the early Sunday night time slot."[73]

The show was aimed primarily at kid viewers with McKeever and his pals engaging in relatively harmless schemes usually trying to solve some perceived problem. For example, in "Hair Today, Gone Tomorrow," McKeever thinks that Sgt. Barnes is upset because Mrs. Warner doesn't like him anymore. The real reason Barnes is disturbed is because he has not received a raise in his latest contract. He ends up telling the Colonel that he has obtained a better job offer and will be leaving Westfield. When McKeever hears that the sergeant will be departing, he concludes it is because of Mrs. Warner. After seeing a TV commercial about how male hair products make men attractive to women, McKeever, Monk, and Tubby purchase a wig for the sergeant. Meanwhile, the Colonel is convinced that Barnes truly does have another job offer, but the school's board representative wants proof. Barnes impersonates his new employer wearing the wig the kids gave him along with sunglasses and a trench coat and receives his raise.

Originally, Four Star contemplated making the series one hour in length, meaning it would have been one of the first hour-long sitcoms. Excluding the *Lucy-Desi Comedy Hour* which did not air on a weekly basis, the first weekly hour-long sitcom was *Fair Exchange* about an American family and an English family who swap teenage daughters for a year. The series, produced by Desilu, debuted September 21, 1962.

In late 1960, Harvey Bullock and Ray Allen wrote a thirty-minute pilot for *McKeever and the Colonel*. In the development of the series, various characters were added and then dropped. For example, the character of Dorothea Barnstable, the granddaughter of General Wellington for whom the school was named and the current owner of the school, disappeared when the school's name was changed to Westfield Military Academy. Mr. Whitlock, a gentleman farmer whose property bordered the school and who had three young daughters, was also deleted as were a group of other cadets including Harvey Danders, who always appeared sloppily dressed; Brian Carter, a prissy and impeccably dressed cadet; and Roger Meadows, a really smart student.

Subsequently, Max Wilk constructed a one-hour pilot script called "Blackwell the Retread." Given the extended length of the planned show, other characters were added such as Coach Hopper, the athletic director at the establishment; Snuffy Olson, one of McKeever's roommates and the smallest kid in the cadet corps; Doc Jeffers, a produce farmer who owns a farm next to the school and provides the school with fruits and vegetables; Nancy Lewis, the school's nurse in love with Coach Hopper; and Don McKeever, one of Gary McKeever's older teenage brothers who is also a cadet at the school..

Of course, McKeever, the Colonel, Monk, and Tubby were characters in the one-hour pilot. Based on the final draft script dated September 17, 1961, the sixty-minute effort involved Gary McKeever and his cohorts attempting to sneak away from watering horses while the rest of the cadets engage in a battle re-enactment ordered by Colonel Blackwell. McKeever and his pals want to see a movie at the local drive-in and get ice cream at the local stand, but the Colonel catches them. Meanwhile, McKeever's older brother Don and his friends try to meet girls from the local girls' school and are also caught by Blackwell. Later, at a regimental reunion, Blackwell gets the idea from his colleagues of making money in the business world. He finds that Tubby's dad has his own electronics business. McGeever plots to get Blackwell a job with Tubby's father's company. When Tubby's dad offers Blackwell the position of plant manager in charge of solving all of the firm's problems, Blackwell decides to leave the school and take the position. He recommends Major Leonard Beadle as his replacement at Westfield. Predictably, the cadets find that Beadle is tougher on them than Blackwell was, and so McKeever and his buddies scheme to have the Colonel return to the school by sending him a cake and recordings to say how much they miss him. At the same time, Blackwell is quickly overwhelmed with his new responsibilities. He resigns his position and returns to Westfield.

A condensed version of this script aired as the twenty-fifth episode of *McKeever and the Colonel* on April 7, 1963. As with other Four Star series, this comedy also, as described below, aired two episodes that were pilots for possible series.

### "Too Many Sergeants"

*Shape up Sergeant*, initially called *Get with It*, was a planned comedy about a female military sergeant, Ann Gruber, played by Ann B. Davis. The pilot aired as "Too Many Sergeants" in October 1962.

In the episode, when the Colonel doesn't think that his assistant, Sgt. Barnes, is being strict enough with the cadets, he calls in Sgt. Ann Gruber. Gruber inspects the honor guard and finds infractions such as McKeever having a frog under his helmet and Tubby with bubblegum in his rifle. She puts the boys on KP for a week. McKeever thinks that Gruber needs a man to make her more easy-going. He and his friends believe that Sgt. Barnes would be ideal for Sgt. Gruber. They plant candy and flowers in Gruber's room and leave Sgt. Barnes under the impression that Sgt. Gruber stole a photo of him. What they don't know is that Sgt. Gruber already has a boyfriend – weight-lifting Sergeant Swatlaski (Mike Muzurki) who is insanely jealous. When Sgt. Barnes asks Gruber on a date, her boyfriend visits and, thinking that Barnes is trying to take away his girlfriend, he proposes marriage, and they elope to Las Vegas.

### "McKeever Meets Munroe"

This pilot took place at Camp Boone where Augie Gitchy (Guy Marks) and Cpl. Ira Bobbit (Jan Stine) are in charge of a trouble-making dog, Munroe, for the K-9 Corps.

Originally called *The Munroe Story*, this 1963 pilot was based on the final episode of *McKeever and the Colonel* titled "McKeever Meets Munroe" about a dog in the K-9 Corps. Scripted by James Poe and produced and created by Harry Tatelman, *Dobie Gillis* director, Stanley Z. Cherry helmed the pilot.

Munroe has a habit of chasing cats including the colonel's mother-in-law's cat. James Flavin plays the colonel and Verna Felton his mother-in-law. Augie Gitchy decides to teach Munroe a lesson by procuring a lion for him to chase thinking that will break the dog of his cat-chasing habit. However, the lion tamer they go to mistakenly provides them with a man-eating lion instead of the tame one. Gitchy puts Munroe in a building with the lion, and the lion ends up chasing Munroe. While this cures Munroe of his habit of chasing cats, Gitchy still has to return the lion to its owner. He tries to trap the lion in a net, but inevitably Munroe, the colonel, Bobbit, the colonel's secretary Selma (Joan Freeman), and he all become caught in the net. Finally, the lion's owner comes to the base and gives Munroe the scent to track the lion. However, the dog finds the colonel's mother-in-law's cat instead. But eventually the mother-in-law locates the actual lion and gets it back into its cage.

CBS expressed some interest in turning *Munroe* into a series but ultimately passed on it.

## *Ensign O'Toole* and Its Back-Door Pilots

Based on books by author William Lederer – *All the Ships at Sea* and *Ensign O'Toole and Me*, this comedy series premiered right after *McKeever and the Colonel* on Sundays at 7:00 pm beginning September 23, 1962. NBC had originally contemplated scheduling the series at 10:00 pm on Thursdays. Dean Jones played Ensign Terry O'Toole with Jay C. Flippen as Chief Petty Officer Homer Nelson. O'Toole was assigned to the destroyer Appleby whose executive officer was Lt. Cdr. Virgil Stoner portrayed by Jack Albertson. Others in the cast were Jack Mullaney as Lt. Rex St. John, O'Toole's roommate and friend; Harvey Lembeck as Seaman Gabby DiJulio; and Beau Bridges as Seaman Howard Spicer.

Screen Gems had planned to debut *Ensign O'Toole* during the 1959-60 TV season, but their pilot did not sell. Bill Davenport created the Four Star pilot, which was completed in January 1962. The company waited until star Dean Jones was free from appearing in *Under the Yum Yum Tree* before the pilot could be made.

On the first episode, "Operation: Kowana," the Navy destroyer Appleby sails into Kowana harbor where the crew is given forty-eight hours leave. CPO Nelson is looking for a poker game. O'Toole gets him into one at an exclusive club after saying that Nelson is an admiral. During the game, Nelson tries to write a check for a wager. When the other players do not understand what he is doing, he attempts to write an IOU on the back of the check with a drawing of the ship to communicate that he has the $200 for the bet back at his ship. His fellow players think that he is wagering the Appleby. When he loses to Kamague (Moko), the latter believes he has won the Appleby. After Kamague and his friends board the ship, O'Toole gives them a tour. He mentions that the Appleby requires about $500,000 in fuel each year. Realizing how expensive up-keep of the ship will be, Kamague decides to settle for the money Nelson owes him instead of the ship.

Head of Four Star, Dick Powell appeared in an October 14, 1962 episode titled "Operation: Benefit" as Chief Richard E. Powell to sing "The Song of the Marines." The sailors want to raise money so they can provide support for all the children at a Korean orphanage and so hold a benefit. When Richard Powell auditions for the show, he sings poorly prompting O'Toole to comment, "What would a guy like that do, if he weren't in the Navy?" The crew has to perform on the show when the female troupe O'Toole recruited doesn't appear because of bad weather. The Kim Sisters, who work at the school, entertain in place of the troupe and sing "Bye Bye Blues" and "When the Saints Go Marching In."

O'Toole was adept at speaking various foreign languages as well as figuring out solutions to problems created by the seamen or senior officers. For example, in "Operation: Jinx" featuring a guest appearance by Soupy Sales as Jerome "Jinx" Johnson, minor disasters happen all over the ship anytime Johnson appears. O'Toole tries to convince the crew that the accidents are their fault because they become nervous around Johnson. The Commander orders Johnson off the ship, but O'Toole secretly keeps him on while St. John poses as Johnson leaving the vessel. The crew unloads a shipment of rocket fuel with Johnson's help and with no mishaps.

NBC failed to renew the series after its initial season. However, ABC began airing reruns of the show during spring and summer 1964 on Thursday evenings. The initial ratings for the repeats were encouraging, and ABC contemplated having Four Star produce new episodes of the comedy. But ratings declined over the run meaning the series was not resurrected. In any event, ABC had another sitcom waiting in the wings for Thursday nights – *Bewitched*, which became one of the network's biggest hits.

*Ensign O'Toole* aired two episodes as back-door pilots.

### "Operation: Potomac"

A December 9, 1962 episode, "Operation: Potomac," was briefly considered by Four Star as a pilot for a new series titled *The Admiral's Daughter*. In the episode, Carolyn Kearny played a female Ensign O'Toole – Tina O'Toole. The Dean Jones character searches the Pentagon for her after he begins receiving a number of gifts such as a box of roses and a cocktail dress from a secret admirer. He eventually bumps into her in an elevator. After the two have a romantic dinner, they try to determine who is sending the gifts. Later, Tina's father calls and explains that he sent the presents to celebrate her promotion to an ensign. But Tina doesn't want to tell O'Toole this so she can continue to see him. When her father stops by Tina's apartment, Terry O'Toole admits that he had already discovered that Tina's dad was the source of the gifts.

On the episode, Tina O'Toole's father was a Chief Petty Officer – not an admiral. If the premise had been developed further, presumably the dad's rank would have been changed to admiral. However, both Four Star and NBC decided not to pursue this possible spin-off.

## "Operation: Geisha"

In June 1962, Four Star assigned writers Ben Starr and Bob O'Brien to develop a situation comedy suggested by movie producer Steve Parker, who had made the motion picture *My Geisha* starring his then wife Shirley MacLaine. The initial idea of the comedy concerned two Hollywood producers and their exploits in Japan. However, by July 1962, the concept changed to two ex-soldiers who had been stationed in Japan after the war, fell in love with the country, and returned as conmen. The proposed series would not only deal with the two men's adjustment to Japanese customs but also with the citizens of Japan desiring to adapt American mores, clothes, and sports.

The pilot for a projected series, *Go East, Young Man* (aka *Two Guys from Tokyo*) aired as the May 5, 1963 episode of *Ensign O'Toole* starring comedian Jack Carter. Set in Tokyo, Lt. St. John's friend Steve Turner (Carter) is about to be deported back to America unless he comes up with $1300 that he owes Mr. Yamada, the victim of his latest get-rich-quick scheme. To raise the money, Turner comes up with the idea of establishing geisha houses for women. Turner is dating Judy (Linda Bennett), the daughter of the U.S. ambassador to Japan. Knowing that Ambassador Cobb (Ransom Sherman) will be away for a few days, he and his partner Al Shrieber (Eddie Ryder) use the ambassador's home for their geisha house. They entertain the women with food and song and give them advice to be less obedient to their husbands which raises the ire of the men in Tokyo. For this scheme, Ambassador Cobb is about ready to deport Turner and Shrieber when Ensign O'Toole steps in as a potential bidder for a franchise of geisha houses for women. To avoid this, Mr. Yamada decides to forgive the money Turner owes him in exchange for stopping the proliferation of the geisha houses.

# Proposed Early Sixties Comedy Projects and Pilots

## The Office

In August 1961, Tom McDermott and Bill Friedberg contemplated a thirty-minute comedy starring Paul Ford as the owner of a mail order business in the Midwest. Ford's character would be an old-fashioned, conventional boss who considers his employees like members of the family. A young, Harvard Business School-type joins the firm and wants to use modern methods in the business. Employees are forced to take sides.

The original idea for this potential series began in 1959 with a script written by Bill Friedberg and Neil Simon called *Mr. Webster*. Webster was a very conservative boss who co-owned a shoe factory in New Haven, Connecticut with his more liberal sister Sonia. Laurie Marshal was Webster's secretary; Oscar Oppenheim, the head bookkeeper; Minnie Whitman, the assistant bookkeeper; Jess Proctor, the sales manager; and Spencer Gribble, everyone's assistant.

The office staff wants Webster to install air-conditioning which he resists doing. Sonia Webster suggests to the staff that Dr. Paul Franklyn, an industrial analyst, be brought in to evaluate the company's management. Franklyn has his staff masquerade as telephone repairmen, electricians, and window washers in order to get a realistic evaluation of Mr. Webster and the shoe company. From his staff's report, Franklyn determines that Webster is a very lonely man and needs female companionship. Sonia has her brother call an old girlfriend for a date. To prepare for the date, Webster dances with Minnie Whitman. The next day, he can't stop talking about how much fun he had dancing. When his old girlfriend cancels the date, Webster takes Minnie out on a date and gives her an electric fan to use in the office.

The concept for the series evolved. In November 1961, Friedberg and David Shaw outlined a revised initial story line for the pilot. In the new outline, Webster has a son named Whitlow who just graduated from Harvard Business School and plans to join his father in the family business which now is the Webster Mail-Order Company specializing in antiquated items like music rolls for player pianos. Minnie Watkins is the company's long-time cashier; Sally Chapman is Webster's secretary; and a young married couple, Coleman Firmery and Jennifer Hill also work at the firm but have to keep their marriage a secret because of Webster's policy of no fraternization among employees. The elder Webster wants his son to begin working in the mailroom like he had done. However, when his father learns that Whitlock had lunch with Sally Chapman, he is fired for violating the no fraternization policy. The firm's staff convinces Whitlock to evaluate the company from the outside using his training as an industrial analyst. Like Dr. Franklyn in the initial pilot concept, Whitlock sends in undercover analysts to determine his father's reasons for desperately clinging to the past. The reason for his father's behavior is the same as in the earlier concept. Vaughn Webster ends up dating Minnie Watkins. Minnie says she would love to go out with him, but she points to the company's no fraternization policy which Webster repeals on the spot. Minnie and Webster go to a restaurant and see Sally and Whitlock at the next table. Webster leans over to his son and rehires him.

Despite all the work on script development, no pilot was ever filmed.

### The Eddie Hodges Show

Neil Simon wrote a script for a comedy pilot featuring teenager Eddie Hodges that was filmed in fall 1960 to be ready as a midseason replacement during the 1960-61 TV season. Hodges played the young son of a widowed father.

### The Shrimp

Four Star entered the field of animated comedy with this co-production with Format Films for a thirty-minute family comedy based on magazine articles by Sy Gomberg. The project began in October 1960, and, at one point, both CBS and NBC considered the series for the 1961-62 season. The characters on *The Shrimp* were to be voiced by Shep Menken, June Foray, and Kathleen Freeman. The pilot was to be produced by Herbert Klynn; Leo Salkin was the story editor.

A script based on Sy Gomberg's writings was done for CBS. It dealt with a boy named Joel and his younger brother Marv, known as the "shrimp." The "shrimp" follows Joel around and rarely speaks. Joel's family lives in a lower-middle class apartment building. His mom wants Joel to go to the butcher's to pick up some ground beef, but he would rather go sled riding. When Joel's friend Frankie asks him to bet on a sled race, Joel tries to shortchange the butcher by a dime so he has money to wager. Meanwhile, Joel pretends to play a game with the "shrimp" by having his young brother stand in place while he and Frankie go to the sled races. After Joel wins the race, he looks for the "shrimp" and finds him frozen standing where he left him. The "shrimp" recovers and wants Joel to give him the dime he won at the sled races.

## The Jimmy Durante Show

This 1961 pilot featured veteran entertainer Jimmy Durante along with Eddie Hodges and Audrey Christie in a comedy about a grandfather (Durante) who, with his younger sister Rose, has to raise his thirteen-year-old grandson, Eddie after the death of the boy's parents.

The pilot, written by Billy Friedberg, Mel Diamond, and Mel Tolkin, involved Eddie just graduating from the eighth grade. Jimmy gives him a contract to co-star with him in a TV spectacular, while Aunt Rose gifts Eddie with a chemistry set. She is against him performing and wants him to consider attending prep school. He is more interested in science than in show business. Rose and Eddie meet with a representative from the school played by John McIntyre who counsels Eddie that he needs to study for the entrance exam. Meanwhile, Jimmy auditions young talent to take Eddie's place. Eddie hears the auditions and decides to do the spectacular while also trying to study. Rose thinks that Eddie is taking on too much. He begins missing his study time and wants to postpone for one year his exam. The prep school representative talks with Jimmy who comes to realize that show business may prevent Eddie from achieving his dream of being a scientist. Jimmy insists that Eddie study for the test and not be on television. Jimmy closes the unsold pilot by singing "Young at Heart."

## The Jane Powell Show

In mid-February, 1961, Jane Powell made a pilot for her own self-titled sitcom written by Michael Morris and Max Wilk from a story by Tom and Frank Waldman and directed by Rod Amateau. Powell played a singer/actress somewhat like her movie star image in the pilot titled "Short Course in Marriage." The actress appears as K. C. McKay, who falls in love with a math professor named Jeffrey Edwards (Russell Johnson, later the Professor on *Gilligan's Island*). Jeffrey, who drives a Duisenberg, had met K.C. at a TV studio while she was rehearsing for a show and he was appearing on an educational program. They know each other for only one weekend before deciding to marry. After the ceremony, the happy couple moves to a remodeled carriage house near Redwood College in California where K.C. becomes acquainted with Jeffrey's colleague and former housemate, Professor Holly Harrigan (Al Checco).

K.C. meets the faculty of her new husband's college at a reception given by Dean Grover and his wife played by Harriett MacGibbon. After singing "My Beloved" for the crowd, some of the faculty engages in a discussion about what motivates entertainers presuming that performers are all exhibitionists. When Jeffrey agrees with them, K.C. becomes irritated and makes him sleep on the couch. Compounding the marital difficulties, K.C. kills Agnes, Jeffrey's queen bee, when it tries to sting her.

The next day, K.C.'s agent Leslie (Elliott Reid) phones about resuming her show business career, but she reluctantly declines. Mrs. Grover stops by and says that K.C. should have spoken up during the faculty discussion about entertainers. After Jeffrey realizes that he should have supported his wife at the get together, he brings her flowers, and she buys a new queen bee for him. Naturally, they make up.

Four Star Television produced the pilot in association with Powell's company, Etoile Productions for the 1961-62 season. Pepsi-Cola planned to sponsor *The Jane Powell Show*, which was initially shopped to NBC and then to CBS. Both networks passed on the series apparently thinking it was too sophisticated for an early time slot and no later time period could be found.

### Flashback

Bill Friedberg came up with the idea of a comedy series starring a man and a woman, each between ages fifty and sixty, who look back on their married lives together. Each episode would show their lives at different times with other actors portraying their children, friends, relatives and associates. Guest stars as well as newsreels, radio transcriptions, and TV kinescopes would be used. Flashbacks would be from the time of World War I to the present. However, no pilot was made, and the concept was dropped by April 1962.

### Low Man on the Totem Pole

Starring Dan Dailey, this half-hour comedy pilot was produced in January 1962 based on the writings and life of H. Allen Smith. Dailey played Smith, and Diana Lynn appeared as his wife Nelle in the proposed series about a writer living in Greenwich Village who struggles to get his works published. Bill Manhoff wrote the original pilot with E. J. Russell scribing the one that was produced. Tom McDermott at Four Star made a co-production deal with Collier Young and John Newland to produce the series with the latter directing.

The pilot finally aired on August 8, 1964. The story line involved the Dailey character first tangling with the neighbor's cat that is after the Japanese radish he planted in his tiny garden. Next Smith butts heads with his publisher, Mr. Turnbull (John McGiver), who is threatening to fire him because a particular Senator objects to being the focus of one of Smith's columns. Throughout, Nelle tries to keep her husband on a steady course distracted temporarily by an encounter with a Mexican prize fighter and his large showgirl wife.

### Lum and Abner

Based on the radio show of the same name, veteran actors Edgar Buchanan and Arthur Hunnicut were featured in this January 1962 pilot written by Palmer Thompson and directed by Hy Averback. The pilot was made for NBC which passed on making it a series.

Lum (Hunnicut) and Abner (Buchanan) own a store in Arkansas called the "Jot'em Down General Store." Lum wants to modernize the establishment, but Abner is against it. Lum hires Steve Parker (Frank Aletter), an efficiency expert, to review the store's operations. Among his suggestions is that the owners remove "Old Betsy," a wood stove in the middle of the establishment. The wood stove is taken out much to the disappointment of Grandpappy Spears (Andy Clyde) who starts avoiding the store. Parker also wants Lum and Abner to collect outstanding bills from customers who owe money. But Lum is a soft touch and can't bring himself to collect the past due amounts. Parker decides that the situation is a lost cause and leaves town. Lum and Abner return the store to its original state.

## Joe and Josie

Joe played by comic Mort Sahl was a cab driver; his wife Josie (Cloris Leachman) operated a beauty parlor. They had two kids portrayed by Trudi Ziskind and Butch Patrick and lived with their uncle (veteran comedian Bert Wheeler) in the suburbs. So was the concept of this thirty-minute comedy created by Garson Kanin. The unsold pilot, made in early 1962, was for ABC.

## Apartment in Rome

Alan Case and Susan Oliver starred on this comedy series attempt as a twenty-eight-year old husband and twenty-two-year old wife from Ohio living in Rome. Steve Adams, the Case character, is an artist. He and his spouse try to survive on his earnings. His wife, Debbie, is from a wealthy Connecticut family.

Created by Sol Saks, the pilot was shot in January 1962 but not aired until August 22, 1964. Saks described the show as a sophisticated *My Favorite Husband* set against the background of the Eternal City. In the pilot, the wife's aunt visits as Debbie and Steve attempt to keep their Bohemian lifestyle a secret from her.

## Parke Levy Projects

Writer Parke Levy, the man behind the TV comedies *December Bride* and *Pete and Gladys*, left his partnership with CBS in August 1962 to join Four Star in developing situations comedies. While at Four Star, he came up with the idea for a family comedy for CBS called *My Daughter's Guys* with George Gobel as one of the actors under consideration for the lead. By November 1962, Four Star became interested in possibly producing a pilot based on a script written by Dick Conway and Roland MacLaine, but no pilot ever resulted.

Levy also developed a proposal for another comedy titled *Mr. Tooley's Mondays*. What it was about is unknown. The proposal may have been an early incarnation of Levy's next comedy series, *Many Happy Returns*, which he developed for MGM-TV after leaving Four Star in May 1963. *Many Happy Returns,* a male-version of Levy's successful *December Bride,* was initially titled *December Groom.* The series concerned a father who lives with his daughter and son-in-law and runs the returns department in a large store.

### *All about Amanda*

Writers Everett Greenbaum and Jim Fritzell along with director Hy Averback developed a thirty-minute comedy to be made by Four Star. Advertisers were interested in the project if Eve Arden would play Amanda. But the project was tabled because of the inability to find a leading lady.

# Chapter 12:
# The Final Star Anthologies, 1960-63

The president of Four Star and one of its founding members, Dick Powell passed away on January 2, 1963. He died from cancer at age fifty-eight. After appearing on television for over ten years, *The Dick Powell Show* would be his final series. Commenting on the company's response to her husband's death, June Allyson wrote in her autobiography:

> Four Star was trying to fill the void left by Richard's death and was holding business meetings, which I attended. I insisted that Aaron Spelling be given the reins of Four Star after Richard died – not just because he was a friend but because he was so talented. I felt the current management would let the studio run downhill but that Aaron, with his fresh ideas, could save it and keep it growing. I was voted down and what I predicted happened.[74]

Instead of Aaron Spelling, Tom McDermott became the president of the company.

## *The Dick Powell Show* and Its Pilots

Dick Powell once said, referring to anthologies, that "There's no reason why every episode can't be a potential pilot – the characters and situation are there."[75] The head of Four Star also commented that he ". . . would never gamble on an hourlong pilot, without a network association, or as a spinoff."[76] Taking into account that only 10 to 12% of pilots sell, he thought the risk was too great to make a pilot without network backing or airing it as a series episode.

Powell thought of his self-titled anthology as a "new experiment in television." He went on to say, "I've been able to sign the best writers and actors in the business because I'm not following the greed principle of the other producers. The actors are coming into my fold because I'm offering them all rights outside the United

States to the shows in which they appear for me. I'm giving the writers every financial break."[77]

Each episode of the anthology opened with photographs of scenes from the upcoming story. Doors would then open to a bare soundstage with Powell entering. Surrounded by camera equipment, he would briefly introduce that week's episode.

As described below, the first episode of *The Dick Powell Show* turned out to be a pilot for *Burke's Law* starring Powell in the role that would be played by Gene Barry in the series. Powell's final series as host and occasional star began September 26, 1961 on NBC.

On a first season episode, "A Time to Die," written by Aaron Spelling and directed by Marc Daniels, the entire Powell family appeared. Powell himself played Steve Burton, a mob boss, who is seriously injured in an auto accident and is near death. Two gentlemen that only Burton can see, played by Edgar Bergen and Ernest Truex, appear in his hospital room. They inform him that he is between heaven and hell and will die soon. The two men decide to give him a chance to escape death if he can find someone to die in his place. They give him a list of three candidates that he cannot let die for three more days. Burton's spirit arises from his bed so he can visit each person.

Leslie Clark (Tuesday Weld), a young woman in love with singer Mike Nelson (Andy Williams), wants to commit suicide since she is depressed that Nelson won't leave his wife to marry her. Burton saves her by turning off the gas in her apartment when he arrives. Pam Powell, Dick's daughter, has a small role as a teen seeking Nelson's autograph.

Next, Burton visits Christopher Stevens played by Powell's son Ricky who is suffering from a bad heart condition. His mother (June Allyson) refuses to allow him to have risky surgery because she is concerned that it may kill him.

Finally, Burton visits Nick Giller (John Saxon), a man who is afraid that he may be killed because he is trying to take over a mob-related business and become the next Steve Burton.

Steve persuades Mike Nelson to convince Leslie that he really has no intention of ever leaving his wife and to break off the relationship. Burton then flies in a top surgeon from the Mayo Clinic to operate on Christopher. He plans to visit Giller thinking that he would be the best candidate to die in Burton's place. However, upon arriving at Giller's apartment, he finds that Giller is already dead. Not wanting Chris to die, Burton decides to die himself. For his final altruistic act, he goes to Heaven.

This episode foreshadowed certain Aaron Spelling's series like *The Love Boat* and *Fantasy Island* by linking three different stories together with an underlying theme.

The first season of the anthology featured an Emmy-winning performance by Peter Falk in an episode, "The Price of Tomatoes." Falk played a Greek truck driver racing to deliver a load of fresh tomatoes ahead of a rival, but his delivery is slowed when he decides to pick up a pregnant and broke hitchhiker played by Inger Stevens.

*The Dick Powell Show* was renewed for a second season on NBC. Powell's last appearance as an actor on the anthology was on a December 11, 1962 episode titled "The Court Martial of Captain Wycliff" about John Wycliff (Robert Webber) accused of killing nuclear physicist Joseph Closter (Martin Brandt) who was leaving the United States for Communist Eastern Europe. Nicknamed the "atomic traitor," Closter was believed to possess secrets about nuclear weapons that he would share with the Communists. Major Ed Clayborn (Powell) prosecutes Wycliff for murder in the court martial; while Major George Torsett (Ed Begley) defends the captain. A witness testifies that Wycliff admitted to him that he had killed the scientist. Another witness for the prosecution states that, during World War II, the captain was trained as a military assassin; while a third person testifies that he saw the captain shoot Closter. The defense introduces Clayborn's married sister, Eve Emerson (Dina Merrill), who says that she was having an affair with Wycliff the night that Closter was killed, but on cross examination, her brother casts doubt on her testimony. When Wycliff takes the stand, he states he did not murder Closter. On cross examination, Clayborn points out that Closter's knowledge of nuclear science was ten years old and that the person who killed the scientist was really a coward. Wycliff finally admits that he executed Closter.

While David Niven did not make any dramatic appearances on episodes of Dick Powell's new anthology series, Powell's other partner in Four Star did. Charles Boyer starred in two episodes of the show. One aired February 6, 1962 with Theodore Bikel, titled "The Prison," about Andreas (Boyer) incarcerated in an island prison guarded by Captain Bellini (Bikel) who insists on following the rules and resists friendly overtures from Andreas raising the question who is really the prisoner. Boyer's second appearance was in November of that year playing Carlos Morell, a deposed Latin American dictator in "Days of Glory," who is returned to power by an ambitious colonel (Lloyd Bochner) and then finds his life in danger when he gets democratic ideas.

After Dick Powell's passing, the title of the show was changed to *The Dick Powell Theatre* and guest stars like David Niven and June Allyson filmed the introductions and endings for each episode. Even after Mr. Powell's death, there was interest on behalf of NBC to do a variation of *The Dick Powell Show* for the 1963-64 season. However, as described in *Variety*, one of the major problems was that Powell ". . . lent far more than his name and face to the hour. He was 'an integral part of the machinery' . . . Powell pampered the show and that it'd be hard to guarantee this same kind of care (in the future.)"[78] Four Star and the William Morris Agency pitched a new anthology hour to NBC hosted by Glenn Ford. The network did schedule another anthology series on Tuesdays for 1963-64 – *The Richard Boone Show*, which was produced by Goodson-Todman – not Four Star.

Several episodes of *The Dick Powell Show*, particularly during its second season, were pilots for potential series.

### "Who Killed Julie Greer?"

The opening episode of *The Dick Powell Show* titled "Who Killed Julie Greer?" turned out to be the pilot film for *Burke's Law*. Written by Frank Gilroy and directed by Roger Ellis Miller, Powell played detective Amos Burke, a fabulously wealthy playboy who is also a member of the Los Angeles Police Department. While he inherited his wealth and was chauffeured around in a Rolls Royce, Burke had started his police career walking a beat and worked his way up through the ranks to become inspector in charge of the Homicide Division. Gilroy's script described Amos Burke as "fifty, good

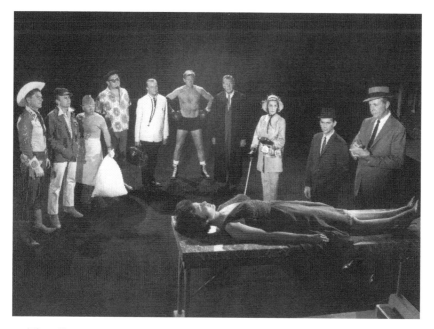

*The all-star cast from "Who Killed Julie Greer?" – Ronald Reagan, Nick Adams, Mickey Rooney, Jack Carson, Edgar Bergen, Lloyd Bridges, Ralph Bellamy, Kay Thompson, Dean Jones, Dick Powell and Carolyn Jones.*

looking, urbane, authoritative, witty, self-contained."[79] Ed Platt portrayed Joe Nolan, one of the detectives under Burke; Dean Jones played Philip Winslow, another detective who had been with Burke for only six months.

Burke investigates the murder of Julie Greer (Carolyn Jones), a model who had dated a lot of men and usually dumped a man after a few months. She was strangled by an unknown assailant. Using Julie's address book, Burke and Winslow interview the different men Julie had dated. In what would be a hallmark of the *Burke's Law* series, several well-known actors played the murder suspects. Ronald Reagan appeared as Rex Kent, a cowboy TV star. Ralph Bellamy was a married judge who had a brief affair with Julie. Other star suspects included Lloyd Bridges as Joe Montana, a boxer; Mickey Rooney as Mike Zampini, who runs a laundry and whom Julie dropped after buying a washer; Jack Carson as Fairchild, a hip bartender, and Edgar Bergen as Dr. Coombs, a veterinarian to whom Julie was talking on the phone when she was murdered. He remembers her yelling the name George Townsend as she was being strangled. Townsend was one suspect the police could not locate. When Burke went to his address, Mrs. Peirce (Kay Thompson), his landlady, said he no longer lived there and that she couldn't describe him since she is blind. A man named George Townsend (Nick Adams) gives himself up to the police but claims he is not the person for whom they are looking. Mrs. Peirce comes to Townsend's apartment to see if she can recognize his voice in a line-up that includes detectives. However, the voice she says she recognizes is that of Philip Winslow. Burke recalls that when he and Winslow visited Mrs. Peirce initially, Winslow said nothing. Winslow is arrested for the murder admitting that he had an affair with Julie using the name George Townsend and that he couldn't accept her ending the relationship and so killed her.

The original script for the premiere episode included other male suspects the detectives questioned about Greer's murder like the chairman of a corporate board, a used car dealer, a jockey, and a musician. But in the interests of time, these characters were not included in the episode. Also, only the character of Mrs. Zampini was described in the original script as being very wealthy. Mr. Zampini had died.

### "John J. Diggs"

On an October 17, 1961 segment of the series, Powell starred as John J. Diggs, a drifter on the border between Mexico and California. He had been shot down while in the military during World War II and his wife had died. He permitted his wife's parents to raise his son. Diggs obtains a job as a bartender working at a hotel in California owned by Margo Haley (Rhonda Fleming) and ends up helping his estranged son who had become part of a car theft ring as well as aiding Haley's college-age daughter.

Although not initially envisioned as a pilot for a series, in September 1962, Four Star considered re-imaging this episode as the basis for a series called *Mr. Diggs* about a U.S. Customs undercover agent working on the Mexico/California border. John Payne was considered for the lead.

## "Goodbye Hannah"

In fall, 1962, Four Star contemplated making a pilot about a detective working in the Missing Persons Bureau of a city police department. Rory Calhoun was sought for the star of the potential series – *Missing Person's Bureau*, which would be based on an episode of *The Dick Powell Show* from November 21, 1961 that starred Carolyn Jones. Jones appeared as Hannah Cole, a wealthy heiress who went missing after her husband had committed suicide. Dick Powell played Lieutenant Smith – "Smitty" for short, who is assigned the task of locating her. When he finds Hannah drunk in a bar, he takes her to his place to dry out. Hannah begins to fall in love with Smitty, and he with her. However, she eventually returns to her uncle's home. A few months later, Smitty sees Hannah again who says that she is not really in love with him – just grateful for his help.

## "A Swiss Affair"

This December 12, 1961 installment featured a tale about three spies each trying to convince a scientist from Russia to defect to their country. The three agents were Hillary Wade (Hazel Court), masquerading as a British secret agent but who is really a double agent working for the Russians; William Gannon (Dick Powell), the American agent; and Maurice Duveaux (Marcel Hillaire), a French agent. Conrad Reicher (Charles Hradilak) is a German scientist kidnapped by the Russians who has escaped that country and is in Switzerland seeking asylum. The three spies are aboard a train to Zurich where they meet each other along with a British citizen, Harry Wilkins (Cecil Kellaway), known as the "Commander." While on the train, Hillary is poisoned by the French agent, but quickly recovers. In turn, the French spy is stabbed and taken to the hospital. Upon arriving in Switzerland, Wade, Gannon, and Wilkins all stay at the same hotel. Hillary is instructed to kill Gannon after she finds the scientist. She drugs the Dick Powell character in order to elicit from him the location of his meeting with the scientist. After Gannon reveals that he will meet Reicher at a café, Hillary can't go through with the killing. When she goes to the café for the rendezvous with the scientist, Gannon and

Wilkins also show up. Reicher announces that he wants asylum in America. Gannon informs him that Hillary is a double agent and that Wilkins is the real British agent, recently appointed to that position by his government. Hillary is arrested for the attempted murder of the French agent.

Evidently, if this episode had been picked up as a series, it would have focused on the William Gannon character with an actor other than Powell portraying him.

### "Squadron"

On January 30, 1962, Dick Powell starred in this segment of his NBC anthology as Col. Luke Harper commanding a squadron during World War II. On a mission, his squadron comes under fire and one damaged plane flown by Bert Evans (Pat Conway) decides to surrender to the Germans signified by releasing its landing gear. However, when one of the plane's engines starts working again, Evans abandons the surrender and returns to base, infuriating the Germans. The Germans demand that Evans and his crew be turned over to them or there will be hell to pay. The enemy concentrates its aerial attacks on Harper's squadron whenever it returns to the air. The airmen in the squadron are extremely upset at Evans for not having surrendered now putting them all at risk. When Evans and his crew return to the air, he plans to surrender to the Germans. Seeing this, the rest of the squadron follow him and beat back the German planes downing the plane flown by the German officer who initially threatened attacks on the squadron until Evans and his crew had been turned over.

If "Squadron" had resulted in a series, actor Pat Conway, who played Bert Evans, would have starred on it.

### "The Hook"

Four Star seemed to like proposing series based on the work of government officials. The company attempted pilots involving judges, a justice of the peace, a public health officer, and this one to be titled *Attorney General*. Starring Robert Loggia as Collin Maese, Attorney General for California, the episode of *The Dick Powell Show* called "The Hook," produced by Arnold Laven, Art Gardner, and Jules Levy and written by Christopher Knopf, aired March 6,

1962. The pilot, based on files from the California Department of Justice, was done in documentary style concerning the head of a drug operation named Magnus Repp (Ray Danton) in San Diego. After a paroled, former drug addict in Repp's employ is murdered, Maese wants to take down the gangster. Learning that Repp was in San Quentin prison with an older guy MacKalaster Thane (Ed Begley), who used to run the drug operation in San Diego, Maese has Thane paroled thinking he will challenge Repp for control of the business. After Maese finds that Thane is senile, he has to make Repp believe that Thane is out to kill him. When Repp learns of this, he, in turn, hires a contract killer to take care of Thane. Maese tails the two when they go on a hunting trip and stops the contract killer from shooting Thane. When Repp tries to shoot Maese, Maese kills him.

### "330 Independence SW"

A truck driver has an accident and police find pep pills as the cause; so opened this potential series that aired March 20, 1962 on *The Dick Powell Show*. David McLean starred as U.S. Health, Education, and Welfare undercover operative Jim Corcoran working out of the Food and Drug Administration who seeks to find who is manufacturing and distributing the illegal amphetamines. Becoming a truck driver himself, Jim buys into the drug operation run by Guts Finley (William Bendix). Finley is shot by his drug contact, but Jim subdues the shooter and finds the supply of drugs.

"330 Independence SW" was a candidate for NBC's 1962-63 line-up. The network considered slotting it at 7:30 on Saturday evenings. NBC was obligated to Four Star to pick up at least one of the company's pilots and ultimately selected *Saints and Sinners* for its schedule instead of "330 Independence SW." However, this pilot about HEW did serve as the basis for the never-aired *Robert Taylor Show* originally slotted on Thursdays for fall 1963.

### "The Clocks"

NBC showed some interest in a Four Star property called *Ghost Breakers*, a thirty-minute adventure-suspense series featuring stories of the occult and supernatural. The production company tried to hire British actor Jack Hawkins for the proposed series but was not successful. Although the network subsequently lost interest in the idea, Four Star aired a pilot on March 27, 1962 on *The Dick Powell Show* featuring a character played by David Farrar who investigates haunted houses.

On the episode titled "Clocks," Valerie Baumer (Joan Fontaine) returns home after a trip and senses an unseen presence in her house – the spirit of her late husband, Curt, who had committed suicide by jumping off the balcony of a clock tower in the mansion. Curt had a priceless collection of clocks which he maintained in the tower. Dr. Leonard Waugh (Farrrar), a professor of parapsychology, is requested by John Bowers (Wayne Rogers), a friend of Valerie's fiancé, Larry Kessler (Charles Drake) to investigate. When the professor and Valerie go to the clock tower, all the clocks are ticking despite not being attended to for six months. Also, Valerie sees a spirit in a mirror. The professor is convinced that something super-natural is occurring in the mansion. When the butler and maid enter the clock tower to see who is winding the clocks, an evil spirit tries to kill the butler. Dr. Waugh concludes that Curt, who had grown overly possessive as he aged, really wanted to kill his wife in the clock tower, but a shadow from a life-sized figure on one of the clocks scared him causing him to fall from the tower. Nevertheless, his evil spirit lingers in the mansion. When the family's cat knocks over a candle into a waste basket, the house catches on fire and burns down eliminating the evil spirit.

"The Clocks" was not one of the better installments of *The Dick Powell Show*. Unsurprisingly, Four Star was not satisfied with the result and so did another pilot in summer, 1962 but to no avail. The second pilot was not picked up as a series either.

## "Safari"

Starring James Coburn as Charlie Allnot and Glynis Johns as Rosie Sayer, this unsold pilot based on the Bogart-Hepburn movie *African Queen*, appeared as the April 3, 1962 episode of *The Dick Powell Show*. Medical missionary Rosie's school in Africa is burned by the Germans, and her students are conscripted to build roads in the jungle at the beginning of World War I. The Germans want to use Allnot's boat, the African Queen, to transport munitions.

Charlie gets away and rescues Rosie from the Germans by distracting them with the sounds of an angry leopard. However, a shoot-out with the Germans as Charlie and Rosie flee injures one of Charlie's crew and damages the steam boiler on his boat. Down river, he stops at a friend's place for repairs. When the Germans put a bounty on Charlie to obtain his boat, an ivory hunter staying with Charlie's friend plots to give the African Queen to the Germans. Rosie and Charlie are able to abscond and sail the boat to an English settlement in Africa. In the course of their adventure, the two begin to become friends.

If the pilot had become a series, the next adventure would have involved taking needed medical supplies to British troops in another town. The pilot was written by Juarez Roberts and directed by David Friedkin.

### "The Boston Terrier"

Airing as an April 10, 1962 installment of *The Dick Powell Show*, Robert Vaughn starred as A. Dunster Lowell, a Boston private detective, in this unsold pilot based on characters created by Blake Edwards and Tom Walden and directed by Edwards. The pilot was shot on location in Boston during the winter. In addition to Vaughn, John McGiver was featured as criminology Professor Mumford who provided Lowell with various gadgets like a panel truck equipped with a transmitter and with a recording device contained in a cigarette holder. Every private eye has a police contact. Lowell's was Lt. Duffy Cardoza (Robert J. Wilke).

Lowell is retained by an insurance company to locate a missing Gattling-type gun stolen from a museum. Wealthy Otis Coots (Russell Collins) owns the gun which is subsequently used to kill four gangsters. Lowell finds that underworld boss Artie Pafko (John Marley) wants to redevelop the entire block on which Coots' museum is located. Coots owns half the block; his neighbor, who has turned up dead, owned the other half of the block. Coots staged the theft of the gun and had the four gangsters killed. Pafko subsequently kidnaps Coots' granddaughter holding her in exchange for the deed to Coots' land. Lowell rescues her and calls the police. In the end, Coots is sent to a rest home.

A second *Boston Terrier* pilot was made called "Salem Witch Hunt," with Elizabeth Montgomery playing a woman (before *Bewitched*) who claimed to be descended from a condemned Salem witch. The plot involved A. Dunster Lowell, still portrayed by Robert Vaughn, being helped by the Montgomery character in the search for a missing young man. This pilot aired on ABC on June 11, 1963.

## "Savage Sunday"

The pilot for Nick Adams' *Saints and Sinners* was filmed in New York City in December 1961 and aired on May 1, 1962 as an episode titled "Savage Sunday" about the activities of the reporters of a major city newspaper on a Sunday. The newspaper's staff deals with several issues: an aging journalist suffering from diabetes, reporter Lizzie Hogan (Ann Blyth), from the paper's Washington office, covering the United Nations, and an accident involving a car and a truck carrying live chickens. But the main story concerns a young woman named Merlee (Carolyn Kearny) arriving in the city from North Carolina to visit her fiancé studying at a Bible college. When he is unable to pick her up at the bus station, two soldiers she met on the bus suggest that they can take her to meet her fiancé, Eldon (Burt Brinkerhoff). On the way, one of the soldiers sexually assaults her, but she is able to escape the vehicle with the help of the other soldier. She goes to a police station where Eldon finally comes to pick her up. When he sees the story in the newspaper with a photo showing her wearing a torn dress, he becomes disgusted. She leaves him and, based on something the soldier who assisted her said, she goes to a dance hall where he is. Meanwhile, Eldon meets Nick, who wrote the story about Merlee, and berates him for his salacious article. Eldon confesses that he let Merlee down. He informs Nick that the paper's editor is toning down the article in the next edition. Nick and Eldon eventually find Merlee, and the soldier who committed the assault is arrested. Nick admits to his editor that he juiced up the story.

## "Borderline"

John Payne and Hazel Court starred on this November 27, 1962 episode set in Tijuana, Mexico. Payne played soldier of fortune

James J. Fitts who returns to Tijuana after trying to find gold with no luck. He considers himself a born loser. He goes back to his old job as bartender at a hotel owned by Pamela (Court) and becomes involved in the case of a missing private eye who was staying at the hotel. The PI was searching for a stolen diamond bracelet. After shaking down a local bar owner, Fitts concludes that the private investigator was killed by one of the bar owner's henchmen who was seeking the bracelet. Fitts subsequently finds that the PI mailed himself a key to a locker where he stashed the valuable jewel. He conspires with Pamela to retrieve the bracelet, sell it, and split the money with her. Fitts gives the key to a shoeshine boy to retrieve the bracelet from the locker because detectives as well as the bar owner's henchmen are shadowing him. When the boy delivers the bracelet to Fitts, detectives from the insurance company take the jewel from him. The shoeshine boy receives the reward for finding the bracelet. However, there is a missing diamond from the jewel that Fitts plans to keep for himself until the local police come to the hotel and he is forced to turn it over.

The episode was considered for a possible series for the 1963-64 season but was not sold to any network.

### "Project X"

A soap opera set against the backdrop of America's early space program was the premise of this pilot starring Michael Rennie as retired Air Force General Conrad Munday who is put in charge of project X – the "X" referring to the personnel working on aerospace projects. In the January 8, 1963 pilot, Munday seeks to help Beth and Roger Canfield. Roger (Steve Forrest) is hard at work on a missile launch which is consuming all of his time to the detriment of his marriage. His wife, played by Gena Rowlands, is drinking too much and thinking of leaving him. She is especially upset that he values his work over his family so much that he wasn't available when she lost their baby in the seventh month of pregnancy. Munday encourages her to accept that her husband is doing important work and go to Vandenburg Air Force Base to witness the launch of her spouse's project. She visits the base. When there is a problem with the missile launch, Roger risks his life to prevent the rocket from exploding. After it is launched successfully, Roger decides to take time off to be with his wife.

Collier Young wrote and produced the pilot. If it had become a series, the show would have been a half-hour drama, but before it aired, it was fairly clear that no network would turn it into a series.

### "The Losers"

On January 15, 1963, *The Dick Powell Theatre* aired a modern reworking of the series, *The Westerner*. Written by Bruce Geller and directed by Sam Peckinpah, this version featured Lee Marvin as Dave Blassingame and Keenan Wynn as Burgundy Smith – two conmen in the present-day West. As Smith says, "(You) can't play poker like it is a game of chance." Smith and Blassingame become involved in a poker game with four other fellows. The duo wins the game thanks to Smith's marked cards. Discovering the cheating, the four other guys pursue Smith and Blassingame in a Keystone Cops-like scene. The pair flees and comes upon a blind man and a boy. Known as Blind Johnny (Adam Luzarre), Johnny does odd jobs and likes to sing at revival meetings. The three guys and the boy stop at a farm in order to work for food and for Smith and Blassingame to obtain transportation. The farmer's daughter, Melissa (Rosemary Clooney) is pretty even though her father doesn't think so, and, of course, she sings. Blind Johnny and the boy perform at a revival meeting where Melissa, Smith, and Blassingame join them. Dave and Burgundy leave the religious event early and find themselves continued to be pursued by the men they cheated at poker.

### "The Judge"

Richard Basehart starred as State Superior Court Judge Dan Zachary in this potential series broadcast February 5, 1963. Judge Zachary dealt with two major issues in the pilot. One concerns finding out about the background of Tony Figlia (Robert Bolger) who has been convicted of manslaughter. The judge wants to know more about the man before he passes sentence. Zachary discovers that Figlia was considered a hot head by those who know him, and, from Figlia's wife, he learns that, in a fit of rage, he hit his daughter's crib with such force that he caused his daughter to lose an eye. The judge sentences Figlia to a term of seven to twenty years in prison.

The other issue Zachary deals with is advising the governor on whether or not the sentence of a convicted killer should be commuted from death to life in prison. His former law partner, Matthews Connors (Edward Binns), now a state senator, is campaigning for commutation and makes the public aware that, much to Zachary's dismay, the judge and he are close. Zachary provides the governor with his recommendation in private. The killer's sentence is commuted to life in prison.

Bruce Geller and Harry Mark Petrakis wrote the pilot which was directed by Bernie Kowalski. Originally, *The Judge* was conceived as an anthology series dealing with different jurists, but Four Star later decided on focusing on one judge – not several. Despite the change in focus, it never became a series.

### "Luxury Liner"

Christopher Knopf wrote this pilot about a cruise ship that aired February 12, 1963. Starring Rory Calhoun as Captain Victor Kilhgren of the S.S. Providence and Carroll O'Connor as Doctor Lyman Savage, this entry interwove stories of various passengers sailing from Barcelona to New York City. Among the passengers was Selena Royce (Jan Sterling) on an around the world cruise given to her as a gift by her boss with whom she had an affair but then he married someone else. Depressed that she hasn't found true romance in her life, she doesn't want to return home. Another passenger, Jan Veltman (Ludwig Donath), served in the German army during World War II. Suffering from ulcers and post-traumatic stress, he is contemplating suicide because he gave orders during the war to attack a ship in the Atlantic not knowing on board were several hundred displaced children. During the cruise, Miss Royce finds a young stowaway named Digo (Michael Davis). First she is friendly toward him but then turns him over to the ship's stewards. When they come for Digo, he flees to the engine room. Veltman convinces the boy to stop running. Eventually, Miss Royce decides to take care of the boy, and Mr. Veltman decides not to kill himself but to continue helping children.

In July 1963, Four Star considered a second effort at a series set on a cruise ship. Titled *S.S. Paradise*, the company contemplated filming the pilot as an episode of *Burke's Law*, presumably with Burke investigating a murder on the ship. By March 1964, the project was terminated.

### "Apples Don't Fall Far"

Michael Kane starred as Mark Brill in this pilot about the work of a parole officer to be called *Parole* or *Man Between*. Written by Les Pine and directed by Joe Leytes, the show, airing February 19, 1963, was titled "Apples Don't Fall Far."

Mark Brill is asked to help fourteen-year-old Peter Jackson (Johnny Crawford), an orphan, who wants to find his father. The father, Alex Johnson (David Wayne), is in prison for killing his wife's friend and doesn't want to see his son. Brill visits Peter's mother, now remarried, with a young daughter and a husband that doesn't know about her son whom she put up for adoption or about her convict ex-husband. She doesn't want to tell him about her past. However, Alex Johnson finally relents and agrees to meet his son. He seeks to become better acquainted with Peter and applies for parole.

### "The Infernal Season"

Another *Dick Powell Theatre* pilot was for a series called *Colossus* to star William Shatner and Robert Brown as immigrants to America. On a March 1963 episode, Shatner starred as Swedish immigrant Eric Tegman who, with his friend, Irishman John Reardon (Robert Brown) purchases a ranch in the San Fernando Valley of California in 1912. Their neighbor Dan Corbett (Frank Overton) holds the mortgage on the ranch and wants to buy it from them to add to his giant spread. However, Tegman and Reardon won't sell. They struggle to maintain the ranch and its cattle, but the lack of water on the property creates major problems. Reardon wants to leave the ranch to pursue his passion – acting. But then it finally rains. Corbett offers Tegman a bet – if the two fight and Eric wins, Corbett will give him an additional piece of land. If Corbett wins, then Tegman must turn over the ranch to him. Naturally, Eric wins, and Johnny leaves to join an acting company.

If the pilot had become a series, the focus would have jumped to the present with both Tegman and Reardon having large families.

Tegman would have become wealthy from land development and oil wells; Reardon would be a motion picture tycoon.

## "The Old Man and the City"

This pilot, titled "The Old Man and the City," airing April 23, 1963, starred Charlie Ruggles as Judge Fairbrother and Bruce Dern as his grandson Hank, a lawyer working in the District Attorney's office. The episode centered on the town of Adamsburg facing the threat of losing a major employer – Ellis-Lathrop that directly and indirectly employed 10,000 of the town's 100,000 residents. The company, which makes jet engines, has been underbid on several contracts by a competing corporation owned by Jake Hollander (Charles Bickford). Hollander has also been purchasing stock in Ellis-Lathrop.

At the Board of Directors meeting for Ellis-Lathrop, Hollander demands that the president resign and that the plant be closed immediately. His motives are unclear, but Hank Fairbrother finds that Hollander's father committed suicide several years earlier because his construction company had remodeled the local public school which then collapsed killing 153 children. After meeting with Hollander about this, the old man has a heart attack. The next day, Hollander announces that he will retool the Ellis-Lathrop factory to make missiles. Hollander confides to his nurse that, when he arrived in Adamsburg, he wasn't sure if he would close the plant for good or re-open it. Apparently, after his cardiac arrest, he decided to do the latter.

There was some discussion that Jackie Cooper may have taken over the role played by Bruce Dern in the pilot. The possible series, *Adamsburg USA*, was a candidate for a spot on NBC's 1963-64 schedule, but ultimately the network passed on it.

## "Last of the Private Eyes"

Bob Cummings starred in this spoof of the private eye genre on the final show of *The Dick Powell Theatre* that aired April 30, 1963. Cummings played private investigator J.F. Kelly who is asked by George Lane (William Bendix) to find a man named Louis Dixon who is blackmailing his wife. Dixon is demanding money in return for not revealing Mrs. Lane's (Linda Christian) past. Kelly speaks with various characters trying to find Dixon, including a bartender (Arnold Stang) at one of Dixon's supposed hangouts and a dancer named Lavern Lavern (Janis Page) who knows where Louis lives. Mrs. Lane is concerned that when Kelly finds Dixon her husband may try to kill him. One night, she calls Kelly to tell him Dixon is at the Lane house meeting with her husband. When Kelly arrives, he finds the police there and George Lane murdered. Kelly's secretary, Elsie (Jeanne Crain) has a boyfriend Detective Duff Peterson (Macdonald Carey) who rounds up possible suspects in the murder case for Kelly to question. The suspects include Mrs. Lane and the Lane's attorney, Frank Jeffers (William Lundigan). Kelly claims that Dixon doesn't really exist and that Mrs. Lane was behind the scheme to create a character named Dixon along with the Lane's butler who impersonated Dixon wearing a disguise. Mrs. Lane killed her husband to inherit his money.

In addition to the stars described above, several other familiar faces appeared in cameos in this pilot. Eddie "Rochester" Anderson played a man shining shoes. Sebastian Cabot and Keenan Wynn were two henchmen who beat up Kelly.

Four Star offered "Last of the Private Eyes" as a series to NBC as a substitute for *Burke's Law* which that network wanted but which went to ABC. NBC evidently thought that the final installment of *The Dick Powell Theatre* would be a pilot for *Burke's Law* starring Gene Barry in the role that Dick Powell had played on the initial stanza of his anthology series. A script was written for another *Amos Burke* installment on the Dick Powell anthology, but the episode was made as the ABC premiere of *Amos Burke*.

### "The Commandos"

One unproduced episode of *The Dick Powell Show*, written by Harry Julian Fink in May 1962, was under consideration as another back-door pilot.

"The Commandos" dealt with an elite group of soldiers formed by Allied forces during World War II. Sir William Kenner, Chief of his Majesty's Imperial Staff, decides that a mission needs to be undertaken to rescue a retired British general, Sir John Roy, with knowledge of British secret codes who is in a hospital in France under German control. If he can't be rescued, then orders are to assassinate him before he divulges the secret information.

Kenner instructs Major Amos Sandell, an American, to put together a group to carry out the mission. Sandell had led a commando unit previously that resulted in nine of his unit being captured and hospitalized in the same facility as the retired general. Sandell forms a group of seven soldiers, all from different backgrounds, to carry out the new mission. They successfully infiltrate enemy lines and free Sir Roy and the nine other commandos but come under heavy enemy fire as they flee to the beach where they meet a British landing craft. Three of the seven are killed, but the British general and the other commandos survive.

## *The Lloyd Bridges Show* and Its Pilots

On this variation of the standard anthology series, Lloyd Bridges starred as freelance journalist Adam Shepherd who imagined himself as the central character in each story he was writing. The half-hour show, originally titled *Johnny Fable* and then *Adam Fable*, began on CBS on September 11, 1962 and lasted for one season. Created and executive produced by Aaron Spelling, Lloyd Bridges appeared in each episode of his self-titled series unlike prior Four Star anthologies where the hosts starred in only a limited number of installments.

*The Lloyd Bridges Show* opened with Bridges narrating: "My name is Adam Shepherd. Over the years, my writing has taken me to many fields – fact as well as fiction, and I've tried to write the truth as I've seen it for papers and magazines and truth as I've wished it to be, short stories and novels."

The debut episode, "Wheresoever I Enter. . .," written by Christopher Knopf, involved a doctor, played by Bridges, vacationing in Greece where he meets his three cousins. The wife of one of the cousins is giving birth, and the doctor steps in to successfully handle a breach birth. The doctor has to leave Greece the next day since he has been offered a position with one of the finest doctor's in Chicago. However, the villagers don't want him to depart since they have no real doctor. When he tries to leave, his car won't start, and he has a brief altercation with one of his cousins resulting in the doctor breaking his thumb. No doctor is around to set the break. His cousin says that now he knows what it is like to have no doctor. A cousin also says that they sacrificed to send the doctor's father to America, and for that reason, he should not leave. The doctor decides to stay and send one of his cousins to America to study medicine for five years. Five years later his cousin saves the lives of three men involved in a mining accident in West Virginia.

About the first episode, writer Knopf described what happened at the first table read of the initial script by the cast. "As he (Bridges) opened his script, we stared in disbelief. The entire teleplay had been rewritten on the blank, left side of each page. Not just Lloyd's dialogue, but everyone else's as well, no warning, no call from Lloyd that he had problems with the material. The script has been approved by the network, Lloyd had approved it."

Knopf went on, "Challenging him about the changes, Lloyd seemed to have a difficult time explaining why they'd been made, but defended them as though defending his wife, which he was. The rewrite had been done by her."[80] In response, the producers suggested to the actor that maybe he would be happier not doing the series. After that veiled threat, no further talk of rewrites was mentioned.

The series incorporated several stories written by Bill Lederer portraying good deeds performed by Americans abroad. Henry J. Kaiser, whose company sponsored *The Lloyd Bridges Show*, had wanted Four Star to develop a series showing a favorable side of Americans overseas, as a counterpoint to Lederer's book, *The Ugly American*.

For example, an October 9, 1962 installment, "Mr. Pennington's Machine," based on a story by Bill Lederer, concerned Bruce Pennington (Bridges) and his wife Ellen (Betty Garrett) touring China and seeing that, in spite of American assistance, the Chinese are malnourished and being exploited by black marketers. The Pennington's are particularly stirred by the sight of a young girl dying of malnutrition. They bring a noodle machine to the girl's village and fight the black marketers.

Other episodes of the series ranged from Westerns to science fiction to comedies. In "The Courtship," a Western, featuring Diane

Baker, Bridges appears as farmer Jonathan Tatum courting a blind woman named Birdie. On their first meeting, they set a wedding date. After the marriage, Jonathan takes her to his farm, but she locks him out of the bedroom on their wedding night. Later, a friend of Jonathan's visits the farm uninvited and assaults Birdie. Jonathan stops the attack which draws Birdie closer to him.

In "Testing Ground," Adam Shepherd imagines that he is one of four astronauts exploring another planet when they discover a diamond cross-like sculpture. The astronauts debate taking a sample of the sculpture back to Earth. One astronaut, a doctor, wants to keep the cross intact. The others fight with him, and he is accidentally shot and killed. They place the dead astronaut in a crypt and agree not to tell anyone that the planet is a diamond, claiming that the doctor's faith was strong enough for all of them to find their true selves.

In a comedy installment, titled "The Sheridan Square," Bridges appeared as Archie Hammond, a writer, living in Greenwich Village with his wife Katie (Gogi Grant), a theater actress/singer. Archie is working on a book about the Civil War while also writing for a daily TV show called *Breakfast with the Baxter's*. Each day he has to come up with a "Thought for the Day" for the husband and wife program. While he is attempting to write during the evening with his wife away at the theater, Archie is continually interrupted by unexpected visitors invited by his wife. When Katie returns, Archie learns that one of the visitors is an important literary agent who is interested in publishing his book. Plus Katie gives him inspiration for the "Thought of the Day:" "Sometimes out of the most blinding chaos and confusion comes a little good."

Written by Lee Philips and Everett Chambers, this March 12, 1963 episode was originally written as a pilot for a possible series starring Lee Philips as Archie.

At mid-season, the show dropped the concept of Bridges playing a journalist who imagines himself at the center of all of his stories and simply became a standard anthology hosted by Mr. Bridges.

Commenting on the pending demise of his series after one season, Bridges remarked, "I honestly believe our initial mistake was the format gimmick of having me play a dual role, my regular Adam

Shepherd role and the different character he assumed each week. We've rectified that by eliminating Adam, but too late, I suppose."[81]

Even though the anthology lasted only a single season, it included certain episodes as pilots for possible series.

### "The Rising of the Moon"

In this episode, Bridges appeared as Michael Curran, a member of the Irish Republican Army in the first half of the twentieth century who, on his wedding day to Nora (Kathleen Nolan) decides to carry out an attack on the British Army using dynamite. Nora wants her husband to give up the fight against the British and go to America with her which he ultimately decides to do.

The inspiration for the story was the Celtic folk song, "The Rising of the Moon" which concerned the 1798 rebellion of the Irish against the British Army. The last verse of the song is, "Death to every foe and traitor, whistle out the marching tune

And hoorah me boys for freedom 'tis the rising of the moon

'Tis the rising of the moon, 'tis the rising of the moon

And hoorah me boys for freedom 'tis the rising of the moon"

During the February 19, 1963 episode, the different verses of the ballad were sung as the story played out with William Schallert (later to play Patty Duke's father on her self-titled comedy series), as the "ballad singer," performing the final verse of the song. If the pilot had been picked up as an anthology titled *Ballad Theater*, each episode would have used a folk song from somewhere in the world as the basis for the story.

### "War Song"

On this episode, Bridges played a sergeant whose platoon comes under fire on D-Day in Normandy, France. His platoon finds an abandoned baby in a farm house. The sergeant wants to leave the baby behind thinking that the baby's crying will get his men killed. His platoon disagrees and takes the infant with them as they come under heavy enemy fire. The sergeant loses most of his men except for himself, one other injured man, and the baby who later grows up to be a beautiful young woman.

Les Pine scripted this episode which was to be the basis for a series about World War II called *Dog Watch*.

## "Tyrees of Capitol Hill"

This potential series, to be called *Capitol Hill*, starred Edgar Buchanan as Andrew Jackson Tyree from Zactly, North Carolina whose grandson, Boford (Phillip Alford) receives a telegram from Senator Guthrie (Bridges) inviting him to Washington to become a Senate page. Boford's grandfather accompanies him to the nation's capital where they both meet Walter Pike (Jonathan Harris) who trains and supervises Senate pages. Mr. Tyree attempts to introduce "improvements" in the work of the pages causing Mr. Pike to become irritated with him and to complain to Senator Guthrie. After Guthrie talks with Tyree, the grandfather decides to return to North Carolina. Bo wants to resign as a page, but the Senator won't accept his resignation. Guthrie has Mr. Tyree become a guide at the Smithsonian so he will stay in DC and keep out of trouble. This episode of *The Lloyd Bridges Show* aired April 9, 1963.

# Early Sixties Anthology Projects and Pilots

### A Dash of Terror

One pilot that Four Star considered making but then abandoned during 1960-61 was for another anthology series, *A Dash of Terror*. The thirty-minute program would have featured stories of suspense. Thought was given to having the pilot air as an episode of June Allyson's anthology series.

### Ida Lupino Presents This Is Murder (aka Theatre of Crime Classics)

This proposed anthology would have featured Ms. Lupino hosting mystery/suspense stories similar to those shown on *Alfred Hitchcock Presents*. As quoted in her biography about the intended series, "It's about when people love too much. Or hate too much. Or lust too much. It's about murder. All kind of murders. In every land. From every time. And the difference is they are all true."[82]

### Comedy/Musical Anthology Project

Attempting to do something different in the way of an anthology, Four Star, as early as November 1960, pondered developing a comedy anthology series. By September 1961, this idea had evolved to presenting a weekly half-hour musical revue featuring young talent. Later that fall, Tom McDermott suggested that a one-hour anthology of light entertainment might be popular on television. McDermott sought Spencer Tracy as the host for the untitled project. The series would include revues, satire, book musicals, and similar types of programming using film, tape, and live segments.

By July, 1962, the idea seemingly was abandoned, and the suggestion was made to devise an anthology based on classic love stories with Charles Boyer, which never transpired.

### Three Star Theatre

This proposed half-hour anthology would have been hosted by Joan Crawford and two other stars. Details beyond this could not be found.

### Dunham, Inc.

One project that Four Star contemplated in the early 1960s was a one-hour series about big business called *Dunham. Inc.* Tony Barrett wrote a script for the pilot which probably would have been an episode of *The Dick Powell Show* if it had been made. If a series had resulted, it may have been more like an anthology about big corporations.

### University Medical Center

Proposed by writers Mort Fine and Dave Friedkin, this medical series would have involved doctors at the UCLA Medical School with apparently a different cast each week. Fine and Friedkin wrote two scripts for the projected series, initially called *The Hospital*. In one script dated February 24, 1961, Dr. James Martin, a resident in neurosurgery at the facility, is attracted to one of his patients who distracts him from attending to others. Dr. Scott Lund, the senior neurosurgeon, attempts to put Dr. Martin on the right track to treat all of his patients professionally. This script focused solely on the physicians and nurses in the hospital.

The second script from October 25, 1961 expanded the concept of the proposed series to include a hospital located on a university campus along with clinics, a medical school, and research center. This script dealt with a typhoid outbreak. The doctors work with public health officials and other agencies to determine the source of the disease. The patients all seemed to have attended the same party a few weeks earlier. Some teenagers left the party, broke into an apartment nearby, and ate some infected grapes the tenant had which led to the typhoid outbreak.

CBS initially expressed interest in the series. As with other pilot concepts, thought was given to filming it as an episode of *The Dick Powell Show*, which never came about.

### Journey into Crime

Based on Don Whitehead's book, *Journey into Crime*, Four Star briefly looked at adapting this book into a dramatic series in September 1961 but dropped the idea after a few weeks. The book dealt with police practices and crimes around the world, e.g., murder in England, robbery and murder in Paris, counterfeiting in Liechtenstein, and piracy in Hong Kong. One can speculate that the resulting series would have been an anthology chronicling criminal investigations in different countries.

### 1600 Pennsylvania Avenue (aka The President)

Tom McDermott pondered making a series based on a book by Bill Davidson titled *Six Brave Presidents*. The book profiled George Washington, John Quincy Adams, Abraham Lincoln, Andrew Johnson, Chester A. Arthur, and Theodore Roosevelt – all Presidents selected by then President John F. Kennedy. Presumably, if the project had become a series, it would have been an anthology about decisive moments in the lives of different American Presidents.

# Chapter 13:
# The Good, the Bad, and the Beautiful
# Dramatic Characters, 1962-67

For the fiscal year ending June 29, 1963, Four Star's net earnings were up slightly compared with the prior fiscal year. The company's earnings after taxes were $793,501 compared to $734,077 the previous fiscal year. A non-recurring item was a tax-free payment of $500,000 from a company-held life insurance policy on Dick Powell.

During this period, the company created Four Star Television International in February 1963 to distribute its productions in foreign countries.

Four Star also released its first theatrical feature, *Dear Heart*, starring Glenn Ford and Geraldine Page. Financed by Warner Brothers, the film was produced in association with Martin Manulis Productions and Biography productions. In addition, the company acquired the rights to fifteen foreign movies for syndication to TV stations in the United States under the title *Four Star Spectacular Showcase*.

From 1962 to 1967, the company premiered a newspaper drama and two detective series – one about a rich police officer and one, the first contemporary detective show to feature a female in the lead. Also, Four Star brought back two of the company's original owners in a roguish dramedy and had the misfortune of making a series with a famous movie star that never saw the light of day.

## *Saints and Sinners* and Its Back-Door Pilot

Nick Adams starred in this newspaper drama as journalist Nick Alexander working for the *New York Bulletin*. His editor was Mark Grainger (John Larkin). Nick worked with staff photographer Klugie (Richard Erdman), copy editor Dave Tabak (Robert F. Simon), and Washington correspondent, Lizzie Hogan (Barbara Rush who replaced Ann Blyth from the pilot). The drama premiered September 17, 1962 on NBC.

Speaking of the series before its debut, creator Adrian Spies remarked "...we're trying for the dramatic quality of 'The Defenders' and from the looks of the first 10 scripts and two completed films, I'd say we're pretty close to what we set out to do." He went on to say, "Every city room spawns its golden boy and Nick Adams fits the role like Bobby Morse in Broadway's 'How to Succeed.'"[83]

The opener, titled "Dear George, the Siamese Cat Is Missing," centered on a woman, Emily Fielder (Lola Albright) who comes to the *Bulletin's* offices on a Saturday desperate to place a classified ad in the Sunday edition. She tells editor, Mark Grainger, that her husband has been kidnapped and that, in order to communicate with the culprits, she needs to place a personal ad stating, "Dear George, the Siamese cat is missing," so that they will respond with instructions for payment of the $25,000 ransom. The FBI is called in and contends that the kidnappers are not professionals based on the small ransom demand. The kidnappers are revealed to be a man and his girlfriend who has a stutter. News of the kidnapping is leaked to a tabloid which upsets the culprits. Vinnie (Gary Lockwood), a new copy boy at the *Bulletin* who wants to be a journalist, leaked the story to the tabloid in return for a news reporter position. The FBI directs the *Bulletin* to write a special story for the kidnappers to read pleading for them not to kill their victim. Nick Alexander is given the story assignment. The FBI is able to locate and free Mr. Fielder. The agents found the kidnapped victim after interviewing employees at the firm he owned and finding that the girlfriend of a janitor that Mr. Fielder had fired had a stutter.

Film actor Brian Donley guest starred on this episode as an aging re-write reporter who had just been hired by the *Bulletin* and initially came under suspicion for leaking the kidnapping story to the tabloid for whom he had once worked.

Actors who did not appear regularly on television, including Irene Dunne, Michael Wilding, and Paul Muni, were featured on several episodes. Muni made his last TV appearance on an episode titled "A Shame for a Diamond Wedding" playing ninety-three-year old Samuel Foss who is about to celebrate his 75th wedding anniversary with his wife Minna (Lili Darvas). Nick is assigned to cover the story in-depth since the Foss' are the longest married couple in

New York City. A few days before the celebration, family members gather to plan the festivities. They include Arnold Foss (Edward Andrews), the eldest son; Ruth (Florence Halop), the daughter who is married to George, a lawyer with a college-age daughter, Jane (Noreen Corcoran); and the youngest son Manny (Alan Hewitt). At the planning event with the family squabbling over preparations, Samuel announces that he and his wife are going to divorce. The family wants to keep this a secret, but Nick witnesses the announcement. The family decides that an objective outsider should try to talk the parents out of the divorce and that Nick should be the one to do this. Samuel remarks to Nick that his marriage to Minna was arranged by their parents and that, after the marriage, he and his wife only had time to care for the children and grandchildren. This is the first time he has had a chance to request a divorce. Later, Samuel admits that the real reason he announced the divorce was because of the family arguing over the anniversary celebration. He takes the initiative in informing his family that he will head up the celebration and that he is calling off the divorce.

The episode aired November 26, 1962. Paul Muni passed away five years after this installment aired.

Despite *Saints and Sinners* short run, the series aired a spin-off pilot.

### "New Lead: Berlin"

*Saints and Sinners'* final episode was a pilot for a series called "New Lead: Berlin" about a foreign correspondent. The episode featured John Larkin in a dual role as the *Bulletin's* editor and as writer Bart King who is doing a magazine article about Berlin, Germany and how it has changed since World War II. Lindsay Hogan (Barbara Rush) accompanies King to Berlin. Before the war, King had lived in the city and then wrote a book about his experiences. In Germany, King is confronted by a newspaper editor named Heller. Heller advises Lindsay that he was part of the anti-Nazi underground and that King published in his book secrets he had learned from the underground which came to the attention of the Nazis who then arrested members of the resistance. King says that his book did not betray the underground but that the Gestapo got the information from other sources. Lindsay and King track down a former acquaintance of the journalist's who confirms that King's book was not the source of the information but rather that the source was a member of the underground, her husband, who was really a Nazi sympathizer.

The episode aired January 28, 1963, the final installment of *Saints and Sinners*. At one point, Rory Calhoun was under consideration for the lead in this project.

## *The Robert Taylor Show*

Robert Taylor's TV comeback was supposed to premiere on NBC on September 19, 1963 on Thursdays at 7:30 pm. Taylor portrayed Christopher Logan, a special assistant at the Department of Health, Education, and Welfare, the precursor to the current Department of Health and Human Services. Initially, actor Robert Loggia played Taylor's assistant but left after filming of the pilot. George Segal was then signed for this role playing Nick Di Canto. According to Mr. Segal, he had been featured on an episode of *Naked City* titled "Man without a Skin" as a tough cop. A William Morris agent saw the show and brought Segal to Hollywood to appear on the Taylor series.[84]

Logan investigated cases under HEW's jurisdiction involving epidemics of disease, illegal adoptions, and mental illness.

Four Star Television had a deal with NBC for thirteen episodes of the series loosely based on *The Dick Powell Show* episode "330 Independence SW." The program was supposed to have been endorsed by the U.S. Department of Health, Education, and Welfare and based on their case files. However, the Department indicated that the scripts were not based on official files. Further, it was concerned that the series did not recognize its role of working through state agencies on problems but instead focused on the Department's investigators directly intervening at the state level. NBC canceled the program because of this lack of official endorsement and because the network was nervous over a series that addressed sensitive social problems like illiteracy and Native American issues.

Scripts written for the show's episodes dealt with infants mysteriously dying at a county hospital which served the Hopi Indian reservation; a boy named Alfred who attended a school for mentally challenged teens with Christopher Logan helping the boy find a job at the local canine society because of his love of dogs; Nick Di Canto investigating forged Social Security checks; Di Canto finding that a disreputable doctor is administering a bogus cancer cure to Di Canto's infant nephew; and the problems an Amish community has in paying Social Security taxes to the federal government.

As with his role in *The Detectives*, Robert Taylor's appearances on the series were basically at the beginning and end of each episode leaving many of the investigations up to the George Segal character. As Mr. Segal noted, ". . . Bob (btw a perfect gentleman) was to book-end and I would in essence carry the show."[85]

NBC's decision to cancel *The Robert Taylor Show* before any episodes aired led Four Star to a financial loss for the first six months of the 1963-64 fiscal year.

## *Burke's Law* and Its Back-Door Pilot

Sophisticated, urbane, and also wealthy, Amos Burke (Gene Barry) was a millionaire police captain who arrived at crime scenes in a chauffeur-driven Rolls Royce. He solved murders with the help of Det. Tim Tilson (Gary Conway) and Det. Sgt. Les Hart (Regis Toomey). Each episode featured cameos by many Hollywood stars who were suspects in a usually bizarre murder case.

The series aired on ABC beginning on September 20, 1963. As noted earlier in this book, the pilot for *Burke's Law* first aired as an installment of *The Dick Powell Show* – an episode called "Who Killed Julie Greer?" with Powell playing the lead character. Aaron Spelling came up with the idea to have multiple guest stars featured as the murder suspects. Each guest star would only work one day filming his or her part.

Before casting Gene Barry in the lead for the series, Four Star considered Jackie Cooper for the Amos Burke role. In 1962, Tom McDermott had the idea of resurrecting the old *Four Star Playhouse* series as a mystery anthology with Dick Powell perhaps playing Sam Spade, David Niven as Sherlock Holmes, and Charles Boyer as a Hercule Poirot-type detective. Jackie Cooper as Amos Burke was considered as a fourth segment of this anthology, but, when NBC lost interest in the concept, Four Star made a new pilot of *Burke's Law* with Gene Barry. Titled "Who Killed Holly Howard?"and written by Al Reich and William H. Wright, the pilot was directed by Hy Averback.

"Who Killed Holly Howard?" concerned a model found shot in the back on a highway construction site. Burke and his detectives interview Howard's former landlady, Mrs. Bowie (Zasu Pitts) who makes the police aware that recently Howard moved to a new house. At the house, the detectives find photos of Howard's one and only modeling job for Nickerson and Green. At that firm, Burke encounters Fred Hopke (William Bendix), an artist for the company, and subsequently learns that the model actually died from drowning and was shot after her death. A colleague of Howard's, Bridget Jenkins (Suzy Parker) reveals that she and Howard would often swim at a private residence owned by Harry Joe Murdock's (Rod Cameron) corporation. Murdock, along with two other men from the company – Vaughn Moore (Will Rogers, Jr.) and Thomas Mathieson (Bruce Cabot) - would often stay at the residence when in Los Angeles. Incriminating photos of the three men with the various models were taken by John Bush (Sir Cedric Hardwicke), the home's butler. The detectives also find that Holly had originally lived in the same building as Fred Hopke who paid to have her teeth capped and for a nose job so Holly could become a model. They also learn that Bridget Jenkins will replace Howard in the advertising campaign. Burke concludes that Jenkins drowned Holly in her bathtub in order to take her place in the advertising campaign and then Hopke, seeking revenge for Holly ignoring him after he paid for her cosmetic surgery, took her body and placed it in the swimming pool at Murdock's house.

*Variety* gave a glowing review to the premiere of *Burke's Law* writing that the show ". . . is a glossy, sophisticated whodunit, a sparkling, zestful series which provides a maximum of escapist entertainment." The paper further stated that "Gene Barry is glib, suave and polished as the millionaire detective . . ."[86]

One episode in the series first season featured two of the original hosts of *Four Star Playhouse*. In "Who Killed Billy Jo," about the murder of a singer similar to Elvis Presley, Ida Lupino played Lynn

Dexter, Billy Jo's manager and president of his company who was embezzling from him. David Niven had a brief appearance as an untalented juggler auditioning for Billy Jo's agent Lou Cole, portrayed by Howard Duff, Lupino's husband, who was also a suspect in his murder. In fact, Marcus DeGrate (Caesar Romero), an astrologer, was the real culprit who killed the singer because Billy Jo found that DeGrate was meeting with the singer's estranged stepfather to get information on him and DeGrate was concerned that his "psychic" methods would be revealed.

Barry not only was the lead on *Burke's Law*, he also recorded an album for one of Four Star's music companies. Titled *Gene Barry Sings*, the album included songs like "Just in Time," "I'll Be Seeing You," and "Make Someone Happy" as well as the "Theme from Burke's Law" with lyrics like "When we make love, it's Burke's law."

At the end of *Burke's Law's* second season, ABC decided to radically change the format of the series. The character of Amos Burke became a secret agent for a U.S. intelligence agency. Gone were his co-stars – Regis Toomey and Gary Conway as well as the many guest star cameos. However, the Rolls Royce remained in the revamped series, only now, Burke had to drive it himself. He was no longer chauffeured. As Aaron Spelling wrote in his autobiography, "I hated it, Gene hated it, we all hated it, and ABC was very wrong to change it."[87] The show expired during the 1965-66 season.

On the first installment of *Amos Burke: Secret Agent*, Burke has resigned from the police force and meets with "The Man" (Carl Benton Reid) on an airliner to receive his mission working for a super-secret agency. Chinese gold is being smuggled into Cuba and then to other Latin American countries to support rebel insurgents. Burke flies to Switzerland, the starting point for the smuggling operation. He poses as an airline pilot implicated in the smuggling operation in order to get to the head of the operation.

Some of the other episodes bordered on the ridiculous such as when Burke goes undercover to thwart a peace group using a special chemical that makes people act like children. The group uses the chemical to subdue government officials so it can retrieve classified information. Burke finds that the group has been infiltrated by foreign agents who seek to sell the information to America's enemies.

The final story of the series unfolded over two episodes in January 1966. Called "Terror in a Tiny Town," the installments dealt with the citizens of a California town who see all outsiders as threats to their way of life. Rooted in the usual insularity of small town life, the residents of Sorrell, California do not like anyone who believes differently than they do. The denizens of the town have been brainwashed by subliminal messages played on the local radio station. The town's judge, a former Congressman, is behind the brainwashing because he wants to make the town the new capital of the United States by building a nuclear bomb made with material from the town's atomic research facility. He plans on detonating the bomb in Washington DC using a supposed Communist front organization he set up as the perpetrator. The judge wants an obedient and disciplined citizenry who depend only on one man as their supreme leader. Burke, of course, foils the plot.

In 1966, actor Paul Henreid filed a law suit against Four Star claiming that the concept for *Burke's Law* was stolen from a treatment for a television series that he had submitted to the production company in 1959 titled *The Two Manhattans*. The treatment concerned a father and grown son who participate as trouble shooters in dealing with intrigues among the international set. The crux of the suit rested on the use of the Rolls Royce automobile in *Burke's Law*. The main character in *The Two Manhattans* had such a vehicle as did Amos Burke. The suit claimed that the Rolls Royce was one of the "stars" of *Burke's Law*. The suit also pointed out some other similarities between Henreid's treatment and the TV series such as the fact that the main character on both *Burke's Law* and Henreid's creation were bachelors who liked women and the fact of the "father-son" relationship between the lead character and the main supporting character in both. The trial court upheld Four Star's contention that the allegations were not sufficient grounds for legal action. The verdict was appealed, but the California Court of Appeal upheld the judgment of the lower court stating that a Rolls Royce is a well-publicized symbol of wealth and, as such, is an inadequate basis to claim material similarity between *Burke's Law* and Henreid's treatment.

In its original format, *Burke's Law* did have a comeback in 1994. Barry, in his seventies at the time, resumed his role as a police captain, this time with a young son played by Peter Barton who assisted in the murder investigations.

One successful spin-off pilot aired as an episode of *Burke's Law*.

### "Who Killed the Jackpot?"

"Who Killed the Jackpot?" introduced the character of Honey West in an April 21, 1965 episode of the detective drama. It featured West (Anne Francis) and her partner Sam Bolt (John Ericson) finding that her client, banker Andrew Selby, has been murdered. She meets Amos Burke for the first time at the hotel room in which Selby had been killed. Separately, Burke and she investigate the murder. They find that Selby was planning to leave his wife and runaway with all of his money. West figures that a skin diver who had been helping Selby with his plan to leave his spouse killed him to steal his money. Burke arrives just as the killer is trying to murder West.

## *The Rogues*

This series brought back two of the three stars that had founded Four Star Productions. Charles Boyer and David Niven starred respectively as Marcel St. Clair, the French cousin of Alec Fleming, his British cousin, in a tale of gentlemanly conmen. Gig Young appeared as Tony Fleming, Alec's American cousin. Robert Coote and Gladys George also played members of the St. Clair family. The Fleming's and St. Clair's were families that dated back to the eighteenth century when Giles Fleming and Countess Juliette St. Clair fell in love when both attempted to steal Marie Antoinette's jewel box. The family's motto was "Honor before Honesty."

There was some discussion of filming *The Rogues* in Europe to accommodate the schedules of Charles Boyer and David Niven, but that never transpired. Gig Young starred on most of the episodes because his schedule was more flexible than those of Niven and Boyer. Niven could only work in the United States for limited periods because of his complex tax situation, and Charles Boyer only wanted to make brief appearances. NBC bought the series for airing Sunday nights at 10:00 pm.

Writer Stephen Kandel, who wrote and/or polished several of the scripts for *The Rogues,* remarked that the series: "...was unique: the stars had executive clout – and were real actors; the cast came out of the theatre – and they simply refused to deliver really lousy dialogue. So I did a lot of trotting down to the set, listen to a fervent diatribe about talentless, unsayable mushy peas (David Niven) or Tripe a la Caen (Charles Boyer) lines – and do on-the-spot patch-work. Really a great pleasure – because when a line worked, they could deliver it brilliantly."[88]

Not every episode of *The Rogues* involved some kind of con game. In "The Pigeons of Paris," Timmy learns that a friend of his, Bruce Cameron, was killed when someone ran his car off a highway in France. Cameron, posing as an artist, was really a MI5 agent investigating industrial espionage. After his death, his Paris apartment was ransacked by persons looking for something. Timmy and Marcel decide to move into the apartment to attempt to find what the culprits were seeking. Marcel finds that a former acquaintance of his, Jena Tate (Jill St. John), owns the apartment building. She invites Timmy and him to a party she is having where they meet Carl Votrian (Gerald Mohr), a wealthy industrialist. Marcel later meets a little girl who posed for Cameron and to whom Cameron gifted with a baby doll right before he died. Marcel concludes that evidence of industrial espionage is in the doll. However, the girl gave her doll to Jena who, in turn, gave it to Votrian. Marcel and Timmy search Votrian's toy warehouse for the doll. While there, Votrian and his men show up with the doll. Timmy and Marcel abscond, and the police arrest Votrian.

Ida Lupino, the fourth host of *Four Star Playhouse*, appeared in one episode of the series as Arlene, a former French underground member and paramour of the Charles Boyer character. Marcel St. Clair tries to help Arlene's son Jamie (George Hamilton), whom he suspects might be his own son, avoid a life of crime.

Lupino also directed two episodes of the series. The first one titled "Hugger-Mugger by the Sea," starred Ricardo Montalban as wealthy ship owner, Marius Konk, whom Tony Fleming tries to swindle. Much to his surprise, Tony's bid for twenty-two old Navy destroyers is accepted, and he comes to own a small fleet of unwanted vessels. He then has to convince Konk that one of the ships contains a fortune in gold. Raquel Welch appeared in the episode as Miss France.

Ida Lupino also directed "Bow to the Master" featuring Gig Young and guest star Zachary Scott in a tale of a jewel thief. To avenge a woman that a jeweler cheated, Tony Fleming substitutes the woman's pearl necklace with a fake, but then Le Chat (the cat), master jewel thief played by Scott, steals the real pearl necklace from Tony. Tony decides to entice "the cat" into stealing a large diamond for which a wealthy buyer from India will pay $500,000. Fleming convinces the buyer that he is "the cat." The Zachary Scott character disguises himself as the man who cleans the case housing the diamond, takes the real diamond, and substitutes a fake. Charles Boyer in a cameo appearance as an appraiser sent by Tony inspects the substitution and declares it a fake so that the potential buyer for the gem knows that the real diamond was stolen. Fleming, pretending he is "the cat," exchanges what the buyer thinks is the stolen diamond but is really a fake for the half-million dollars. The cat, upon learning that the buyer for the diamond has already left the hotel, gives the real diamond to Fleming to return to the British government.

About *The Rogues*, Tom McDermott felt that the series sharp, sophisticated manner would make it a major hit and would again make the type of dramatic shows Four Star was known for in great demand by the networks. He bemoaned the networks seeming obsession with situation comedies at the time saying, "Who's going to write them? Good comedy writers are the hardest things to find in this business. The year after there's going to be a swing away from comedy, perhaps toward the anthologies – and foreign locations."[89]

*The Rogues* ended after one season. Despite critical acclaim and being positioned after NBC's hit Western *Bonanza*, the series was not renewed by the network. According to Stephen Kandel, *The Rogues* was not regarded with favor by NBC. The network felt that viewers were not ready for literate high comedy, and McDermott did not fight for the series renewal.[90] Also, Mr. McDermott was not correct about anthologies coming back the following television season, but Four Star did have success with one genre that they were famous for – the Western, as described in Chapter 16.

## *Honey West*

This spin-off from *Burke's Law* starred Anne Francis as private detective Honey West who, along with her partner Sam Bolt (John Ericson), ran a detective agency she inherited from her dad. West was proficient in karate and judo, had devices like a radio transmitter in various items including a lipstick tube, martini olive, and sunglasses, and owned a pet ocelot named Bruce. Premiering September 17, 1965 on ABC, the series ran for one season. Originally, the program was conceived as a sixty-minute comedy-drama and submitted to CBS for consideration before ABC picked it up.

The Honey West character originated in a series of novels with titles such as *This Girl for Hire* and *Honey in the Flesh*, written by Forrest Fickling and his wife Gloria beginning in 1957.

The thirty-minute pilot for *Honey West*, "The Gray Lady," was broadcast on December 6, 1965 as the show's thirteenth episode. Written by William Link and Richard Levinson, the story concerned a jewel thief named Abbott (Cesare Danova) who steals from celebrities. After letting the thief get away with jewels stolen from a French actress who had hired Honey to protect her valuables, Ms. West believes that Abbott will strike again to rob the "gray lady" a $250,000 diamond owned by the Ivar's. Honey catches Abbott in the act of stealing the jewel but is interrupted when Mr. Ivar (Kevin McCarthy) unexpectedly returns to his hotel room. He takes the gun away from West revealing that he conspired with Abbott to steal the valuable diamond so he could collect the insurance money. When Honey convinces Abbott that the diamond he has is really fake, Ivar shoots him. Using judo and karate, Honey knocks Ivar unconscious.

Ida Lupino directed one episode of the series – "How Brillig, O, Beamish Boy," written by Don Ingalls and guest starring John McGiver as Brillig who holds Sam hostage after he picks up a package for a client, Mr. Fancher (Norman Alden). Brillig wants to exchange the package, which contains $500,000, for Sam. Honey

*John McGiver as Brillig and John Ericson as Sam Bolt in a scene from
"How Brillig, O, Beamish Boy."*

gives Brillig eyeglasses to give to Sam that contain a homing device.
Brillig discovers the device and uses it to trap Honey. She and Sam
are both able to escape. Fancher contacts the duo to turn over the
package to him in a ghost town. Honey is followed by Brillig to
the meeting place where she learns that Brillig and Fancher were
partners in a gambling deal. Fancher stole the half million in oper-

ating funds which Brillig wants back. Honey is able to knock out Brillig's men when Sam arrives with the sheriff to arrest Brillig and Fancher.

Anne Francis was nominated for an Emmy for *Honey West* for the 1965-66 TV season but lost to Barbara Stanwyck for *The Big Valley*.

# Other Sixties Drama Projects and Pilots 1962-67

### Flight Surgeon

In 1962, writer Tom Gries scripted a pilot called *Fight Surgeon* that was supposed to air in the final season of *The Dick Powell Theatre*. The pilot concerned the activities of the Military Transport Service (MAT) that was involved with such responsibilities as medical evacuation flights, military cargo service, rescue of downed military service members in enemy occupied areas, and humanitarian relief to citizens in emergency situations. At the time of the projected pilot, an international crisis existed and so MAT planes were not available for filming. Subsequently, Sam Peckinpah bought the rights to the teleplay from Four Star and thought of making it as a theatrical film.

### The Adventures of Father Brown

*Father Brown* was another classic fictional detective that Four Star attempted to develop into a series. Based on the stories by G.K. Chesterton, the pilot for *The Adventures of Father Brown*, titled "Not Wanted on the Voyage," was scripted by Marc Brandel in 1962.

Father Brown, a Catholic priest who has a knack for solving crimes, and his confidential secretary, Flambeau, a reformed jewel thief, are on a ship headed to America to attend a conference in Chicago with other priests. Among other passengers on board are fashion model Cindy Jones and her photographer husband David Dexter; chemistry professor Briggs, Joe Miller, a sculptor and his wife Lady Claire, sailing to attend her daughter's wedding; Harold Pearson, a chemical engineer delivering a high-compression helium cylinder to a client in Ohio; and interior decorator Hilda Moore.

While on the ship, the passengers learn of the theft of a Grecian statue from the castle of the Duke of Sussex, Lady Claire's former husband. The theft was only discovered because the castle opened earlier in the season for visitors because the weather had turned warmer.

Dexter and the Miller's recognize Hilda Moore since she attempted to blackmail each of them – Dexter for his supposed involvement with another woman and the Miller's because Moore found that Lady Claire's daughter had had a nervous breakdown over a previous love affair. At night, passengers hear a splash into the water and a lady scream. Hilda Moore is missing, and the Captain wants Father Brown to investigate before the ship reaches New York. Father Brown determines that Moore was not pushed into the water because no one could have heard her later scream since the ship, based on its speed, would have quickly left that spot in the ocean. Rather Brown finds that Moore's body had been placed in a bulkhead on the ship and then taken to a storage hold. Moore was murdered after she screamed when she saw a man toss what looked like the body of a young girl into the ocean. The "body" turned out to be the stolen Grecian statue thrown into the water because the thief knew that it couldn't be sold given the wide publicity over the theft. The culprit had originally planned to sell the art work in the United States before the news of the crime had become known.

When Father Brown and Flambeau find Moore's body in the storage hold, the criminal locks the door and turns on the water to flood the compartment and drown the two investigators. However, the crew frees them. Father Brown figures that when everyone disembarks from the ship in New York, the culprit will be identified when he reacts with horror to seeing that the Father and his assistant are still alive. As the passengers leave the vessel, the only one who reacts to the sight of Father Brown is Harold Pearson – a master criminal who had smuggled the statue aboard the ship in the high-compression cylinder.

### Happy Island

For the 1963-64 TV season, Four Star considered filming a sixty-minute pilot based on a New York City excursion boat. The project, titled *Happy Island*, created by Jule Styne was to be written by Henry Garson.

## Arena

Harry Julian Fink created the concept for a series called *Arena* concerning a small-town district attorney in May 1963 but by September of that year, the project had been abandoned by Four Star. NBC expressed some interest in the idea, but the network's interest appeared to be more with Fink as a creator than it was with Four Star.

*Arena* was later made as a two-part episode of *The Richard Boone Show*, an anthology produced by Goodson-Todman, that replaced *The Dick Powell Show* on NBC for the 1963-64 season. The pilot starred Lloyd Bochner as Joseph Campbell, a district attorney with wants to run for the U.S. Senate. The two-part episode aired March 10 and 17, 1964.

In the two-parter, Campbell attempts to retain his integrity while seeking a Senatorial nomination against the late incumbent's widow. At the same time, he is involved with the case of Jeanette Brown (June Harding), a teenager charged with murdering a sailor. Campbell has to decide if Brown should be tried as an adult for the crime or as a juvenile. Whether he obtains the nomination or not may very well depend on his decision in the Brown case with potential supporters wanting him to decide in favor of trying Brown as an adult. The teenager claims that another man actually killed the sailor, but juvenile records from other states show that Brown was previously involved with shaking down and assaulting sailors. Campbell speaks before the nominating convention saying that he will not be corrupted and asks the attendees to vote their conscience. His opponent wins the nomination by acclamation. Subsequently, Campbell makes the decision to try Brown as an adult.

Richard Boone directed these two installments of his anthology and appeared as the judge considering the Brown case.

## Burden of Proof

In May 1963, Milton Raison presented Four Star with the idea of a legal show involving a District Attorney's office. Raison researched the files of the Los Angeles District Attorney's office as the basis for the series. Most legal series on television at the time like *Perry*

*Mason* and *The Defenders* presented court cases from the perspective of the defendant's attorney. As a news article at the time put it:

> You may never have heard of an hour long series called "Burden of Proof," but don't fret too much about it – you are not alone. Nobody else has heard of it either – largely because it exists only as an idea in the skull of Milton Raison.
>
> Even so, it is receiving favorable attention from a group of sorely put-upon gentlemen: the district attorney's of the United States.
>
> This distinguished group earnestly hopes that "Burden of Proof" will be bought and aired. They need it –mainly because of the terrible beating they have taken during the past six years (referring to Perry Mason who hadn't lost a case in six years).[91]

Tom McDermott was unable to arouse interest in the proposal, and by October the idea had been rejected.

### Gabe Savage

Writer Richard Alan Simmons came up with the idea for a one-hour Western dealing with the cavalry. A ninety-minute pilot was to be made with Robert Redford in the lead. In June, 1963, ABC expressed interest in the project. However, by September, not only ABC had passed on the concept but also CBS and NBC did as well.

### Dragon's Ocean

Late in the 1962-63 television season, Four Star pursued development of a series titled *Dragon's Ocean* about San Pedro fisherman. Richard Alan Simmons wrote a script for an action-adventure show about two men of the sea. Alejandro Rey was considered for one of the roles; Peter Falk was sought for the other role but was not available. Castings problems prevented a pilot from being made.

### Sam Durrell - C.I.A. Agent

Four Star had a tentative deal with ABC in July 1963 to make a pilot called *Sam Durrell – C.I.A.* featuring a combination James Bond –Mickey Spillane type character. Writer Christopher Knopf was set to develop the series. By September 1963, Knopf had left

Four Star and the project was assigned to Tom Gries. However, the writing team of John Pickard and Frank Provo did a treatment for the proposed series that had the lead character being briefed on a new mission, "Venus of Venice." An elderly Contessa, who also happens to be an agent, discovers a secret formula to permit chemical brainwashing and then disappears. Durrell saves the Contessa and would have lived to fight another day if the concept had been turned into a series. The project was tabled in October 1963.

### Omaha

Keeping with the production company's desire to build a series focusing on residents of a particular locale, Four Star considered another proposal from writer Alan LeMay in August 1963 about the development of Omaha, Nebraska. The story involves a group called the Claim Club, an organization that intended to stake out land claims west of the Missouri River and secure their claims by becoming an unofficial law enforcement group in the area. Townspeople are upset at Miles Overton, a steamboat captain, over his land claiming activities. The U.S. Marshal informs Overton that, in a private vote, he has been expelled from the Claim Club and that he owes a hefty amount of fines. However, the town populace comes to believe that Overton is a fighter on their behalf when he prevents a man from taking over a land claim from a homesteader while the homesteader and his wife are away. The townspeople pledge to continue leasing land from Overton.

A pilot based on this proposal was never made.

### The Four Lions

Martin Manulis was behind this one-hour family drama about three brothers and a sister living in different sections of the United States. The pilot script, written by Tad Mosel, focused on Margaret "Maggie" Lion, an Oscar-winning actress living in Beverly Hills; Alex Lion, the oldest sibling and president of Walden College in Ohio who is married with two children and living in the Lion family home; Mark Lion, the middle brother, an unmarried defense attorney residing in New York City; and John Lion, the youngest brother who travels around the world trying to find himself.

Actresses suggested for Margaret Lion included Hope Lange, Eva Marie Saint, Jean Simmons, Diana Lynn, and Barbara Rush. After cancelation of *The Robert Taylor Show*, Taylor was one of the possibilities for the Alex Lion role. Others considered for the role of Alex were Stuart Whitman, Cliff Robertson, and Van Johnson. Rod Taylor, Hugh O'Brien, and Robert Wagner were among those in contention for Mark Lion; actors thought of for the youngest brother included Gardner McKay, Patrick Wayne, and James MacArthur along with Brandon de Wilde.

All four leads would appear together in six episodes. Each of the leads would be the primary star of six other shows with either one or two of the other actors in supporting roles. In addition, each star would play three supporting roles in episodes during the season. The proposed series would feature action-adventure stories usually centered on the youngest brother, women's stories featuring the Maggie character, suspense dramas highlighting the activities of criminal defense attorney Mark Lion, and family dramas featuring all four leads as well as Alex Lion and his family.

The pilot script focused on the Lion's being chosen Family of the Year with a journalist interviewing the family about the honor. John remarks to his sister that he has been awarded a grant based on a competitive examination that will permit him to travel to South America after he graduates. The newspaper reporter brings up a letter to the editor sent in by an elderly professor at Alex's college stating that John won the grant by dishonest means. The American Family Institute that named the Lion's the Family of the Year also has questions about the letter. Alex thinks that the professor, soon due for retirement, is senile. However, John divulges that the professor actually took the examination for him in order to show that his mind was still intact. John's grant is taken away, and he decides to go out on his own.

By December 1963, the concept for the series was dead with Four Star thinking of focusing just on Taylor and Wagner as Los Angeles police officers. When the *L.A.* idea never came to fruition, Tom McDermott at Four Star considered reactivating *The Four Lions* premise for the 1964-65 season, but by October 1964, the project was tabled.

### Settlement House

Jackie Cooper Productions along with Four Star planned an hour-long dramatic series with the pilot to be directed by Cooper in 1963. Norman Lessing wrote a script for the potential series called "The Street" in which a character named Johnny Barth, a graduate of Settlement House, a boys' school, returns for a visit. When he arrives, he finds that Stanley Page, a classmate of his when he attended the school, has been convicted of murder. The convict's younger brother, Mike, a student at the school, is upset over his brother's incarceration. Johnny decides to help both of them by convincing Stanley to appeal his death sentence and by making sure that Mike does not follow in his brother's footsteps. In the end, Johnny decides to teach acting at the school.

Earlier, Four Star had made a deal with Jackie Cooper Productions in 1962 for Cooper to star in a situation comedy but that project never got off the ground. Also, apparently, *Settlement House* never went beyond the script.

### K.E.Y. (aka The Ninth Key)

The writing team of Ivan Goff and Ben Roberts developed a one-hour action-adventure drama for Four Star in spring 1964. Consideration was given to having Robert Taylor as the star of this vehicle. CBS had expressed some interest in the project. However, Taylor seemed uninterested. By July 1964, Goff and Roberts reconceived the series as featuring a trio of investigators who accepted difficult assignments from any strata of society, but this project never went forward.

### The Survivors

ABC made a deal with Aaron Spelling to produce a drama-suspense pilot in June 1964. The project was compared to the movie *Guns of Navarone* in style, but would not have dealt with war, which presumably meant that the drama would focus on a team of undercover operatives carrying out special assignments. By October, both Four Star and ABC dropped the idea.

### Focus on Adventure (aka *The Photographer*)

Created by James Michener and to be produced by Martin Manulis, this adventure series was to star Robert Wagner and would be filmed abroad in Istanbul. ABC and then CBS initially expressed interest in the property. However, by September 1964, the project was dead. Michener was unable to work on the series due to other commitments. Wagner then teamed up with producer Sheldon Reynolds for the half-hour detective adventure series, *Area Code 212*.

### Willie Cannon

The producing team of Gardner, Laven, and Levy came up with the concept for a one-hour legal drama concerning a law officer and the criminals he has known. The series would have a contemporary look with the stories told in flashbacks. By July 1964, both CBS and ABC had rejected the idea.

### Territory North Atlantic

In July 1964, a pitch was made to CBS about Four Star developing a one-hour adventure/suspense series concerning security on the high seas. No pilot was ever made after CBS lost interest in the idea.

### The Adventurer (aka *The Playboy*)

In the spring and summer of 1964, Four Star's Tom McDermott wanted to develop a modern version of the classic, *The Scarlet Pimpernel*. Ivan Goff and Ben Roberts scripted a one-hour pilot for ABC. When that network passed on the project, CBS considered it but then rejected the show as well.

The writing team of John Pickard and Frank Provo also developed treatments and scripts for this potential series. Their work centered on millionaire David Nelson Michael Harrington who appears in newspapers as a typical playboy but actually uses this persona as a cover for fighting crime. Based in San Francisco, David has a sister named Janet, married with two children and a mother named Elinor. Assisting David in his crime fighting is an ex-safe cracker turned valet, Herbert Giles Bagnold.

In a pilot script written by Pickard and Provo titled "Roses Are Red, Cobalt Is Blue, and I Love You," David has an alternate identity as Percy Blakeney, whose mission is to disrupt the crimes of a Greek villain named Spiridou. In the Percy persona, David is suave and effective, but as himself, he is shy and clumsy. David frees a woman named Nicole from Spiridou and defeats his criminal plans, but Nicole is killed in the end.

## Royal Bay

This drama pilot was a reworking of the 1963 effort titled *Adamsburg, U.S.A*, with ABC considering turning it into a series.

Joan Crawford made a guest appearance in the pilot, which featured Paul Burke as Barney Stafford, a young lawyer in the seaside town of Royal Bay. Charles Bickford appeared as Burke's father, Hugh. Bickford's character had three other sons including a psychologist played by Richard Carlson. The concept of the proposed series was that each episode would feature the exploits of one of Stafford's four sons.

In *Royal Bay*, Crawford, who helped produce the pilot, plays Della Chapelle. Della has a daughter, Jenny (Diane Baker) suffering from a rare skin disease that causes extreme sensitivity to daylight which is why Della conducts most of her business at night. Although Crawford appears in the pilot, she apparently would have made only recurring appearances if the project had become a series. When the pilot didn't sell, *Royal Bay* was titled *Della (*aka *Fatal Confinement)* to focus on Crawford's character and released as a movie which is probably why some think that this film was an unsold pilot for a Joan Crawford television series.

## Hell Cats

Aaron Spelling created this sixty-minute comedy/adventure pilot about a group of barnstorming aviators. George Hamilton starred as Lee Ragdon, one of three stunt flyers, part of an aerial circus, in the pilot filmed in October 1964 for the 1965-66 season for ABC. His buddies were Rippy Sloane (Warren Berlinger) and Buggs Middle (John Craig). Ragdon performed stunts in his World War I biplane. The story concerned an attractive balloonist (Barbara Eden) talking the three men into joining a revolution in South America. The pilot was eventually broadcast by ABC on *Off to See the Wizard*, a 1967-68 anthology series.

## Area Code 212

Produced, written, and directed by Sheldon Reynolds, this pilot, made in late December 1964, starred Robert Wagner as a New York private eye who hires himself out for $75 a day and expenses provided there's no danger involved in the case. If danger is involved, he suggests the client contact the police. The private detective can do anything, but doesn't want to be in harm's way.

Talking about the pilot, Wagner said: "If the show is bought and wins high ratings, we can then work on strength. The possibilities and situations are numerous. He can go to Europe, the far and/or middle east, the orient, anyplace. We want to be slightly removed; but entertaining. We do know that, when the character does get involved, the audience knows he can handle any situation in a most honest and human way."[92]

## Three for Danger

Three soldiers of fortune – Larry Pennell as Chris, Alejandro Rey as Alan, and Charles Carlson as Simon, sail the seas on the "Quest," a ninety-five foot, two-masted schooner in search of adventure. The trio becomes involved in a woman's (Joanna Petit) plot to help her husband (Jason Evers) steal $10 million in gold bullion. The unsold pilot, made in 1965, aired on September 8, 1967.

## Pursue and Destroy

For ABC, this pilot, originally called *Sea Wolves*, starred Van Williams as Capt. Russ Enright, the commander of a submarine in the Pacific during World War II and Paul Comi as Lieut. Barney Redesko. While on a mission to take out Japanese destroyers, Enright finds that his sub's torpedoes are missing their targets causing his vessel to receive heavy enemy fire and be destroyed. After rescue, Enright claims that the torpedoes are faulty but subsequent tests show that they hit their marks.

Enright is assigned command of a new sub, the Blue Fin, to go on a special mission to rescue British citizens stranded on a Pacific island. Arriving at the island, the crew finds that a wounded soldier needs special care meaning the Blue Fin will not be able to leave under cover of darkness. Coming under enemy fire, the rescue party barely escapes.

The sub's next mission is to take out a Japanese convoy hoping that the torpedoes will be more effective this time. They aren't. The crew finds that the weapons run too deep passing under their targets. Adjusting the depth settings allows the torpedoes to hit their mark.

Produced and directed by Don Taylor and written by Ivan Goff and Ben Roberts, the pilot aired August 14, 1966.

### High Noon

This 1966 pilot, based on the Gary Cooper motion picture *High Noon* and written by James Warner Bellah and Robert Enders, starred Peter Fonda as Will Kane, Jr. returning to the town where his father had been sheriff. Marshal Will Kane had just been killed by the sons of Frank Miller, the man Kane had rid the town of years earlier. Kane Jr. wants to find his father's killers.

He meets Helen Ramirez (Katy Jurado) who gives him one of his dad's old guns for protection. Will Kane Jr. meets the town's current marshal and helps him take care of some local outlaws. The marshal gives Kane his father's old badge with Will deciding to stay in the town to wait for Miller's sons.

### The Savages

Actor Robert Pickering starred in this 1966 unsold pilot, produced by Collier Young and written by Betty Andrews, as a young unmarried attorney who, after eight years of touring the world, returns to his home town to start a law practice. This family drama focusing on the Savage family featured Jeanette Nolan and her husband John McIntyre as the attorney's parents and Nancy Olson as his love interest. The proposed series was described as an anatomy of an American family.

### Red Rover

Written by Dan Ingalls and Richard Newton, the script for this pilot, titled "All the Wild Decembers," set in 1870, focused on a young boy searching for his father. The boy's dad had drawn the fire from Indians attacking a way station where he and his son, Red Rover, were holed up. The father escaped in one direction; his son in another direction. Now Red Rover is roaming the West to find his dad. An elderly man named Adam comes upon Red's campsite. He has a bullet wound in his shoulder, and Red tries to help him. The man says he was wounded because he caught a man cheating at cards. Three men – Griff, Tate, and Mr. Boley, are pursuing Adam. When Adam's wound begins bleeding again, he and Red visit some friends of Adam's – an orphaned brother and sister, who try to help the old man. Feeling stronger, Adam decides to leave on his own, but Red has to accompany him. Griff, Tate, and Boley spot them as Adam and Red head for a town where Adam's wife, whom he hasn't seen in years, lives. Delirious, Adam confesses to Red that he was shot for trying to steal a horse – not because of discovering a man cheating. The two come upon the outskirts of the town when Adam passes away. The place is a ghost town having been abandoned years ago. The three men trying to catch Adam see Red burying his body.

No pilot was ever made for this proposed half-hour series.

# Chapter 14:
# More Four Star Sitcom Attempts, 1963- 67

In the mid-to late-1960s, Four Star tried again and again to launch a successful comedy series on network television. They only succeeded in premiering one sitcom which lasted for one season.

## *The Smothers Brothers Show*

Not to be confused with the brothers' various variety series, this comedy, which premiered on September 17, 1965 on CBS, dealt with Tommy as an apprentice angel trying to help people and often asking for assistance from his brother Dick, an executive at Pandora Publications. Leonard J. Costello (Roland Winters) appeared as Dick's boss. Harriet MacGibbon, most remembered for her role as Mrs. Drysdale on *The Beverly Hillbillies*, was Mrs. Costello, and Marilyn Scott played the Costello's daughter.

Produced by Four Star and Knave Productions, Aaron Spelling and Richard Newton created the comedy. Shortly after the show premiered, Spelling left Four Star to form his own production company with United Artists in 1966. As he remarked, "I left Four Star in 1966 after some idiot decided to wipe Dick Powell's name off the masthead. I didn't want to work there anymore, and just walked out . . ."[93]

Spelling decided to develop a series for the Smothers Brothers after they appeared as the Rafer Brothers on an episode of *Burke's Law* titled, "Who Killed the Richest Man in the World?" However, the brothers were used to working in front of a live audience and improvising – something that a filmed one-camera comedy did not permit.

Writers Alan Burns and Chris Hayward wrote the original pilot script for the series when it was titled *The People Watchers*. In that pilot, Dick worked as an administrative assistant for Amalgamated

*Dick and Tommy Smothers in a scene from "Halo in the Ring," a November 12, 1965 episode of* The Smothers Brothers Show.

Consolidated Ltd. Alan Bunce appeared as his boss, Leonard Costello, and Julie Parrish had the role of Costello's daughter, Diane. The unaired pilot concerned Tom attempting to break up a gambling ring of little old ladies.

Phil Sharp, the initial producer of *The Smothers Brothers Show*, did not blend well with the brothers' personalities. A veteran comedy writer, Sharp had authored scripts for *The Phil Silvers Show*, *I Married Joan*, and *The Donna Reed Show*. As Tommy Smothers put it:

> Sharp was our producer, and there was a personality conflict the first time we met. He was once a comedy writer, and they are all frustrated comedians. Maybe we came in cocky, but we did have seven years experience in our particular brand of comedy, which wasn't commercial for a long time – until we made it commercial. Phil had definite ideas on how we should do the show. We came in, and we didn't pretend to be actors. But we were confined by the scripts, there was no latitude, we couldn't ad lib. This was his interpretation of comedy. Our problem was that what we were doing was not what we were hired for. They could get any two comedians for that. We felt we were losing our identity, and it got to the point where we couldn't work together.[94]

Because of the problems the brothers had acting on a filmed series, at one point CBS considered scarping the sitcom and have the Smothers Brothers appear on a half-hour variety show. Fred de Cordova replaced Sharp as producer. He along with Aaron Spelling and the director gave the brothers more leeway to rewrite the sitcom scripts and ad lib.

In the first regular episode, Tommy appears to Dick as an apprentice angel "to help people when they get in jams and such stuff." His first assignment is to reunite two lovers who have been separated by thousands of miles and the U.S. Navy.

Episodes usually began with Tom and Dick doing a comedy routine and then telling viewers what to expect in this week's installment. For instance, in "The Boss Who Came to Breakfast, Lunch and Dinner" which aired March 25, 1966, the episode begins with Tommy looking at a TV set as Dick enters declaring that now is no time to watch television. Tommy, referring to the viewers, responds "Don't tell <u>them</u> that . . . or you'll be an unemployed S.B. S.B. is for Smothers Brothers . . . of which we are each one. Sometimes I wish Mom had named me 'Which' instead of Tommy . . . so people could say, 'Which is Which Smothers?'"[95]

On the episode, Dick Smothers boss' Leonard J. Costello attempts to avoid a process server who wants a deposition from him to try to prevent his wife from realizing stock options worth $1 million. Costello hides out in the Smothers brothers' apartment. This installment demonstrates Tommy's attempts, as an apprentice angel, at magic. In one scene, trying to hide Costello in a trunk, Tommy closes his eyes and makes a squeezing gesture for a trunk to appear. Initially a bare tree trunk materializes. He tries again, and a midget elephant comes up. On the third try, a trunk large enough for Mr. Costello finally appears.

Other shows had Tommy trying to un-haunt a supposedly haunted house and helping to unseat a corrupt mayor.

On the haunted house adventure, Dick is attempting to persuade Chloe O'Brien (Mary Ann Mobley) to find her late uncle's manuscript for a mystery novel to which Dick's company owns the publishing rights. Chloe's cousin, a bookstore owner, doesn't want her to sell the uncle's house which everyone thinks is haunted and which contains the manuscript. Dick and Tommy find the missing manuscript in a wall safe in the house and discover that the cousin is behind the strange happenings. The cousin wanted to retrieve the uncle's rare book collection to sell at his store.

"His Honor, The Crook" episode, written by Lila Garrett and Bernie Kahn, dealt with Mayor Link of Kipsleyville who has been in office for a number of years. Tommy meets with city officials to share information on how corrupt the mayor is, but the officials are all the mayor's relatives. Tommy's revelations fall on deaf ears. He decides to run for mayor of the town as Farmer Jones against Link. Link tries to bribe Tommy to drop out of the race, but the angel refuses. In a debate, Tommy points out how the sister city of Buntley has thrived, while Kipsleyville has not. When, in response, Mayor Link offers a "tax rebate" to all the citizens, they see it as a bribe and vote for Tommy. However, Tommy learns that there was a proposition on the ballot to incorporate Kipsleyville with Buntley, and so Kipsleyville now has no need for a mayor.

Despite the initial behind-the-scenes issues and a relatively low number of CBS affiliates airing the series, the first ratings looked promising. The show landed in the top 10. However, as the season wore on, the ratings declined leading to its cancelation.

Of course, the brothers Smothers would have much more success on CBS in a one-hour variety series beginning in 1968.

# Comedy Projects and Pilots 1963-67

### Jugger

In 1963, Four Star optioned the book *Jugger* by Sterling "Red" Quinlan as the basis for a possible comedy series. Jugger is an old rascal who lives on the outskirts of Crater Village in upstate New York. He loves to drink applejack and lives by his wits often appropriating food and other items from the good citizens of the community. The town's welcome sign to visitor's states: "Crater Village: Where You Will Want to Die."

Four Star may have decided against developing a comedy around a not-so-lovable character who, among other transgressions, steals from churches, and would rather get drunk than work for a living.

### Mimi

Four Star worked very hard to come up with a comedy vehicle to display the talents of Mimi Hines and her partner Phil Ford. Initially, Mac Benoff was enlisted to write a script for the comedy team as ex-vaudevillians who couldn't make it in show business and so open their own restaurant. The Ford character has a heart-of-gold and can't turn away his deadbeat actor friends. Tom McDermott shelved this idea and contracted with Everett Greenbaum and Jim Fritzell to develop a new pilot about the operation of a modern motel. This script didn't pass muster either, and so Artie Stander was enlisted to write yet another pilot. This one was filmed in October 1962. ABC expressed some interest in the pilot but ultimately rejected it.

In November 1963 a new pilot was written and directed by Phil Rapp. This pilot, "The Garden of Eden," had Phil Ford and Mimi Hines working at a summer health resort and attempted to display Mimi's physical comedy to its fullest extent. Ford played a therapist at the resort; Mimi was a dietician.

On the pilot, Mimi's character annoys a famous French ballet master named Monsieur Quibideaux (Thomas Gomez) by dancing into his room with a flying tourjette. She jumps on his sofa and continues dancing clumsily falling onto the man causing him to hurt his back.

Later, a jockey registers at the resort. His manager advises the head of the Garden of Eden that the jockey can have only kelp juice to maintain his weight for an upcoming race. When Mimi and Phil are instructed to deliver a large dinner to the ballet master, the inevitable happens. The large meal is delivered to the jockey who consumes it with gusto; the ballet master receives the kelp juice much to his displeasure. Mimi and Phil try to smuggle the jockey into the exercise room so he can lose some weight and then take him back to his room. In the process, Mimi accidentally ends up in the ballet master's room where, in the darkness, she trips and lands on him while he is sleeping in his bed. Near the end, Mimi and Phil take the jockey to the race track. When the jockey passes out from exhaustion, Mimi dresses as the jockey but then finds out that the jockey's horse has been scratched from the race because it injured itself by over eating.

Mimi Hines and Phil Ford never did get their own sitcom.

### The Dean Jones Show

After the demise of *Ensign O'Toole*, Four Star pursued another comedy for Dean Jones. Sheldon Keller and Howard Merrill, who wrote several *Ensign O'Toole* episodes, came up with the idea of Jones as the owner of an apartment building who becomes involved in the lives of his tenants. An alternative title considered for the possible series was *Bungalow Court*. The pilot was shot in December 1963.

### George Gobel/Carol Channing Project

In the mid-sixties, Four Star also looked at the possibility of pairing Carol Channing and George Gobel in an untitled comedy, but nothing came of this endeavor.

## Comedy-Western project

In spring 1964, Four Star thought of developing a one-hour comedy Western based on an idea from producer Henry Kleiner. No title for the project was ever given, and it never got to the pilot stage.

## *Poppy*

Tom McDermott was pushing the company to film a thirty-minute teenage sitcom called *Poppy* in April 1964 but again nothing appears to have developed from this idea.

## *Apartment 3-G*

Gene Barry sought to create a half-hour comedy with Four Star based on the syndicated newspaper cartoon strip called *Apartment 3-G*. The comic strip, which began in May, 1961, had three main characters: Margo Magee, a brunette secretary, who held other positions over the life of the strip, Abigail "Tommie" Thompson, a redheaded nurse, and Lu Ann Powers, a blonde art teacher. They all lived in apartment 3-G in Manhattan. Irving Cooper was to write the pilot script for a possible ABC series. However, by early September 1964, the project was in limbo.

## *Malcolm (aka The Johnny Crawford Show)*

After *The Rifleman* ended, Four Star attempted a series starring Johnny Crawford. Produced by Gardner, Laven, and Levy, the idea initially was to star Crawford in a comedy Western. But by January 1964, the concept changed to feature Crawford as Malcolm, a nineteen-year-old husband with an eighteen-year-old wife played by Sandra Descher and the father of a new baby. Jeff Donnell and Paul Reed appeared as Malcolm's parents, and Tom D'Andrea was Malcolm's boss at the gas station where he worked. If it had become a series, it was intended to premiere as a mid-season replacement in January 1965.

## *The Dean Jones Show (aka Alec Tate)*

Trying to find yet another vehicle for Dean Jones' talents, during fall, 1964, Four Star piloted the actor in a comedy in which he played Professor Alec Tate, the head of research and development for a think tank, Magna Dynamics Corporation. Alec, age thirty, is a swinging bachelor who becomes the guardian for his teenage sister Bunny (Robyn Millan). To be the appropriate role model for his sister, he attempts to give up his playboy lifestyle and uses a computer named "CLARA" as a guide on how to raise his sibling. Bunny sets him up with her friend's cousin, an attractive blonde named Sherry who, after he kisses her, thinks they are engaged. Alec pretends that he wants to marry Sherry for her money, but the plan backfires when her wealthy dad confesses that he also was a fortune hunter. Sherry calls off the wedding when she finds that Alec is really a playboy.

Starring with Jones in the pilot was Jay C. Flippen as Captain Skidmore, Alec's landlord. Four Star thought the pairing of the two actors from *Ensign O'Toole* might be a good selling point for the pilot.

This Dean Jones project appears to have grown out of an idea titled *1088 and Bonnie Tate*, a half-hour comedy dealing with an electronics engineer and a computer that had been rejected both by CBS and ABC in summer 1964. Before this premise came about, Jones was to play a young, bachelor lawyer whose life is interrupted by his young sister named Kelly.

### Oh, Nurse!

In September 1964, Four Star looked at the feasibility of making a pilot written by Norman Hudis about the misadventures of hospital nurses. Hudis had written several of the popular British *Carry On* films including *Carry On Nurse*, which chronicled the antics of the female nurses and male patients in a hospital ward. The sitcom proposal was submitted to CBS which passed on it.

### Our Man in Suburbia

Also in fall 1964, writer/producer George Axlerod, who wrote the screenplays for *Breakfast at Tiffany's*, *The Seven Year Itch*, and *Will Success Spoil Ross Hunter?*, among many others, developed a project at Four Star for CBS that would star actor Eddie Mayehoff. The proposed comedy was to be a co-production between Four Star and Axelrod's company, Charleston Enterprises. However, no pilot materialized.

### The Bette Davis Show (aka The Decorator)

Starring none other than screen legend Bette Davis, this late 1964 pilot was produced by Aaron Spelling for Four Star. In the pilot, Davis plays an interior designer named Liz who lives briefly with her clients in order to become accustomed to their tastes as she redecorates their homes. Richard Kinon directed the effort from a teleplay by Cy Howard and Matt Crowley based on a story by Cy Howard. Mary Wickes played Viola, Liz's assistant.

A wealthy judge (Ed Begley) from Oklahoma wants to hire Liz for $10,000. Since she is heavily in debt, Liz takes the job with two conditions – she must be given carte blanche when decorating and must live with the client during the redecorating process so that the home will reflect the client's personality. The judge's daughter Missy (Davey Davison) is to be married, and the judge wants Liz to redo the farm house he and his wife lived in when they were first married. He is giving it as a wedding gift to his daughter and her fiancé, Jim (James Stacey). The judge hopes that Liz will show his daughter the good life so she will decide not to marry her less-than-prosperous fiancé. However, Liz encourages Missy and Jim to elope to avoid Missy's father planning all details of the wedding. Liz does redecorate the farm house like it was when the judge and his wife Mabel lived there. Naturally, the judge likes what she has done.

If the pilot had gone to series, each week a new guest star would appear as Liz's client. CBS first considered buying this property and then ABC thought about scheduling it for the 1965-66 season, but never did.

### Tell Aggie

Ben Roberts and Ivan Goff developed this comedy for NBC about a female newspaper editor based on Aggie Underwood, editor of the *Los Angeles Examiner*. By the time the pilot was scheduled to be shot in December, 1964, the setting changed from a newspaper office to a television station with the main character being an advice columnist for a television program who wants to help people who ask for her opinions on personal problems. Marlyn Mason portrayed the lead character. Brett Somers co-starred in the pilot playing a chef who had a cooking segment on Aggie's TV show.

Reminiscing about the pilot, Ms. Mason remarked that "There was a not unusual upbeat feeling about the show as we were doing it; I was a natural for comedy as were all my cohorts, so it was disappointing when it didn't make the list (of pilots picked up as a series)."[96]

### Which Way to the Beach?

In conjunction with Teen-Age Fair Inc., headed by Al Burton, Bart Ross, and Frank Danzig, Four Star sought to develop a teen-age sitcom called *Which Way to the Beach?* The script for this 1965 pilot was written by Paul Rapp.

### Ace of the Mounties

This never-sold 1966 pilot concerned a strait-laced Royal Canadian Mounted Police Constable, Wade Terhune (Ron Hussman) with a lazy St. Bernard named Ace who never obeyed his master. Terhune thought the world of the dog. Ace was the dumbest dog in the Mounties' kennel, but he had a strong jaw and sharp teeth. The dog would only move when told to "sit."

Joan Blondell was featured as Ma Devereaux, the owner of the local trading post, in this comedy take-off of *Sergeant Preston of the Yukon*. Others in the pilot included John Williams, as Inspector Nigel Fairchild to whom Terhune reported and Gabby Devereaux (Susan Yardley), Ma's daughter and potential love interest for Terhune. Written by Chris Hayward and Allan Burns, the pilot episode titled "Call of the Mild" was produced by Four Star for ABC.

The story line involved Terhune dealing with fur traders trying to cheat the Indians and the traders' boss, Dirk Sangler (Simon Oakland). The Mountie has the traders pay up and leaves the money with Ma Devereaux for safekeeping, but he soon learns from Gabby that Ma needs help fending off Sangler and his men who want their money back. Terhune spots explosives and asks Ace to carry the dynamite to the stove in the saloon where Dirk and his boys hang out. Instead, Ace puts the dynamite in Ma's stove just as Dirk and his gang enter the trading post. After the explosion, Terhune captures the men and thinks that Ace, buried under some wood, is dead. But the dog is just sleeping. Subsequently, Terhune learns that Spangler is one of the most wanted criminals in that part of Canada, thereby making Terhune a hero.

The pilot was shot in a canyon near Los Angeles which the production company sprayed with artificial snow to look like Canada in the winter. It never became a series because it was aimed for an early time slot on ABC's schedule, and the network had no openings for a comedy of this type aimed at youngsters.

### Robin Hood Jr.

Written by Arnold Margolin and Jim Parker, this proposed series about Robin Hood's son was to be produced by Fred de Cordova.

### The King and Me

Created and written by Lila Garrett and Bernie Kahn, this comedy project centered on a fictional movie actress who marries the king of a principality. Any similarity to the marriage of Grace Kelly to Prince Rainier of Monaco was purely intentional. Zsa Zsa Gabor was to play the actress with Peter Lawford under consideration for the role of the king in this potential 1966 series.

### Klutz's Pirates

This proposed situation comedy about clumsy pirates was written by Alex Gottlieb in 1966. However, no pilot resulted from the script.

### I Married a Bear

Developed for the 1967-68 season, *I Married a Bear* concerned Fran Loomis (Michele Lee) and her husband Roger (Stephen Young), parents of a son named Rover (Ron Rich) and a daughter, Julie. Roger is a baseball player for the fictional Bears. In the pilot, Roger's hand becomes stuck in a garbage disposal when trying to retrieve Fran's wedding ring. Unwilling to lose the ring, Roger misses a game. In the end, the wedding ring turns up in the couple's bedroom where it was all along. The ring he was trying to retrieve was a plastic toy that Julie had lost. However, Roger didn't lose out on playing with the team since the game had been rained out.

General Foods had backed the pilot but, upon viewing the completed project, abandoned sponsoring the potential series.

## The Pickle Brothers

Written by Gerald Gardner and Dee Caruso, this 1966 comedy effort starred the three Pickle Brothers – Baxter Pickle (Ron Prince), Buddy Pickle (Mike Mislove), and Bobo Pickle (Peter Lee). The Pickle Brothers were really a comedy team dubbed "The Uncalled for Three," that performed in clubs and on college campuses in the 1960s. In the pilot, the "brothers" tried to replicate the antics of the Marx brothers' films.

The premise of the series was that each week the brothers would attempt a new vocation. In the pilot, the three checked into a hotel in New York City called the Manor House to produce a movie, *Moses Takes a Wife*. They work with the hotel staff for seven weeks rehearsing with very mixed results. The hotel manager demands they fork over the seven weeks of rent they owe. Since they don't have the money, they spend a lot of time avoiding the hotel detective. Baxter Pickle, the Groucho Marx wannabe of the group, barges into a meeting with Mrs. DeWitt (Carol Veazie), the owner of the hotel who is trying to sell the place. Baxter says he will purchase the hotel for $2.5 million and is given two weeks to raise the money. When he fails in this attempt, the brothers try to come up with a publicity stunt that will draw guests to the hotel. While the brothers are also unsuccessful in this endeavor, guests do start arriving – all part of a princesses' entourage. The princess had been impressed by Bobo's comedic efforts.

Dee Caruso and Gerald Gardner had written several episodes of *The Monkees*, and the humor in *The Pickle Brothers* pilot was very similar to that of *The Monkees*. The pilot was directed by William Friedkin who later helmed films like *The French Connection* (1971) and *The Exorcist* (1973).

About the pilot, Peter Lee remarked that it was very close to getting picked up. "It was real network cowardice. Supposedly they were afraid that we couldn't keep it up, but I think they thought it was just too out there."[97]

## Manley and the Mob

In 1967, Four Star head Tom McDermott announced two half-hour comedy projects – *The King Thing* and *Flat in London*. Details on the premise of each of these potential pilots could not be found, but one pilot the company did make in 1967 was *Manley and the Mob*.

Another effort written by Dee Caruso and Gerald Gardner, it starred Paul Lynde as a dim-witted private detective named Manley Toombs with actor Nehemiah Persoff playing a mob boss named Big Mike Corbo.

The pilot for ABC involved the murder of Benny Cosgrove, a mob boss competing with Mike Corbo who runs a nightclub and casino. When Cosgrove's body is found in Corbo's office, he attempts to plant the corpse on Manley to frame him for the murder. Manley finds the body and tries to get rid of it only to have one of Corbo's men find it. Eventually, the police become involved in the case. Manley explains to the police that, through a process of elimination, he knows who killed Cosgrove. The murderer is not Corbo but instead is a woman named Toby Clarice (Arlene Golonka) that Cosgrove knew.

*Manley and the Mob* was not picked up as a series by any network.

# Chapter 15:
# Four Star's Game, Variety, and Reality Shows, 1963- 67

By the mid-sixties, Four Star started to turn away from producing series for ABC, CBS, and NBC and focused more on syndication not only of reruns of its network series but also distributing first-run game and variety shows to local stations. Producing game shows was not really a new endeavor for the company. In the mid-fifties, Four Star attempted to make a game show, *Pass the Buck*. Nothing is known about the format of the show, and, apparently, no pilot was made.

In September, 1961, Dick Powell and Tom McDermott decided to purchase Heatter-Quigley Enterprises in order to diversify the company's participation in live television. Acquiring the services of Merrill Heatter and Bob Quigley to create and develop game shows led to Four Star having its first successful shows in this category. Both Heatter and Quigley had worked with Tom McDermott when he was at Benton & Bowles.

In November 1961, NBC showed some interest in Four Star attempting to update the long-running radio show *Information Please* where people submitted questions to a panel of experts. Dave Garroway was under consideration as the moderator. The suggestion was that the proposed series be developed as a world-wide quiz program using an international panel. But the project did not get to the pilot stage.

The new videotaped series Four Star introduced from 1963 to 1967 are profiled below.

### *People Will Talk*

Partnering with Bob Quigley and Merrill Heatter, Four Star made its first daytime game show, *People Will Talk*, hosted by Dennis James.

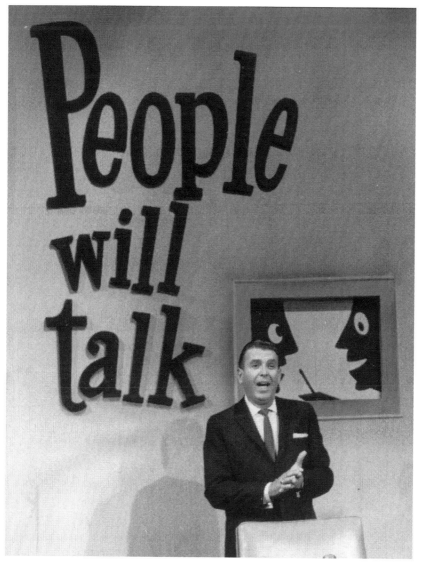

*Dennis James on* People Will Talk.

The series, appearing on NBC, ran from July 1, 1963 to December 27 of that year.

Contestants argued both sides of a question like, "Should a woman lie about her age?" After considering both sides of the argument, a panel of celebrities would then vote "yes" or "no." The contestants would try to choose a celebrity that they thought agreed with their argument. If the contestant and celebrity matched, the contestant would win $25. If they didn't match, the other contestant would win the money. The first contestant to win a total of $100, won the match.

The pilot for *People Will Talk* was made in August 1962 with Arthur Godfrey as host. It had an eighteen-member panel with each contestant selecting three panelists hoping the panelists would support his or her position on the topic. At the time, Heatter and Quigley also planned a children's version of the show to be called *Small Talk*.

## *The Celebrity Game*

Four Star brought its first game show to prime-time TV hosted by Carl Reiner and produced by Heatter and Quigley. The show replaced *The Judy Garland Show* on CBS on April 5, 1964.

Somewhat similar in format to *People Will Talk*, *The Celebrity Game* had a panel of nine celebrities who would lock in their "yes" and "no" answers to questions like "Can most women keep a secret?" The contestants would then try to guess how each celebrity responded and why. Correct guesses won the contestant money.

## *Shenanigans*

Four Star got into the children's TV business in conjunction with Heatter-Quigley Productions with this Saturday morning program hosted by Stubby Kaye. The show premiered on ABC September 26, 1964. Kaye, dressed in straw hat, bow tie, and plaid sports jacket would open the show singing the *Shenanigans* theme song. Kenny, the Cop (Kenny Williams) would assist Kaye with the game. Kids competed on a game board moving space by space as determined by two children called "pressers" who pressed a button to determine the number of moves (from one to four) that a contestant could make. Depending on the square on which the contestant landed, he or she would win a prize, accumulate "shenaniganzers" money which could be used to trade for prizes, or sometimes had to go to the doghouse and be temporarily out of the game. The first contestant to the finish line won the game and additional prizes.

## Hollywood A Go Go

This music variety series originated in Los Angeles on station KHJ-TV in 1964 and was initially titled *Ninth Street West*. The show was similar to ABC's *American Bandstand*. Four Star began syndicating its fifty-two episodes nationwide in January 1965. Hosted by Sam Riddle, the regular music group on *Hollywood A Go Go* was The Sinners (Tony, Vic, and Manuel) and dancing was performed by The Gazzarri Dancers.

The series featured acts such as The Platters, Freddy Cannon, The Everly Brothers, The Byrds, Tina Turner, Lesley Gore, Simon & Garfunkel, Glen Campbell, Rick Nelson, Chuck Berry, Sonny & Cher, and The Rolling Stones.

On the initial syndicated offering the guests were Round Robin, the show's answer to Chubby Checker; singer Carol Connors; The Serendipity Singers; Joe and Eddie, the Walker Brothers; Skip Batten, formerly part of "Skip and Flip;" and the new singing duo of Rick and Donna. The young audience members clapped and danced to every performance which ranged from soul, to rock 'n roll, to folk songs. Like Dick Clark, host Sam Riddle had a photogenic smile throughout the program. Riddle later became a producer and announcer for the talent show, *Star Search*.

## P.D.Q.

Four Star syndicated the Heatter-Quigley game show, *P.D.Q.* that ran for four years beginning fall 1965. Hosted by Dennis James, the show involved two teams trying to guess words or phrases from letter clues. One member of each team was placed in a soundproof booth, the other was shown a phrase and then placed the first three letters on a game board for his/her partner to see. The partner had to correctly guess the phrase or have letters added one at a time until he or she figured it out. The other team then got a chance to work with the same phrase. The team using the least amount of letters before a correct guess won. One team had two celebrities; the other team consisted of one celebrity and a contestant.

## *Winchell-Mahoney Time*

Written by ventriloquist Paul Winchell, his then-wife Nina Russell, and Tom Dagenais, this children's show, originally broadcast on KTTV in Los Angeles, was syndicated by Four Star from 1965 to 1968.

Winchell had pioneered new techniques in ventriloquism by placing his dummies in front of a backdrop painted on loosely woven cloth – a scrim, which appeared solid when viewed from the front. While he provided the voices and worked his dummies' heads, his assistants would operate the dummies' arms through the scrim backdrop. Winchell's cast of characters included his most famous dummy, Jerry Mahoney; Knucklehead Smith; Tessie O'Shea; Scats the Scarecrow, a bird that isn't really scared; and Mr. Goody-Good, a combination of man, costume, and trick photography.

As writer Tom Dagenais commented about the show, "Our own kids watch this show, so we have something personal at stake here. We try to incorporate a lesson or moral into the show. Something they can take with them."[98]

## *Showdown*

Premiering on NBC daytime on July 4, 1966, this game show, hosted by then controversial talk-show host, Joe Pyne, featured two teams of three contestants each competing in a question and answer game. The members of each team would have something in common such as a male team consisting of three fighter pilots and a female team made up of models. Each team would have to lock in an answer to a multiple-choice question with four possible answers only one of which was correct. An incorrect answer would cause a player to literally drop out of the game through a trap door underneath their seat. When all members of a team were eliminated, the other team would win $100 and play a "Triple Threat" bonus round. In the bonus round, the team had to answer one question correctly to win a vacation. If they answered wrong, they continued on the show against a new team.

A rock n' roll group called The Bantams played music during the show and sometimes provided musical clues for certain questions. The series was produced by Heatter-Quigley Productions and Four

Star. It lasted only thirteen weeks and was replaced by another H-Q Production, *Hollywood Squares*.

## *Hollywood Squares*

In 1965, Four Star Television and Heatter-Quigley Productions filmed the pilot for what would become the long-running game show of tic, tac, toe with nine celebrities sitting in cubicles arranged as a tic tac toe board. Two contestants competed to obtain an "X" or an "O" by determining if a celebrity correctly answered a question posed by the emcee. Bert Parks was the host of the pilot presentation that was done for CBS. The nine celebrities were Wally Cox, Gisele MacKenzie, Abby Dalton, Jim Backus, Robert Q. Lewis, Rose Marie, Morey Amsterdam, Vera Miles, and Charlie Weaver.

A year went by and, in 1966, NBC picked up *Hollywood Squares*. Heatter-Quigley wanted a fresh face to host the series. Peter Marshall was in contention with Dan Rowan as the new host and secured the job. Four Star was associated with Heatter-Quigley in producing the game show from its premiere in 1966 until 1967. Apparently, in 1967, Merrill Heatter and Bob Quigley were no longer affiliated with Four Star. Their production company merged with Filmways in 1969.

## *Go!!!*

In spring 1967, Four Star helped to produce a special titled *Go!!!* for ABC which starred Ryan O'Neal, Donna Douglas, Noel Harrison, and Herman's Hermits. Rudy Vallee, John Cameron Swayze, Eddie (Rochester) Anderson, and Dear Abby (Abigail Van Buren) made cameo appearances on the program. The show focused on trends in fashion, music, and transportation and other items of interest to young people. Highlights of the special included a paper clothing fashion show, a dune buggy ballet, and a surfing sequence. Al Burton's Teenage Fair, Inc. made the show in conjunction with Four Star Television.

## *Malibu U*

Hosted by singer and actor Ricky Nelson, this summer replacement series for the canceled *Green Hornet* aired on ABC from July to September, 1967. Nelson was the so-called "Dean of Malibu U" where various music acts performed on the beach. Given that the show was not filmed in a studio but outdoors, the vocalists had to lip synch to their recordings. Musical numbers were usually staged like primitive music videos. In addition to Nelson, other regulars on the program were Robie Porter as the "President of the Student Body" (i.e., she had a nice body), Bill Callaway doing comedy bits, and the Bob Banas dancers. Canned applause and laughter were inserted into the show. Guest stars ranged from actors like Leonard Nimoy and John Astin to middle-of-the-road singers including Don Ho and Engelbert Humperdinck to rock stars such as The Doors and Chad & Jeremy.

Reviewing the second episode, *Variety* noted: "At last week's class it was learned that Bobby Rydell is a real pro, even while lip synching and leaping around a beach location; Mrs. Eva Miller can't sing, but has a comedic flair which hints broadly at a vaudeville background; Leonard Nimoy, Mr. Spock of ABC's (sic) 'Star Trek,' can't sing either, except within a range of a couple of notes, and doesn't have pointed ears either."[99]

The series was produced by Four Star Television in association with Robert E. Petersen Productions and Teen-Age Fair, Inc.

## Something Special

*Something Special* featured singers like Pearl Bailey, Buddy Greco, Peggy Lee, and Julie London hosting their own musical hours that were syndicated to local stations.

Four Star also produced eleven one-hour musical specials with the same format for the Celanese company during 1967.

## Entertainment Projects and Pilots

### Great Ideas

Four Star filmed a pilot for a series, *Great Ideas*, for the 1964-65 season which was hosted by Clifton Fadiman. The pilot, a joint venture with the *Encyclopedia Britannica*, had, as regular panelists, Dr. Mortimer Adler and Robert M. Hutchins. Guest experts on a different subject for each episode would also appear.

Produced by Heatter and Quigley and first titled, *It's a Great Idea,* the proposed show was designed to tackle broad topics like art, democracy, education, family, religion, science, and immortality in a conversational setting. The series would deal with philosophical-type issues and not with daily current events.

Two pilots were made in 1963. A narrator began the series with a voice over: "Man communicates through conversation as he has done for thousands of years. And though his spoken word is lost forever in the soft winds of time, his ideas, his great ideas live on."[100]

Each week, the plan was for the host to provide viewers with the subjects of upcoming shows so they could submit questions for the panelists. If a question was used on the air, the submitter would receive a set of the *Great Books of the Western World.*

Topics considered for the pilot episodes were "Family," with guests including Dr. Benjamin Spock and John Cogley; "Love," with Julie Harris, Ann Landers, and Margaret Mead; and "Automation," with Walter Reuther and Thomas Watson, Jr.

## Way Out

This half-hour musical variety pilot hosted by Joey Paige and featuring guests Ian Whitcomb, Brenda Holloway, and Mel Carter was produced by Teen-Age Fair, Inc. and Four Star. The 1965 pilot couldn't find any buyers and so never became a series.

## Allen Ludden/Betty White Project

In August 1967, Four Star pitched the idea of a ninety-minute variety/talk show for daytime hosted by Allen Ludden and his wife Betty White. While this project never came to fruition, a few years later Ludden did host his own talk show, *Allen Ludden's Gallery,* which was produced by Metromedia.

## The American Fashion Awards

Also in 1967, Four Star, in association with Procter & Gamble, came up with the idea of producing a special focusing on the world of women's fashions. High fashion designers and critics as well as name talent were to participate in the special.

For the fiscal year that ended in June 1966, Four Star reported a net loss of a little over $1.5 million. The loss was attributed to not only the higher costs of developing and producing network series but also to the depreciation of the company's inventory of series episodes to be rerun given that virtually all the shows Four Star had produced were in black and white with color programs now being demanded by networks and stations. Reportedly, in 1966, because of its inability to launch new network TV series, Four Star was looking for prospective buyers.

The company also had a loss of about $1.5 million for the fiscal year ending June 30, 1967. One bright spot in Four Star's revenue stream during 1966-67 was money raised by its music company based on Frank Sinatra's recording of "That's Life." However, for the company's fiscal year ending June 1967, Four Star's gross income was about $11,000,000 – a sharp drop from the prior fiscal year when income was over $20,000,000.

Given its financial situation, it was probably no surprise that the company was purchased on August 15, 1967 for $1,000,000 by members of a syndicate of investors headed by David Charnay. Charnay had been a newspaper reporter in New York City for several years and then became a powerful Washington lobbyist. The syndicate included a realtor, a lawyer-industrialist, and a newspaper conglomerate head. It first bought up the Four Star stock from the estate of Dick Powell, and then Tom McDermott sold the investment group his interests in the company. Boyer and Niven sold all of their stock except for 36,000 shares that each retained.

After the acquisition, Tom McDermott remained for awhile as president announcing that the company would continue to explore making feature films including *King of the Rainy Country* from a book by Nicholas Freeling. The film was never made.

# Chapter 16:
# Four Star's Final Western Series, 1965-69

Four Star's final series for network television was fittingly a Western starring a legendary film actress and produced by the men who made *The Rifleman.*

### *The Big Valley* and Its Back-Door Pilot

On *The Big Valley,* which premiered September 15, 1965, actress Barbara Stanwyck played Victoria Barkley, the widowed matriarch of a family that included her three sons – Jarrod (Richard Long), Nick (Peter Breck), and seldom-seen Eugene (Charles Briles), her daughter Audra (Linda Evans), along with her deceased husband's illegitimate son, Heath (Lee Majors). Stanwyck thought that the Heath character should have been her illegitimate son instead of her husband's, but producers believed that this would spoil her mother image on the show. The series ran for four seasons on ABC.

*The Big Valley* was a rare adult Western with a female as its lead. The only other TV Western, *Annie Oakley,* with a heroine as the main character, was primarily aimed at juveniles. Created by Lou Edelman, the producer of Stanwyck's one-season anthology show on NBC and one of its writers A.I. Bezzerides, Stanwyck's character was originally conceived as a tougher female, but potential advertisers were leery of women in Westerns. Edelman sold the show to producers Levy, Garner, and Laven, who had produced the successful *The Rifleman* for ABC. They made a deal with Four Star Television and ABC to make and air the series.

In his book about the rise and fall of the TV Western, J. Fred MacDonald describes *The Big Valley* as the epitome of the "domestic" Western – the type of series characterized by a focus on family and not on the lone-rider heroics of other adult Westerns. He goes on to state, "Set in the San Joaquin Valley of central California,

*The Barkley family cast: From left to right – Linda Evans, Barbara Stanwyck, Richard Long, Peter Breck, Lee Majors, and Charles Briles.*

this series was headed by a woman. Matriarchy was not unknown in the real West, but in the video West women were almost always subordinate to men. After all, the Western was a masculine genre, and the principal audience for the TV Western was male. Thus the appearance of Barbara Stanwyck as strong-willed Victoria Barkley, ruler of the vast Barkley ranch, was unprecedented."[101]

Before ABC picked up the series, it was offered to both CBS and NBC. Early in the development of the show before Four Star became involved, it was conceived as a possible back-door pilot from CBS' *Rawhide*, but ultimately that network rejected the project.

Christopher Knopf, who wrote the pilot for *The Big Valley*, had come up with a series idea called *The Cannons of San Francisco* about a wealthy California family involved in the freight-hauling and transportation business in the 1850s. The Cannon family included father Thomas, who had moved his wife and children from Ohio to San Francisco to start a new business; Mary Gavin Cannon, the strong, caring mother; Michael, the oldest son who would one day takeover the family business; Lize, the second oldest son, who liked to gamble; Audra and Francis, twins, with Audra prone to getting into various misadventures and her brother Francis, the scholar of the family; Marcy, the youngest sister; and John Patrick, the youngest brother who liked the sea. Tom McDermott rejected the proposal since it was similar to a project he had already had been working on - the concept for *The Big Valley*. However, he wanted Knopf to write the pilot for that Western series. Knopf initially rejected the offer, but producers Jules Levy, Arthur Gardner, and Arnold Laven convinced him otherwise. They asked Mr. Knopf what it would take for him to scribe the pilot. He replied, "Get me out of my contract with Four Star, pay me $10,000 and I'll do it, with one proviso. That I get to bring my characters from my project into the script... I wrote the pilot, agreeing to write the second show as well if it sold so that the two could be linked together for an overseas motion picture sale."[102] Knopf patterned the characters portrayed by Barbara Stanwyck and Linda Evans in *The Big Valley* after Mary Gavin Cannon and Audra Cannon that he described in his treatment for *The Cannons of San Francisco*.

In the pilot, Heath Barkley arrives at the Barkley ranch. The railroad seeks to take over the land of local farmers and ranchers near Stockton, California. The landowners want to fight the railroad, but Jarrod suggests handling the issue through the courts. Heath reveals to the family that he is the bastard son of the late Tom Barkley. His mother had died a month earlier, but, before her passing, she told him whom his father was. Heath wants what he is entitled to. His siblings would like him to leave. However, Victoria and her offspring eventually come to accept him. Meanwhile, the railroad is intimidating the landowners by burning down their homes. The Barkley's decide to side with the landowners and fight the railroad. The railroad sends an army of men to face off against the farmers and ranchers. A gun battle ensues with the railroad's men retreating.

As they did with Robert Taylor in *The Detectives*, Levy, Gardner, and Laven freely used the co-stars on *The Big Valley* as the leads on several episodes with Barbara Stanwyck appearing in only a few scenes. Although Ms. Stanwyck's character was not the central focus of each weekly episode, her presence was always felt on the set. As *TV Guide* put it referring to a scene in an episode featuring Richard Long, ""Missy (Stanwyck) is not even in the scene. But she rules it. She rules everything and everyone. She rules the grips, the gaffers, the guest stars, her co-stars, the directors, the camera operators, the wardrobe people, the sound men."[103]

Stanwyck won an Emmy in 1966 for her performance on *The Big Valley* and was also nominated as best lead actress for the series in 1967 and 1968.

In somewhat a change of pace episode for a Western, actor/singer Sajid Khan, who had been a regular on the NBC series *Maya* with Jay North, starred in a season four episode of *The Big Valley*, originally titled "Paper Prince" but then called "The Royal Road," in which he played a Punjabi Prince named Ranjit Sigh visiting Stockton and falling for Jarrod's ward Laura Hayden (Kathy Garver). The Prince's attaché Captain Crawford (Harold Gould) is recognized by a waitress at the hotel as Harry Davis, a man wanted for murder in San Francisco. Crawford murders the waitress so she does not divulge his true identity. Heath finds her body and thinks he saw Crawford fleeing the murder scene. Jarrod looks into Crawford's background and finds that he is indeed a conman who rescued the supposed Prince from deplorable conditions in India and the two are running a confidence game to swindle the good citizens of Stockton out of money that the town's residents think will be used to buy food for starving people in India. After the sheriff questions

Crawford about the murder of the waitress, Crawford informs the Prince that they need to leave town immediately but not before taking the jewels Laura Hayden's mother left her. The two go to her house, confiscate the valuables, and take Laura hostage. The sheriff and a posse including Jarrod go after them. When Crawford shoots Jarrod, the Prince rebels and demands that Crawford leave by himself. The Prince and Crawford fight. Laura retrieves Crawford's rifle and shoots him. In the end, the Prince is released on probation in Jarrod's custody to work on the Barkley ranch.

Four Star thought that Sajid Khan would be the next great teenage idol and so signed him to a contract in 1969 to star in an hour-long variety special, *Holiday Dream*, but the special was never produced. Also, in that year, the company announced that Khan would star in a pilot for a children's show but that project also never got off the ground.

The final episode of *The Big Valley* was typical for the series. On "Point and Counterpoint," from prison, a dying man asks his son to seek revenge on Victoria and Stockton banker Otis Clark (Russell Thorson). The man's son, Rich Stokely (Clifford David), robs the bank and kills Clark. He then goes to the Barkley ranch where he asks Jarrod to defend him proclaiming his innocence. Jarrod is considering a run for Attorney General of California, and Nick thinks that his brother's defense of Stokely will prevent Jarrod from being elected to that position. During the trial, the sheriff testifies, as an eyewitness, that Stokely is the murderer, but Jarrod casts doubt on his account. Jarrod also produces a witness that says Stokely was working for him on the night of the murder. The jury acquits Stokely. Subsequently, Stockton's sheriff receives a telegram that another man named Stokely passed part of the money stolen from the bank at a saloon in Modesto. The other man turns out to be Rich Stokely's twin brother Billy. Victoria recalls that twenty years earlier she and Otis Clark were witnesses at a robbery trial that convicted the Stokely's father and that is why the Stokely twins are after revenge. Billy Stokely is being transported to Stockton. His brother frees him, and they both go to the Barkley ranch and hold Victoria at gunpoint. Jarrod is able to shoot the twins and free his mother. He decides to turn down the nomination for Attorney General.

*The Big Valley* never ranked among the top thirty series during its four-season run but performed respectably for ABC on Monday nights at 10:00 pm. The series is still seen today on certain "nostalgia" channels.

In 1969, film rental income from *The Big Valley* represented 70% of Four Star's income.

Four Star International, the successor to Four Star Television, announced, in 1987, plans to revive *The Big Valley* beginning with a two-hour TV movie intended as the pilot for a reboot of the series. Peter Guber, Jon Peters, Jules Levy, and Arthur Gardner would serve as executive producers of the project. CBS was reported as interested in the reboot, but it never came about.

*The Big Valley* did air one episode that served as the basis for a potential spinoff.

### "Rimfire"

Van Williams starred as Dave Barrett, sheriff of a town named Rimfire, in this February 19, 1968 back-door pilot. The sheriff has a young son named Daniel (John Daniels). In this respect the pilot reminded viewers somewhat of *The Rifleman* with a strong central character – a widower, raising a young boy in the West.

Jarrod arrives in Rimfire to meet with Sydney Glover (Robert Middleton) to finalize a deal to merge the Barkley silver mine with the Glover mine. However, a Chinese couple, Wong Lo (Mako) and his wife Ling (Lisa Lu), have laid claim to the abandoned mine in between the Barkley and Glover mines. Glover seeks the mine claimed by the couple in order to expand his tunnels for cross ventilation to bring more air into his mine as his workers have to dig deeper for the silver. Although Glover wants to use force to take over the abandoned mine, Jarrod first offers the Chinese couple money to buy the mine. The couple refuses Jarrod's offer. When the circuit judge visits, he finds that the claim for the abandoned mine was filed after a law was passed preventing non-citizens from owning property. However, Ling, born in San Francisco, is a citizen. Jarrod calls off the merger when Glover uses force to take over the disputed mine. Glover's men want to hang Wong Lo after he kills one of the men who attacked his wife. Sheriff Barrett takes Wong

Lo into custody with Jarrod's help. Jarrod and Barrett then have to fight off a lynch mob who wants to take Wong Lo from the jail and hang him. In the course of events, Barrett is shot. He is not seriously wounded, but his young son pleads with the mob to allow his father to do his job, pointing out how his dad had helped all of the town's citizens. The mob disburses. Wong Lo goes off with the marshal for his trial. Jarrod plans to represent him, and Wong Lo agrees to sell his mine.

"Rimfire" was Four Star's second pilot with actor Van Williams that failed to become a series. The first was 1966's *Pursue and Destroy*.

# Chapter 17:
# Four Star International's Syndicated Entertainment and Game Shows, 1968-89

On November 14, 1967, Four Star Television became Four Star International with David B. Charnay assuming the presidency of the company succeeding Tom McDermott. Charnay indicated that the company would continue to develop programs for the networks as well as for syndication. In a November 1969 stockholder meeting, Charnay elaborated on his opinion about making pilots for consideration by the networks:

> The day of deficit financing is over. I'm not going to speculate with company money on a show that may show a return on investment three or four years from now. I'm not going to make programs for network television unless I can break even going in. I'll just stay off the networks and if the stockholders disagree with me they can just vote me out of office.[104]

Most of Four Star's efforts under Charnay were directed toward first-run syndication of entertainment and game shows and other genres.

## Variety Specials

Between 1968 and 1989, Four Star International syndicated several variety specials to local television stations. Included among the programs were:

### Holiday-Themed Specials

The company syndicated holiday specials in the late 1960s - a show celebrating Thanksgiving with Burl Ives and one focusing on Christmas in 1968 titled *The Magic of Christmas* with Ann Miller and Howard Keel. In 1969, the shows included *Frankie Avalon's Easter Holiday*, *Jack Cassidy's St. Patrick's Day*, and *Buddy Greco's Funny Valentine*.

In 1989, Four Star International syndicated a live two-hour special, *Search for Haunted Hollywood*, in time for Halloween. Hosted by John Davidson, the show featured a séance summoning legendary stars from the past, a professional ghost hunt, re-enactments of paranormal events reported in Hollywood, strange gravesites and mansions, and personal ghost stories provided by celebrities. Appearing on the special where Patrick Macnee, magician Harry Blackstone, Jack Carter, and Norm Crosby.

## Music Specials

In 1970, Four Star syndicated *The World of the Seekers* – a musical revue starring The Seekers produced by General Television Corporation in Melbourne, Australia. In 1976, *The San Francisco Serendipity Singers Special* featuring songwriter Hal David and *The Great Fairs Special* with Roy Clarke, Jim Nabors, The Fifth Dimension, The Guess Who, and Helen Reddy were made available to TV stations. A concert titled, *Alice Cooper and Friends*, aired in 1977. Along with Cooper, The Tubes, Nazareth, and Sha Na Na performed.

Also, two specials had singer Vic Damone visiting the countries of Australia and New Zealand: *Australia – For the Fun of It* and *New Zealand – For the Fun of It*. Both 1979 shows featured local talent in various musical performances.

## *Here Come the Stars*

Hosted by legendary comedian George Jessel, nicknamed the "Toastmaster General of the U.S.," this syndicated series saluted famous show business personalities like George Burns and Bob Hope in the form of a roast in a hotel ballroom with a dais made up of lesser-known celebrities reading scripted material satirizing the guest of honor. The series, initially titled *George Jessel Salutes the Stars*, aired for twenty-four episodes beginning September 7, 1968.

*George Jessel and guest of honor, George Burns, on* Here Come the Stars.

## Can You Top This?

This re-working of the radio show and early 1950s television show featured a panel of comedians trying to top a joke a viewer sent it. Morey Amsterdam executive produced the series which was syndicated for eight months by Four Star International beginning January 26, 1970. Amsterdam was also a regular panelist along with two guest comedians. Host Wink Martindale would have presenter Richard Dawson relate the joke the viewer submitted. The TV studio's reaction to the joke would be registered on an applause meter up to 100 points. The viewer would win $25 for the joke submission. The panelists would then relate their own joke on the same topic (e.g. stories about dentists). If the audience reaction to a panelist's story showed less applause, then the viewer would win an additional $25 up to $100 and a prize, if none of the panelists' jokes topped the one sent in by the viewer.

Reportedly, the show received about 20,000 joke submissions a week from home viewers. Four Star's vice president of production, Dick Rosenbloom, indicated that "... we get a lot of blue material and surprising enough 80% are from women."[105]

# BBC-TV Specials

Beginning in January 1971, Four Star International syndicated a series of thirteen entertainment specials that aired originally on the BBC. Six of the shows starred the British comic duo of Morecambe and Wise. Other programs in the package included those hosted by singer Cilla Black, singer-comedian Harry Secombe, pop singer Lulu, song-and-dance group Young Generation, and singers Vera Lynn and Cliff Richard.

## Juvenile Jury

In August 1970, David Charnay entered into an agreement with veteran game show host and producer Jack Barry for the creation, production, and sell of video properties. One result of that agreement led to Barry bringing back *Juvenile Jury* that originally aired in the late 1940s and early 1950s as a syndicated offering beginning on January 9, 1971. The once-a-week thirty minute show featured a panel of youngsters giving advice to solve problems presented by other kids.

A celebrity guest showed up each week for one segment of the program. For instance, Zsa Zsa Gabor talked about love with one four-year-old panelist asking the star why she had been married so many times. On another show, one of the five children on the "jury" asked a casually-dressed Janet Leigh why she didn't look as attractive as she did in the movies. Ms. Leigh explained that when she is not working in a film, she does not wear glamorous outfits.

## The Reel Game

Four Star partnered with Jack Barry in producing this game show for ABC that began on January 18, 1971 and ran for five months. Three contestants bet a portion of their money starting with $250 each on their ability to correctly answer a question whose answer would be illustrated with a film clip. After bets were placed, the question was posed and the right answer revealed by a film clip. For example, a topic on one show was "Howard Hughes" and the questions were: Did his plywood plane ever fly? If so, did it land safely or crash? After the bets and answers were placed, newsreel clips showed the Spruce Goose taking off and landing safely.

## The Wonderful World of Magic

Hosted by Bill Bixby, this syndicated series featured magicians from all over the world performing feats of legerdemain. Four Star syndicated twenty-six half hours. On the pilot, magicians are shown performing tricks that involve slight-of-hand with cards, birds, top hats, metal loops, fire, and clocks. The entire series was filmed in Paris, France.

## Lohman & Barkley

Four Star syndicated this variety series starring radio personalities Al Lohman and Roger Barkley in 1976. Twenty-six hour-long episodes were made.

The show featured segments like "The Swiss Family Door Slammers" and a recipe for Duck A L'Orange with ingredients - a pot of water, a duck, an orange, and an iron. On one episode, actress/comedienne Martha Raye spoke of a new French avant-garde movie she made with a scene from the film showing Ms. Raye being chased by a gorilla and the actress hitting the gorilla with a custard pie. In another segment, the hosts request celebrity Barbi Benton to take questions from the audience. One audience member asks her "How much magnesium ore does Brazil produce in a year?"

## Peter Lupus' Body Shop

This exercise/interview show was hosted by former *Mission: Impossible* star and body builder Peter Lupus. Produced by Davilup Corporation, the daily series had two guest interviews per episode along with Lupus demonstrating various exercises for viewers. Interviewees included celebrities and experts on health, nutrition, and beauty. Four Star began syndicating the series in 1978.

## Metro Productions Syndicated Series

In 1979, Four Star International attempted to syndicate several first-run videotaped series produced by Metro Productions, Inc. which made about 500 hours of syndicated programs in 1977 and

1978 as a tax shelter for its investors. Most of the financing for the various series came from the Mormon community. The shows covered a variety of subjects such as sewing, cooking, music, comedy, and children's programs. Some of the shows that Four Star tried to sell to local stations included:

*Up for Grabs*

This weekly half-hour – a satire of morning television programs - was meant to be aired in late night. In addition to sports, music, and interview features, segments included "Gardening with Mother Dirt," "Nancy's Household Tips," "Cooking with Lenny," and "Mr. Fix-It." Thirty-nine episodes were offered to TV stations.

*Sew What's New?*

Hosted by Los Angeles fashion designer and sewing authority George Trippon, this instructional series used *Vogue* patterns to complete a garment on each episode. Seventy-eight installments were made. *Sew What's New?* was probably the most successful Metro Productions series.

*The Melting Pot*

This five-day-a-week ethnic cooking show was hosted by Orson Bean. The series featured celebrity guest hosts and guest chefs. One hundred thirty episodes were made.

*Master Bridge with Edwin Kantar*

This show featured a celebrity guest and three others playing a hand of bridge with commentary by Eddie Kantar, a world team bridge champion.

Other series made by Metro Productions and syndicated by Four Star International in 1979 were *Country Serenade*, a musical show; *Imagine That*, a children's show; and *Pinkiny Canandy*, a comedy series, as well as shows titled *Remarkable* and *Success*. *Pinkiny Canandy* was created and produced by Michael Chain who recorded an album of the same title and portrayed the pink-spandex-clad rock star named Pinkiny Canandy. His 1969 album included songs like "Sadie Godiva" and "Christopher Centipede."

## *Matchmaker*

Hosted by Dave Hull, this was one of Four Star's final series airing in syndication from September 1987 to September 1988.

The game involved three men and three women looking for dates. Hull could not see the contestants, and they could not see each other. Based on their thoughts and opinions, the host would determine the perfect date couple.

At the beginning of the show, Hull would interview each potential date about his or her hobbies and profession while supposedly making notes about the answers. He would then eliminate one man and one woman. Next he asked the four remaining contestants about love and romance. Hull would then eliminate one more contestant leaving one person of one gender and two of the other gender. The one person became the "romantic lead," and Hull would determine which of the two remaining contestants would be his or her best match. The lucky pair would have a chance to win prizes of increasing value. Each contestant had been asked to answer questions before the show like "What is your favorite color?" If the pair matched answers on one question, they would win a basic prize. If they matched on two questions, they would get a better prize, and, if they matched answers on the third question, they would take home the grand prize.

Game show producer and announcer, Bill Armstrong created the series.

## *The New Liars Club*

Four Star's final game show was a reboot of a program on which three celebrities suggest false definitions or descriptions of an unusual object while a fourth celebrity describes the object correctly. Contestants have to determine which celebrity is giving the accurate description.

The series was originally hosted by Rod Serling in the late 1960's and was brought back again in the mid-seventies. The Four Star version, produced in Canada, was hosted by Eric Broadman and ran during the 1988-89 season.

# Entertainment and Game Show Projects and Pilots
# 1968-87

## Blast

In 1969, Ernest Glucksman, Tony Hendra and Nick Ullett were signed by Four Star to develop a half-hour satirical revue for television called *Blast*. The program would have satirized a different topic each week.

## Lee Majors Specials

Four Star signed Lee Majors in 1969 to host a series of five one-hour country and western musical specials for syndication in association with Majors' Hangtown Productions.

## Sydney Omarr's World (aka Your Sign . . . and Mine)

This 1969 entertainment program, proposed as a daily half-hour daytime show centering on astrology, featured astrologer Sydney Omarr along with actress Janet Blair as host. The program would have covered such topics as astrology in fashion, astrology in cooking, and audience participation in readings.

## The Honeymoon Game

If this 1969 pilot had become a series, it would have been the first ninety-minute game show on TV. Hosted by Jim McKrell and produced by Jack Barry, the pilot, initially titled *The Love Game*, featured six newly-married couples participating in different games. The first game involved a round with the spouses of each of three couples attempting to guess the answer to questions like "What is his favorite hobby?" Another round would then be played with the other three couples. The lowest scoring couple from each round would be eliminated with the other four couples playing the semi-final game.

The semifinal game was played like a version of Barry's *The Joker's Wild* with two couples playing a slot-machine-like device with three wheels spinning simultaneously. The wheels would indicate the category of the question with the possibility that some of the three wheels would indicate "bonus." If the same category appeared on all three wheels and the couple answered correctly, they would earn three points; if only two wheels had the same category, two points could be won, and so on. If the word "bonus" appeared on a wheel, the husband and wife team would earn one point. The added twist for this game was that celebrities would pose the questions based on the category each celebrity represented. In the pilot, actor Bob Crane asked questions about show business, former California Governor Pat Brown posed questions about politics, singer Jay P. Morgan's category was music, child actor Marc Copage's category was "kid's stuff," and former baseball player Don Drysdale had the sports category. When the first two couples completed their round, the second two couples would play the same game with the highest scoring couple from each round participating in the next game.

The final game still used the *The Joker's Wild* slot machine, but this time, the left wheel showed a category for a question, the right wheel, the dollar amount of the question, and the middle wheel was titled "take a chance." If a couple answered the query correctly, they would earn the dollar amount for that question and then could decide to "take a chance" meaning they could win a prize, another spin, or a dollar amount added to or subtracted from their winnings. The top winning couple would then proceed to the bonus game.

In the bonus game, the couple could spin the wheels up to three times deciding to take the prizes indicated on the wheels with the first spin or go on to another spin to see if they could win better prizes.

If the *Honeymoon Game* had become a series, Barry indicated that the first game would be eliminated and the other two games extended along with more in-depth interviews of the couples in order to still have a ninety-minute show. The pilot was made by Barry's company and Four Star International in association with Metromedia.

### Celebrity Circus

This half-hour program offered for syndication by Four Star in 1972 involved famous people performing as clowns in a circus. Each episode would have featured two regular circus acts with the rest of the installment devoted to comedy performances of the celebrities dressed as clowns.

### Shadow and Substance

Another John Newland project, this proposed thirty-minute series focused on psychic phenomena using film and videotape to dramatize scientific findings with actual case histories. About the potential show, Newland noted, "We believe this series will help to close the creditability gap between growing scientific evidence and a lagging public acceptance of the fact that there is more substance than shadow in the world of psychic phenomena."[106]

### The X Factor

This half-hour effort was also created and produced by John Newland. The 1974 syndicated project dramatized the psychic experiences of famous people. Hosted by Ed Mitchell, a former U.S. astronaut, the program focused on the ESP and supernatural experiences of celebrities with William Shatner appearing in the pilot. Future celebrities planned for the unsold series would have included Carolyn Jones, Clint Walker, and Burl Ives.

### Laugh Line

This 1974 effort appears to have been a reboot of the 1959 game show that had been emceed by Dick Van Dyke involving a celebrity panel creating funny captions for skits acted out by a stock company of actors.

### You Bet Your Life

Four Star acquired the rights to this long-running game show that had been hosted by Groucho Marx for several years on NBC and attempted in 1974 to update it. No doubt the company was attracted to this idea given the success of the syndication of the original *You Bet Your Life*. However, the reboot attempt failed.

### Star Cluster

Jim McKrell emceed this pilot for a comedy game show featuring a panel of six celebrities sitting on a three-tier set. The game involved two contestants answering multiple-choice questions about the celebrity panel. If a contestant matched the answer given by the celebrity, the player received $25 plus $25 for each celebrity who agreed. A round was completed when a contestant completed a cluster (a triangle) of stars or when six questions had been asked. A second round was played for higher stakes. The contestant who had the most money at the end of two rounds moved on to the bonus game. The bonus involved true/false questions where four celebrities answered "true." If the contestant identified all four panelists answering "true," then he or she would win a car.

The celebrities on the pilot included Abby Dalton, Bob Ridgely, Jm J. Bullock, Doug Davidson, Shelley Taylor Morgan, and Linda Blair. The 1986 pilot was produced by Bill Armstrong and Four Star and offered for syndication with apparently few takers.

# Chapter 18:
# Four Star International's Kids Shows, 1968-1989

Most of the company's programs aimed at children were animated shows made in Europe, Japan, and Australia and repackaged by Four Star for syndication in the United States.

### *Arthur and the Square Knights of the Round Table*

Four Star International began syndicating this Australian cartoon series in 1968. The thirty-six episodes were a take-off on the legend of King Arthur of Camelot. For instance, one cartoon, "Old Moody," had the King's jester inheriting a "treasure" from his uncle. When the jester has to travel to Moody Mountain to claim it, Arthur orders Sir Lancelot to follow the jester to protect him. In so doing, Lancelot wards off various animals that attempt to attack the jester. When he arrives and opens the treasure chest, the jester finds that his uncle has left him some old joke books so he could become better at his work.

### *Treehouse*

Co-produced by American Intertel Corp. and Joe Camp's Mulberry Square Productions, *Treehouse* was a thirty-minute talk show hosted by teenagers interviewing other teens who have succeeded in various fields as well as interviewing adult entertainment and business professionals. The series was taped at KTVT-TV in Dallas, Texas and was syndicated in the early 1970's.

Set in a tree house, the show was hosted by teen Britt Langford with Craig Lackey handling the announcing. "Regal Eagle," a comical-looking baby bird puppet had a nest on a limb outside the tree house. On the pilot show, guests included the yo-yo champion of the world and two teen girl singers. The Treehouse Orchestra, a seventeen piece group of teenage instrumentalists, provided music for the show.

Joe Camp, who produced *Treehouse*, is best known for his series of movies about the dog, Benji.

## Children's Specials

Nine TV specials, mostly based on fairy tales and produced by Martin Tahse, were syndicated by Four Star in 1974. The specials were *Pinocchio, The Emperor's New Clothes, Aladdin, Jack and the Beanstalk, Cinderella, The Midnight Ride of Paul Revere, Sleeping Beauty, The Cricket on the Hearth,* and *The Canterbury Ghost*.

## *Boomerang*

Made by Seattle TV station KOMO, this children's show featured singer Marni Nixon, who was living in Seattle at the time with her then husband. Nixon was most famous for dubbing the voices of Audrey Hepburn in *My Fair Lady* and Natalie Wood in *West Side Story*.

Using three puppets – Norbert, a green-nosed, yellow puppet; a red-haired, pink-freckled puppet named Melinda; and Libby, a dreadlocked brown puppet, Nixon would teach lessons to preschoolers. Apparently, the show's budget was so meager that Ms. Nixon couldn't do rehearsals before an episode aired.

Four Star syndicated the series 172 half-hour episodes and three seasonal specials from 1975 to 1981.

## *Kidpiz Showcase*

Four Star used this umbrella title to syndicate six animated series that were originally made outside the United States. The shows were *Dr. Snuggles, The Magic of Dr. Snuggles, Ninja the Wonder Boy, Robby the Rascal, Timefighters,* and *Timefighters in the Land of Fantasy*.

### Dr. Snuggles

This cartoon concerned a madcap scientist creating unusual machines like a robot helper, a wormmobile, a time machine, a gadget to fight depression, and a diamond-making machine. A co-production between British and Dutch producers, the show was narrated by Peter Ustinov who voiced Dr. Snuggles. The doctor's arch enemy was Professor Emerald, a crazy magician.

In a typical episode, the doctor, who travels by using his umbrella as a pogo stick, finds that the Earth is running out of water. Someone has been stealing big blocks of sea water, and the doctor sets out to retrieve the liquid.

*The Magic of Dr. Snuggles,* produced in Holland, was a sequel to *Dr. Snuggles.*

*A drawing of Dr. Snuggles.*

### Ninja the Wonder Boy

As the theme song for the series says, "he fights for right; he's a bundle of dynamite." Duke is a young boy in training to be a Ninja warrior. He is learning his magical Ninja powers mentored by Master White, who, in the opener, gives the Wonder Boy a chance to earn his Ninja certificate by testing his courage. Duke earns his certificate and sets off to keep his land free.

### Robby the Rascal (aka Robby the Robot)

From Japan, this cartoon featured the antics of a lovable, mischievous robot with a television set in his stomach. "When you need a good friend, call Robby, the rascal robot," so went the theme song for the series. Robby inadvertently causes trouble but is always willing to help people.

On one episode, an arch villain named Horace wants to acquire Robby created by Professor Art Deco. Horace decides to kidnap the professor and make him build a robot just for him.

### Timefighters

This Japanese cartoon show focused on the adventures of time travelers in their insect-shaped time machines created by scientist Dr. Keilat. The time travelers always encounter time skeletons, a group of villains, who thwart their efforts to find the scientist. The good doctor disappeared after his maiden voyage in a time machine. In their search through time, the timefighters meet famous historical figures.

### Timefighters in the Land of Fantasy

This series had the timefighters encountering fairy-tale characters instead of historical figures. Not having found Dr. Keilat in historical time, the time fighters decide to search for him in a different kind of time, i.e., fantasy time. In this effort, they encounter characters like Snow White and the Evil Queen.

# Kids Show Project

## *The Kids USA-Supershow*

Four Star International tried to launch a weekly hour-long series that sought to focus on the "wholesome side of the world of children" according to producer J. Orion Brunk.[107] CBS showed some interest in the show for Saturday mornings presumably for the 1969-70 season. Indian singer/actor Sajid Khan, who had guest starred on an episode of *The Big Valley*, was supposed to host the series which never saw the light of day.

# Chapter 19:
# Four Star International's Documentary and Reality Shows, 1968-89

Under President David Charnay, Four Star International formed a news and documentary department.[108] The company produced and/or syndicated several documentary specials including three documentaries made by French director Frederic Rossif - *Encore Paris,* about the Paris of yesterday and today; *Fall of Berlin*, dealing with the final days of the Third Reich; and *The Russian Revolution*, concerning the fall of Tsarist Russia and the Soviet takeover. Other documentaries involving Four Star were:

*Maharishi* - This 1968 documentary film about Hindu Monk Mahesh Yogi followed the Maharishi on his world tour presenting his solutions to the world's problems.

*Howard Hughes* – A 1968 film about the reclusive American billionaire was made by Four Star. When Hughes found out about the project, he dispatched one of his senior aides and an attorney to scuttle the project. Reportedly, Hughes acquired the film for between $50,000 and $60,000, and it was never shown.[109]

*Fastest Man on Earth* – This 1972 auto racing documentary featured drivers from the early days of electric and steam engine autos to contemporary rocket-powered racers. The special was culled from seventy hours of archive footage with new film from Europe and the United States.

*A Child's Garden of Pollution* – The program featured Bill Bixby and Brandon Cruz from *The Courtship of Eddie's Father* taking an ecological tour of Southern California.

Other documentary and reality series syndicated by Four Star International are profiled below.

## Portrait

Produced by Rick Spalla, this program profiled individual motion picture stars and was syndicated by Four Star International beginning in 1968. Stars highlighted included Omar Sharif, David Niven, James Mason, Robert Mitchum, and Barbara Stanwyck.

## The Seven Seas

In November 1968, Four Star announced a documentary project, *The Seven Seas* – a series of seven specials produced by oceanographer Bruno Vailati. The programs included segments on the Atlantic, Pacific, and Indian Oceans as well as the Mediterranean Sea, the Polar Seas, and the Red Sea. Norman Corwin narrated the documentaries.

The episode about the Atlantic Ocean focused on the activities of countries and islands that surround the ocean such as sky fishing in Iceland, sardine fishing off Morocco, penguins on the Cape of Good Hope, and a dive to explore the sunken Andrea Dora off Nantucket Shoals.

## News Feature Service

In 1970, Four Star International came up with the idea of offering local television stations brief, two or three minute, segments that a station could insert during its newscasts. The features included Dr. Randolph Alseben reporting on medical trends, attorney Melvin Belli discussing legal issues, Sue Cameron offering Hollywood gossip, and Teresa Drury talking about consumer protection issues.

Also, producer and on-air host Jack Douglas in association with Four Star offered a ninety-second news insert to local stations called *After Apollo* exploring the world of scientific and technical developments and the people who created them. If any stations actually bought this program is unknown.

## Towards the Year 2000

This series from Canada looked at innovations anticipated during the 1970s. Episodes covered such topics as "Mass Transit: Up, Up and Away" focusing on vehicles of the future that will move commuters at incredible speeds signaling the death of the automobile by the year 2000; "Medicine: Living to Be a Hundred" dealing with the role of automation and computerization in medicine; and "Genetics: Man the Creator" concerning cloning and methods of preventing the birth of genetically defective children.

## Target the Impossible

This was another Canadian documentary series syndicated by Four Star International in the late 1970s that was a sequel to *Towards the Year 2000*. Unlike the latter series, *Target the Impossible* looked at scientific breakthroughs of both the past and the future. Titles of episodes included "Jetspeed at Ground Zero: Super-Cool, Superconductors," "To Build a Smog-Free Car: The Steam Machine Dream," "To Capture the Power of the Sun & Tide: Unlimited Energy," and "To Halt Man's Physical Collapse: Fitness in an Unfit Age."

## Thrill Seekers

Reaching back to the company's glory days, Four Star hired Chuck Connors, former star of *The Rifleman*, to host a syndicated reality series called *Thrill Seekers* featuring people who perform dangerous stunts. The series ran in 1973.

Connors introduced each episode explaining that the show is about "men who don't wait to meet danger; they chase it, they challenge it, they lick it . . . They're Thrill Seekers." He closed each installment stating, "Our location is the planet, our aim – to entertain you, our promise to make you a thrill seeker too."

The pilot presented motorcycle riders training for stunts involving ramps and then performing their stunts with the motorcyclists describing what they were thinking as they executed each feat of daring do. The next segment featured hang gliders with one man attempting to beat a hang gliding record near Lake Tahoe. The final sequence showed stunt pilots performing maneuvers with Connors describing each stunt by name as it is shown.

## Secrets of the Deep

Hosted by former astronaut Scott Carpenter, this syndicated series probed the Earth's oceans and seas. The thirteen episodes covered topics like Great White sharks, the Zabair Islands in the Red Sea where there are submerged mountains, and the Great Barrier Reef in Australia.

## Backstage in Hollywood

David Sheehan, KNXT film critic, hosted this 1975 series focusing on movies and television. The first installment, "The Disaster Movie Mania," included interviews with Paul Newman and Faye Dunaway from the motion picture, *The Towering Inferno*, Charlton Heston from *Earthquake*, and George C. Scott, one of the stars of *The Hindenburg*. Other episodes were titled "The Other Side of Stardom," "1975's Oscar Hopefuls," and "The Movie Star and His Image."

## Millions to Inherit

Produced by Hoelscher Teleshows, Four Star syndicated *Millions to Inherit* – a show that attempted to find missing heirs. The series sought to tap the dream of inheriting a fortune.

## The Achievers

This thirteen episode documentary series profiling the lives of famous people like Carole Lombard and Joe Louis was offered for syndication in 1986. The show was advertised as offering little-known facts and private glimpses of celebrities.

# Reality and Documentary Pilots and Projects

### Spartan Safaris

This project, intended for first-run syndication in 1968, documented outdoor adventures taken by movie and television stars. It was to be produced by Spartan Productions owned by actor Christopher George and syndicated by Four Star. Richard Boone starred in the pilot filmed in Hilo, Hawaii involving Hawaii's International

Broadbill Tournament, one of the largest fishing competitions in the world.

## Athlete

Tom Harmon was set to host a documentary series on sports to be produced and syndicated by Four Star in 1968. The pilot featured football player Gary Beban.

## The Motion Picture Hall of Fame

This thirty-minute series proposed to chronicle the history of motion pictures from the beginning of the industry to current day focusing on stars, directors, writers, and producers. Twenty-six episodes were planned. Four Star International was not sure if the projected series would be marketed to networks or to local TV stations directly.

## Anatomy of...

In 1971, Four Star announced that it was developing a half-hour nonfiction series titled *Anatomy of...* in association with National Education Media. The program would take an in-depth look at topics of current interest.

## Sports to Remember

Films of memorable sporting events would be intermixed with contemporary interviews of the participants in this sports documentary series. The pilot had boxers Joe Louis and Billy Conn being interviewed about their famous boxing match with clips from the fight shown. Chick Hearn was the interviewer. The series was offered for syndication in 1972.

## The World of Medicine

This 1974 project of ten to twelve minute segments featured updates on mental and physical health. Four Star offered the series as a thirty-minute program or the option for TV stations to use the segments as part of their own program with studio discussions by local medical experts using suggested script outlines provided by the production company.

## Courthouse

A proposed 1974 weekly syndicated series, *Courthouse* centered on a reporter who would take viewers into the courtroom for trials of the century.

## Land of the Brave

*Land of the Brave*, a planned 1974 nature adventure series, was to be hosted by a Native American.

## The Movie Scene

Helmed by Hollywood journalist and critic David Sheehan, this proposed 1974 weekly half-hour series would have focused on movie reviews, previews, and behind-the-scenes interviews of stars.

## Portrait: The New Breed

Four Star attempted to follow-up their prior series of celebrity profiles with a syndicated thirty-minute show looking at new talent after their breakthrough on television, movies, stage, or in music. A pilot was made late in 1979 and marked Four Star's return to active production. In a news studio setting, the show's host was John Gavin with entertainment reporters Bob Thomas, James Bacon, Vernon Scott, and Carol Hemmingway who provided the celebrity profiles.

The pilot presented Vernon Scott's profile of Lynda Carter explaining how she became Miss World USA and her lucky break starring in the *Wonder Woman* television series. Carol Hemmingway next covered a portrait of Ron Howard with Garry Marshall, producer of *Happy Days*, Andy Griffith, and Tom Bosley talking about the actor/director.

## The New Millionaires

One of the final syndicated efforts to be proposed by Four Star was a new weekly thirty- minute program produced in association with Photoplay Productions to feature success stories about wealthy people who started from almost nothing. Jamie Farr was to host the series set for a fall 1989 debut.

# Chapter 20:
# Four Star International's Comedy Series, 1968-89

After the many unsold pilots that were made under the presidency of Tom Mcdermott, Four Star's new management in the late 1960s adopted a new, cautious approach to making pilots for consideration by the networks. Management labeled as a "kamikaze approach" the method previously used by Four Star with respect to preview episodes of potential series which used deficit financing. The company was much more conservative in developing possible series, but, nonetheless continued to consider comedy projects for the networks and for first-run syndication.

However, Four Star International was never able to launch a situation comedy – either on the networks or in syndication despite many attempts. The only comedy show that the company had any success with was one composed of old movie clips with fresh dialogue.

### Mad Movies with the L.A. Connection

Twenty-six episodes of this spoof of classic movies were syndicated by Four Star during the 1985-86 television season. Each episode satirized a feature film using the video from the movie edited to a thirty-minute length and then dubbing humorous dialogue written and voiced by the comedy troupe, the L.A. Connection. About the series, Four Star remarked that "The whole purpose of this is to try to develop a comedy format slowly so that after two or three years, we'll be totally acceptable to the audience and it can play as a strip."[110] This never happened since the show lasted only a single season.

Movies spoofed included the original, *A Star Is Born* about an aspiring actress played by Janet Gaynor whose career is on the rise and a matinee idol whose career is in decline. In the spoof, the Janet Gaynor character becomes an unfortunate little girl who needs a date. *Sherlock Holmes and the Secret Weapon* had Holmes helping a scientist escape the Gestapo, but in the *Mad Movies* version, Holmes and Watson try to stop a conspiracy from stealing library books and selling them on the black market. Another motion picture spoof was *The Stranger* starring Orson Welles and Edward G. Robinson in which the latter was hunting a Nazi war criminal played by Welles. In the edited version by the L.A. Connection, a tabloid editor wants to do a feature article on hunchback Quasimodo.

The L.A. Connection turned the film noir *D.O.A.* about a man who has been poisoned and has only twenty-four hours before he dies to find the person who poisoned him into an *I Love Lucy* spoof. Edmond O'Brien, the star of *D.O.A.*, becomes Latin bandleader Rico Bicardo, who finds that his wife Ruthie is missing with landlord Ed Nertz. He searches for her but eventually confesses his love for Ed's wife, Ethel.

## Comedy Projects

Four Star International considered many situation comedy proposals. However, none of these projects ever became a pilot, let alone a series.

### Quixote

Based on the classic story by Cervantes, Four Star sought to develop a comedy series called *Quixote* in 1969. Lewis John Carlino was reportedly writing the initial script.

### Call Me a Cop

This 1969 comedy proposal for NBC, written by Walter Kempley, concerned the antics of cops in a Bronx police station. At one point, Four Star thought of developing this project as a feature film called *Cops and Robbers* instead of as a television series, but neither version ever materialized.

### Dr. Livingston, I Presume

Written by Bernie Orenstein and Saul Turteltaub, this project, intended for NBC for the 1970-71 television season, was to star stand-up comedian Stanley Myron Handelman.

## Charley Weaver's Tales of Mount Idy

Set in the fictional town of Mount Idy, this 1972 animated project would feature the voice of Cliff Arquette as Charley Weaver with others portraying the citizens of the town. The planned series, based on Arquette's "Letters to Mama," was offered to both networks and local stations, but none took up the offer.

## The Magic Eye

This thirty-minute situation comedy was created by Lou Derman and David Levy for the 1972-73 season. While the details of the project are not known, comedy writer Lou Derman was also a magician who frequently performed a comedy/magic act at the Magic Castle. This proposed comedy may have centered on magic.

## The Richest Man in the World

Created by Ed James and developed by David Levy, this comedy project was intended for the 1972-73 season. The title sounds very close to the premise of a pilot produced by Goodson-Todman in the late sixties called *Rhubarb*, about the wealthiest man in the world.

## Me and Homer

Designed to star Peter Breck and Jack Elam, this project, a comedy Western, had a script written by Warren Douglas and was earmarked for the 1972-73 season for ABC. Breck and Elam were to play a pair of ne'er do well cowboys who ride roughshod over every town they visit.

## Mr. Perkins

This fantasy comedy was created by Dorothy Cooper-Foote for the 1972-73 season. Specific details concerning it are not known.

## Precinct No. 13

*Precinct No. 13*, presumably about a police station, was to be made by Four Star and Comedy Store Enterprises in 1973. Sammy Shore and his wife Mitzi along with comedian Pat McCormick were the principals behind Comedy Store Enterprises.

## This Is No Place Like Home

Another project between Four Star and Comedy Store Enterprises, this 1973 comedy was about life in prison with Pat McCormick playing one of the leads.

## The Traipsers

This proposed series for ABC, an hour-long comedy Western, was to be co-produced by Alan Jay Factor for Four Star International in 1974.

# Chapter 21:
# Four Star International's Dramatic Series, 1968-89

After *The Big Valley* ended, Four Star never had another dramatic series on network television despite repeated attempts as described in this chapter. In a 1971 interview with UPI Hollywood correspondent Vernon Scott, David Charnay bemoaned the lack of creativity (and the lack of demand for Four Star's projects) on network television stating:

> The trouble lies with the lack of imagination and integrity among agents and packagers who sometimes wear the same hats. There is chicanery involved, too. One of the greatest television crimes is that two or three studios dominate the prime time of the three networks. That's one reason the shows have a similar look about them. I've written the networks to say the programming is dull because they concentrate their dollars in a couple of places for a plastic product.[111]

Although Four Star International had some success with dramas for first-run syndication, the company relied mainly on videotaped game and entertainment programs in syndication as well as reruns of its vast library of dramatic shows produced during the Powell/ McDermott era.

One of the first drama projects that David Charnay announced after taking over Four Star was a feature film version of *The Rogues* stating, "Mr. Boyer and Mr. Niven are both excited about the project; they have agreed to reactivate their old roles and we're going into production just as soon as the screenplay is finished."[112] As with other announcements about movie versions of Four Star series, such as a planned film with David Jansen in his role as Richard Diamond and a motion picture focusing on the Dante character, *The Rogues* project was never realized.

The company did dabble in releasing low-budget independent feature films during the early seventies. One such movie was 1970s' *The Hard Road*, originally produced by Jack Valie Enterprises and Ed De Priest Productions. The motion picture concerned a middle-class suburban high school girl who becomes pregnant, is too embarrassed to return to school after giving birth, and ends up living with a prostitute and a drug addict.

Another 1970 movie the company distributed, *Madron*, starred Richard Boone as a grizzled old gunfighter who teams up with a nun played by Leslie Caron, the only survivor of a wagon train massacre, to fight for survival. The motion picture was filmed in Israel.

In 1971, Four Star distributed *Okay Bill* produced by Cake Co. Productions and directed by John Avildsen, who helmed the movie *Joe*, about middle America meeting the seventies counterculture. *Okay Bill* told the story of Bob Brady, a young, married stock broker in his father's business who is fascinated by hippies, modern art, and artists. One day, Bob decides to go to Fire Island with a fashion photographer and his model, but he misses his wife and returns to her. Avildsen later directed *Rocky* and *The Karate Kid* movies.

In 1973, Four Star released a Challenge Films production called *Tom* about a Vietnam veteran torn between a premarital crisis and a desire to improve race relations. In its review of the film, *Variety* wrote that "Its woeful incompetence manages to make both whites and blacks seem such thoroughgoing idiots, however, that the two races will unite in laughing the Alvin L. Fast production off the screen."[113]

Four Star International did contemplate producing a movie itself in 1983 by purchasing the rights to a sequel to *Butch Cassidy and the Sundance Kid*. Based on a British novel, *Whadda We Do Now Butch?*, the book posited that the two bandits didn't die in a Bolivian tin mine shootout but rather got away to England and France. In Europe, they become involved with Mata Hari, Kaiser Wilhelm, and a young Winston Churchill. The film was never made.

Concerning the company's involvement with TV during this period, in 1981, Four Star announced that it pioneered a breakthrough in cable TV for its library of early 1960s dramas with Theta Cable which picked up reruns of *The Dick Powell Theatre* and other Four Star series for its "Classic Television" channels.

In 1987, the company attempted to capitalize on the popularity of actor Steve McQueen after his Four Star series ended by colorizing the black and white episodes of *Wanted: Dead or Alive* and offering them in syndication to local stations.

## Movies of the Week

During the 1970s, ABC and CBS had regular weekly series consisting of ninety-minute made-for-television films which, in many respects, were the latest iteration of the anthology series. Being a master at producing anthologies, Four Star attempted several such projects but apparently only two were ever made. Some of the movie project attempts were *The Captive* to star actor Christopher George with a script written by Andre Stojka and *The England Game*, a World War II spy drama – both projects for ABC. Other ABC potential movies were *The Secret Witness* by David Westheimer and *The Tycoon* by Luther Davis.

For CBS, the company announced that it would film a movie based on a novel by Julian Symons, *The End of Solomon Grundy?* about an advertising executive suspected of murdering a young woman with whom he had an affair. This project never came to fruition and neither did a movie based on another book titled *Dark on the Other Side* concerning the wife of a writer who thinks she is losing her mind but whose husband may be behind the mysterious happenings on their estate.

The two made-for-TV movies that Four Star actually produced were:

### In Search of America

Starring a young Jeff Bridges as Mike Olson, a student who drops out of college to learn more about himself and the world, this 1971 *ABC Movie of the Week*, originally titled *The Road Gang*, was directed by Paul Bogart and written by Lewis John Carlino. Mike persuades his father Ben (Carl Betz), mother Jenny (Vera Miles), and his grandmother Rose (Ruth McDevitt) to join him "in search of America." He buys a 1928 Greyhound bus for the trip and refurbishes it with the help of his dad. The family's first stop is a hippie retreat where Mike and his parents encounter an expectant mother, a guitar-playing singer, and a man doing incantations around the bus. The expectant mother gives birth after finally agreeing that Jenny and Rose can help with the delivery. The family also meets a mother and father trying to locate their daughter who is ill with kidney disease. Mike knows the daughter but, obeying her wishes, refuses to make her parents aware of where she is. Finally, when she becomes very ill, the girl is airlifted to a hospital. The Olson family leaves the encampment and continues on their journey.

The movie pilot was filmed entirely on location. Producer William Froug remarked about the pilot that "It is not a message show but (it has) the objective of bringing people together in search for love and truth."[114] While Four Star hoped that it would become a series, that goal was never achieved.

## Deadly Hunt

Airing October 1, 1971 on the *CBS Friday Night Movie*, *The Deadly Hunt*, filmed in Vancouver, Canada, starred Jim Hutton, Tony Franciosa, Peter Lawford, and Anjanette Comer in a story about

*Tony Franciosa and Peter Lawford in a scene from* Deadly Hunt.

a $100,000 contract put out on a couple. Initially titled *Autumn of the Hunter*, Cliff (Hutton) and his wife Martha (Comer) own a company that plans a merger, but Martha's uncle is opposed to the plan. The couple goes on a camping vacation in the Sierra Mountains not realizing that they are being followed by Ryan (Franciosa), the hit man, Mason (Peter Lawford), his associate who plans the assassinations, and their driver Danny (Thomas Hauff). The pursuers stake out Cliff and Martha's campsite. All are unaware that a forest fire caused by lightening has re-ignited. Ryan begins shooting at the couple, downing Cliff but Martha runs away followed by her assassin. The forest rangers in the area hear the shots and see Martha fleeing. Ryan catches Martha who pretends to faint. She then knocks Ryan unconscious with a rock. Cliff, uninjured, appears and says that he put the contract out on his wife. A local Native American helps Martha flee before Cliff has a chance to murder her. Mason is caught in the re-ignited fire; while Danny, who had driven to another location to pick up Mason and Ryan, continues to wait for them to appear as the fire rages.

## *Monty Nash*

Starring Harry Guardino in the lead role, this syndicated series involved a quasi-government agent who goes undercover to catch criminals. The show debuted in September 1971 and ran for fourteen episodes.

The character of Montgomery Nash came from a series of novels authored by Richard Jessup using the pseudonym of Richard Telfair. Each installment was made for around $35,000 about half the cost of a network half hour. Two episodes were made over six days. Stories dealt with nontraditional subjects such as Nash protecting the right of a neo-Nazi to speak even though he disagreed with everything the guy had to say, tracking down vigilantes disguising themselves as cops, and protecting the rights of Jesus freaks to practice their religion their own way.

The premiere episode had Nash assigned the task of sneaking a gangster from an Indiana detention center to one in Chicago so the guy could testify before a Senate committee on crime. A $500,000 contract is put on the hood by the syndicate to make sure he doesn't appear before the committee. Someone in law enforcement, enticed by the money, attempts to kill the gangster.

NBC financed the series for the TV stations it owned scheduling the program for 10:30 pm on Fridays – thirty minutes that the FCC had turned back to local stations.

## Police Surgeon

Four Star International syndicated this Canadian police drama from 1972 to 1974. *Police Surgeon* starred Sam Groom as Dr. Simon Locke who worked for the police department's emergency unit usually assisting officers in solving crimes with the help of medical research. Groom previously played the title role in *Dr. Simon Locke*, as a new doctor in the rural town of Dixon Mills helping veteran physician Andrew Sellers (Jack Albertson). *Dr. Simon Locke* had aired during the 1971-72 season.

Dr. Locke, accompanied by a paramedic, would drive around the city in a black and white emergency vehicle labeled "Police Surgeon" with the radio call identification, 3MD9.

Also appearing on the series were Larry D. Mann as Lt. Jack Gordon, Locke's superior and, on the early episodes, Len Birman as Lt. Dan Palmer. Working for the police, Locke got involved in everything from mad bombers and street gangs to escaped convicts and kidnappers.

An early episode, "Lady X," from 1972 showed how Locke helped police in tracking down suspects. A bomber is threatening the city, setting off bombs all related to a particular conglomerate. Locke finds that the bomber is taking medication for iritis, an inflammation of the eyes. The bomber is difficult to identify since he assumes various disguises – an elderly woman, a construction worker, and a priest. After receiving the medical records of current and former employees of the conglomerate, the doctor identifies the perpetrator as a recently laid-off security analyst. Locke and Lt. Palmer track down the culprit who confesses that he was planting the bombs to show the company's lack of security.

However, some episodes strayed from medical research. In "Time Bomb," a December 1974 installment, Locke accompanies police on a drug bust and testifies at the drug dealer's trial. The dealer is being defended by Lt. Gordon's girlfriend who contends that her client was entrapped by the police. Gordon and Locke believe that the dealer's boss will try to free him during the trial before he is taken to prison. His boss plants a gun in the defense counsel's briefcase which the dealer uses to try to escape with his attorney as a hostage. The police shoot the dealer who finds the gun is not loaded. His lawyer is wounded in the shoot-out and subsequently dies despite Dr. Locke's best efforts to keep her alive.

The series was created by Chester Krumholz and Wilton Schiller.

# Drama Projects

Four Star International attempted to develop several dramatic projects, none of which resulted in pilots.

### The Dusters (aka Blassingame and Company)

Four Star International's most ambitious undertaking was with Sam Peckinpah, who had started with Four Star in the 1950s, and had become a major film director. A proposed action-adventure series for CBS for the 1970-71 season, *The Dusters* was to be a sixty-minute show about two airplane pilots who love to fly. Peckinpah planned to write the pilot script and serve as executive story consultant.

An undated treatment for *The Dusters* by Peckinpah and James R. Silke introduces the characters of Matt Blassingame, a fighter pilot from World War II, who would like to start his own airline, and Dave Breckenridge, a Korean War pilot. For the two lead characters, Peckinpah re-used the first and last names of the drifter from *The Westerner*.

A wealthy rancher, Ed Robinson, wants to hire the pair to hunt wild horses from planes in the High Sierras. Robinson seeks to rid the high country of wild horses that are using up good grazing land, and seeks to sell their carcasses for dog food.

Before the hunt begins, Matt and Dave become acquainted with the Tilford clan who live in the area and want to preserve the wild mustangs. The Tilford's attempt to destroy Matt and Dave's planes but without success. After their first hunt for the horses, the two flyers become disenchanted with the slaughter of wild mustangs.

Seeing that they no longer want to co-operate with the hunt, Robinson breaks his contract with them and orders them to leave. Matt and Dave then decide to help the Tilford's save the horses. They learn that Robinson has hired two new, expert pilots to carry on with the hunt. Matt and Dave secure two old airplanes to go up against Robinson and his men. The ensuing dogfight between Robinson's planes and Matt and Dave's results in Dave's plane crashing with him dying. Matt is arrested and then given the choice by Robinson to either stay in jail or leave town. He leaves town a loser.

Presumably, in developing the actual pilot script for the possible series, the downbeat ending would be changed to have Dave survive and the horses saved from slaughter. CBS expressed interest in filming the pilot as a two-hour movie for its *Sunday Night Movie* series that premiered in fall 1971. But, even with the title change to *Blassingame and Company* and modifications to the script, the movie pilot was never made. Four Star subsequently tried to interest NBC and ABC in the potential series to no avail.

### The Horse Traders

In the early 1970s, Peckinpah also attempted to have Four Star and CBS produce a pilot called *The Horse Traders*, based on a treatment by Max Evans. The project concerned two old cowboys in the West in the 1950s who buy a gasoline station, but the two had no idea on how to run a business. As Evans remembered, "I wrote down a five thousand-word outline and asked Sam if he'd like to see it. To my surprise, he stood up and read the whole damn thing while he kept barbecuing. Then he said, 'I'll give you $5000 for this if you work on the script with me.' He gave me a check for $5000, and it turned out to be good! One thing I respected about Sam was he never pulled that old director/producer thing where he bullshitted you about a project."[115] However, the project ended when Peckinpah found out that Evans' agency, MCA, was going to take 10% of the revenue from the possible series.

Other dramatic series Four Star International proposed included:

### Gothic Place

Developed by *One Step Beyond's* John Newland, this 1968 project would have featured spooky stories from yesteryear.

## The Guardians

Developed by Steven Kandel, who had worked on *The Rogues*, this proposed 1970 series concerned psychic phenomena and ESP.

## Dateline: Danger

Lewis John Carlino, who had written the Four Star TV movie, *In Search of America*, was signed by producer John Newland to do the pilot script for this series that may have been a candidate for the 1973-74 season.

## Amex-7

Writer Bob Barbash, who had scripted episodes of *Zane Grey Theatre* and *The Dick Powell Theatre*, was enlisted by Four Star to develop this sixty-minute dramatic series whose pilot would have been a movie of the week. The series was projected for the 1974-75 season.

## Dynasty

Not to be confused with the ABC and more recently CW soap opera of the same title, this proposed 1974 series would have focused on the Oklahoma oil fields at the turn of the twentieth century. Bob Barbash would have written the pilot as a ninety-minute movie of the week.

## Dateline

Created by Four Star International's president, David Charnay, a former journalist himself, with a pilot script written by Bill Davidson, *Dateline*, a 1974 project for NBC, focused on the adventures of an investigative reporter.

## The Sea Rovers

This proposed 1974 action-adventure show, developed by Louis "Deke" Heyward, involved a guy and a girl, boat owners, who worked out of San Pedro, California.

## Mochilla

A "mochilla" refers to the mail bag used by the Pony Express. This projected 1974 Western would have chronicled that mail delivery service.

*Appointment with Fear*

Long-time producer Sheldon Reynolds was set to star in this prime-time access series planned by Four Star in 1975. Reynolds had previously made a pilot in the late fifties with the same title starring John Dehner as an American soldier-of-fortune traveling around Europe. Like the 1975 project, the prior pilot never became a series but if it had, evidently Richard Burton would have starred in the lead role instead of Dehner.

## Actors Studio Specials

In 1976, Four Star International and Twentieth Century Fox TV signed a deal with the Actors Studio to televise at least three Broadway plays a year featuring actors who were members of the studio. The plays would first be presented on Broadway in limited runs before airing on television. Initial plans were to have a play in September 1976, December of that year, and March 1977. Some of the stars mentioned as possibilities for appearing in these presentations were Anne Bancroft, Bruce Dern, Dustin Hoffman, and Steve McQueen, but the specials never materialized.

Four Star had attempted the same project with the Actors Studio earlier – in 1967, but without Twentieth Century Fox, seeking to produce ninety-minute or two-hour specials but such specials also never came to fruition.

# Drama Pilots

Not including the TV movie, *In Search of America*, Four Star International made only two drama pilots.

## On Trial

This projected anthology series dealt with court proceedings of various types like criminal trials, divorce proceedings, and preliminary hearings. Made in 1969, the pilot featured MacDonald Carey as a lawyer in a murder case in which a defense attorney seeks to show that his client's wife was killed by an unknown intruder. The series was to air in syndication with the novel idea of using local TV talent as witnesses in the different cases thinking that this element might increase viewership for the anthology if it had become a series.

## Hunted

Described as a cross between *The Fugitive* and *Lassie*, this 1972 syndicated offering involved an eighteen-year-old boy, Dale Somerfield (Jim Henshaw) on the lam with his dog, a Briard – a French herding dog. The boy's father, Arthur Somerfield (John Gardiner), had been convicted of murdering a woman named Lydia Morgan (Jean Templeton) who is actually alive. Sought for questioning by the police, the boy and his dog elude the cops and pursue the woman as syndicate killers attempt to hunt them down.

The pilot for the series aired March 5, 1972 as an episode of *Dr. Simon Locke* called "The Wanderer." As noted above, *Dr. Simon Locke* was the precursor to *Police Surgeon*. A man named Scott (Arch McDonell) brings Dale Somerfield to Dr. Locke for treatment after Scott had tried to kill the teenager. Dale tricks his pursuer into fleeing and then, following a clue, visits a blind man who had worked with Lydia Morgan. Lydia has refused to make herself known to authorities because she has a black book containing a list of syndicate members, and the syndicate is out to kill her. Dale is not only searching for Lydia but is also wanted by the police as a suspect in the murder of a news reporter, Edward Zane, who had been working on an expose about organized crime. Dale had taken possession of Zane's dog after the pet was injured in the attack on his master. With Locke's help, Scott is captured and, understanding that Dale is on some type of mission, the doctor lets Dale escape.

The potential series, in association with CTV of Canada, was to be produced by Wilton Schiller and Chester Krumholz who had worked on *The Fugitive* and *Police Surgeon*. Schiller had also written for *Lassie*.

# Chapter 22:
# Drama at the Top, 1968-89

While the takeover of Four Star by David Charnay meant a new direction for the company, the period between 1968 and 1989 was not without its share of drama in the boardroom – the type of events that could have made a good mini-series.

Charnay began signing contracts with top-flight talent to act in and/or produce series for the company. In late 1970, Four Star executed a two-year deal with Anthony Quinn for his services as actor and consultant. Four Star also acquired Quinn's independent production company, The Franior Company, in exchange for 285,714 of Four Star preferred stock. However, a few months after the deal was reported, Quinn sued Four Star and David Charnay for fraud and breach of contract in the amount of $2.2 million plus another $5 million in punitive damages.

In 1973, Charnay was among those indicted along with billionaire Howard Hughes in connection with Hughes' 1968 purchase of Air West airlines. The defendants were accused of conspiring to pressure the directors of Air West to sell the company to Hughes by depressing the value of the airline's stock and threatening lawsuits against Air West's directors. Charnay was a former Air West stockholder. The indictments were dismissed in January 1974 only to have them reinstated and subsequently dismissed again by the same judge. A federal appeals court re-indicted the officials in May 1976, a month after Hughes' death. The case dragged on and was eventually settled in 1979 with charges dropped against the individual defendants but with two of Hughes' corporations agreeing to pay at least $30 million to certain former stockholders of Air West.

In the 1974 fiscal year, Four Star reported a net loss of $364,000, a downturn from profits of $856,000 from the year before. Charnay indicated that the loss was due to a decline in syndication of prime-time access shows and discontinued participation in the production of *Police Surgeon*.

In September 1982, Henry Harrison Kyle became president and CEO of Four Star International when he purchased about one-half of the stock owned by Charnay. Kyle was a Dallas attorney and businessman who made his fortune in real estate, coal, and construction. He started investing in films in 1968 and had been on Four Star's Board of Directors since 1970. When Kyle became president, Charnay remained chairman of Four Star's board. Kyle hoped to have Four Star begin producing series again. Early in 1983, he commenced talks with his former Marine buddies about a television series based on their experiences as prisoners of war during the Korean conflict. He also contemplated doing a documentary on former NFL player, Art Schlichter.

However, Henry Kyle was shot in the back and died in his Bel-Air mansion on July 22, 1983. His twenty-year-old son Rick was wounded in the elbow by, as reported at the time, an unknown assailant. Kyle and his son had gone downstairs to investigate noises that had awakened them. Police said that two guns had been found in the house but would not say if either one was the murder weapon. Rick Kyle was later indicted for his father's murder. The son had reportedly told his half-sister and her boyfriend that he had killed his father and had thrown the murder weapon into a neighbor's yard. His dying father had shot his son in the elbow. The shooting was prompted in part by Henry Kyle's intention of changing his will, deleting his eldest son from inheriting anything.

Rick Kyle's first trial ended in a hung jury on April 29, 1985. He was tried again in July 1985. In his closing argument, the prosecutor in that trial told the jury that Henry Kyle had solved his own killing when, after his son had shot his father, the senior Kyle fired a wild shot that struck Rick Kyle on the arm. The prosecutor, Lewis Watnick, remarked, "Without that shot, fired in the dark by a dying man, we would probably not have had this matter before us. To me, this is almost like the hand of God."[116] The jury in the second trial convicted Rick Kyle of involuntary manslaughter in the death of this father. He was sentenced to five years in prison.

In November 1983, Four Star International entered into an agreement with Technicolor, Inc. to purchase its subsidiary Gold Key Entertainment. As part of the purchase agreement, Four Star issued 360,000 shares of common stock to Technicolor. Technicolor also bought over 360,000 shares of stock from the estate of Henry Kyle as well as an additional 163,767 shares from David Charnay and 18,000 shares from Four Star vice president Martha Arnold giving Technicolor a majority interest in Four Star International. Gold Key syndicated shows like Dick Tracy features and Abbott and Costello cartoons.

Not surprisingly, a few months later, in March 1984, Joseph A. Fischer succeeded Charnay as the new board chairman and CEO of Four Star International since Technicolor, Inc., owned by the McAndrews and Forbes Group was the majority stockholder in the company. For a time, Charnay remained on Four Star's board. Billionaire investor, Ron Perelman had purchased MacAndrews and Forbes in 1980 and Technicolor Inc. in 1983.

In June 1986, Alfred Markim was named chairman-president-CEO of Four Star International replacing Fischer, who resigned. Markim's appointment was part of a deal with Compact Video to takeover Four Star as well as VidAmerica, a video cassette distributor headed by Markim. Both Four Star and VidAmerica became part of a new Entertainment Group of Compact Video. Ron Perelman had acquired Compact Video in 1986. Markim indicated that Four Star, now a subsidiary of Compact Video, would continue to look at producing game shows and specials for syndication.

Alfred Markim had started out as an actor appearing in the early 1950s science fiction series *Tom Corbett, Space Cadet* before venturing into TV production and video cassette duplicating.

In 1989, Perelman bought New World Entertainment with Four Star becoming a division of New World. Four Star International, in essence, ceased existence as a production company and syndicator of television shows. Subsequently, it became part of Rupert Murdoch's News Corporation (now called 21st Century Fox) as a result of a buyout between Murdoch and Ron Perelman in the late 1990s. 21st Century Fox now controls distribution of most of Four Stars productions.

After thirty-seven years in business and multiple changes at the top, Four Star came to an end. During the late fifties and early sixties it had been one of the major independent television production studios in Hollywood. The company was most famous for making anthology series and Westerns – two television genres that have all but disappeared from network television.

While some of the Westerns the company produced, such as *The Rifleman*, *Wanted: Dead or Alive*, and *The Big Valley* are still rerun today, the question remains what, if any, lasting impact did the company have on the business of television? Four Star never made what could be called "cutting edge" television, nevertheless, it did impact television series in certain ways after its demise.

One obvious effect was felt in the television series subsequently produced by writers, directors, and producers who had worked at Four Star before venturing off on their own. The best example is that of Aaron Spelling who went on to produce numerous series after he left Four Star. He made several made-for-television movies for ABC in the 1970s. The weekly made-for-television films were basically a reincarnation of the anthology genre done so well by Four Star. Spelling also adapted this genre for certain shows like *The Love Boat*, *Fantasy Island*, and *Hotel* by making each series regulars, both literally and figuratively, the hosts of the weekly stories starring numerous motion picture and popular TV actors.

Moreover, Spelling appears to have been influenced by Four Star shows like *The Detectives* and *The Big Valley* that paired veteran actors with young unknowns in a mentor/student type of relationship where the veteran actor would appear in a few scenes with the younger ones carrying out most of the story line. This arrangement can be seen in Spelling's series like *The Mod Squad* about a group of undercover young detectives supervised by actor Tige Andrews from *The Detectives*; *The Rookies*, young police officers under the command of Lt. Riker (Gerald S. O'Loughlin); *Charlie's Angels*, created by Ivan Goff and Ben Roberts who had worked at Four Star, that featured the exploits of three young female private investigators given their assignments by the unseen Charles Townsend (John Forsythe); and *Dynasty*, somewhat like a modern patriarchal equivalent of *The Big Valley*.

Producers and writers, Richard Link and William Levinson, who worked on Four Star detective series like *Michael Shayne, Burke's Law,* and *Honey West,* later created and wrote such classic mystery shows as *Mannix* (which they created with Four Star alumnus Bruce Geller), *Ellery Queen, Columbo,* and *Murder, She Wrote.*

Vincent M. Fennelly, who produced the Westerns *Trackdown* and *Stagecoach West* for Four Star, went on to produce other Western series – *Rawhide, Daniel Boone,* and *A Man Called Shenandoah.*

Another impact of Four Star on the television business is seen in its use of pilots airing as episodes of established shows to launch potential new television series. Four Star was a pioneer in incorporating back-door pilots into established series – something that continues to this day. *Wanted: Dead or Alive* was the first television show to have its pilot air as an episode of another continuing character drama – *Trackdown.* Four Star also attempted to launch a comedy series – *Teenage Idol* by helping to produce the first back-door sitcom pilot as an episode of *Mr. Adams and Eve.*

As illustrated in the profiles of Four Star drama and comedy series, the company made extensive use not only of back-door pilots in continuing character programs but also of regular pilots as episodes of various anthology series. *Dick Powell's Zane Grey Theatre* aired at least nine pilots during its run with five becoming regular series – *Trackdown, The Rifleman, Black Saddle, Johnny Ringo,* and *The Westerner,* probably a record for any TV anthology.

Finally, Four Star led the industry in having actresses as the main characters in television dramas. Before *Honey West* and *The Big Valley,* females were, for all intents and purposes, consigned to lead roles in situation comedies and as hosts of anthology series. Those two Four Star series from the mid-sixties changed that and led to female character dramas like *Police Woman* in the seventies, *Cagney and Lacy* and *Murder, She Wrote* in the 1980s, *Dr. Quinn, Medicine Woman* in the nineties, and *Alias* in the 2000's with actresses playing the central character.

# Endnotes

1   Tim Brooks and Earle Marsh, *The Complete Directory to Prime Time Network and Cable TV Shows*, 1946-Present, Ninth Edition, New York: Ballantine Books, 2007, xv.

2   Murray Schumach, "Hollywood Stirred by Death of Powell," *The New York Times*, January 4, 1963.

3   Larry Swindell, *Charles Boyer: The Reluctant Lover*, Brattleboro, Vermont: Echo Point Books & Media, 1983, 243.

4   Dave Kaufman, "On All Channels," *Variety*, December 30, 1955.

5   Swindell, *Charles Boyer*, 243.

6   Bill Davidson, "Deadeye Dick from Little Rock," Part 2, *TV Guide*, March 31, 1962, 25.

7   "An Actor-Turned Producer Appraises TV Film Problems," *Broadcasting*, July 22, 1957.

8   William Hawes, *Filmed Television Drama*, 1952-1958, Jefferson, North Carolina: McFarland & Company, Inc., 2002, 134-35.

9   Herman Rush, "A View from Hollywood – A 65 Year Overview of the World of Television," The Caucus for Producers, Writers, Directors, Caucus Journal, Summer 2015, retrieved September 6, 2017.

10  "Four Star Theater," *TV Time*, undated.

11  "Don Sharpe Resigns 2 of His 4 Star Posts; Partners Demand Fulltime Exec at Helm," *Variety*, November 28, 1955.

12  "Sharpe Sells New One to Cal Standard Oil," *The Billboard*, November 5, 1955.

13  "The Double Cross," Telepix Reviews, *Variety*, November 23, 1956.

14  "Roommates," Telepix Reviews, *Variety*, October 22, 1956.

15  William and Milarde Brent, *Grand Motel*, London: Rich & Cowan, 1956, 51.

16  Ibid., 159.

17  Hal Humphrey, "Jeannie Not Too Happy, But Dick Is Plain Mad," *Los Angeles Mirror-News*, May 1, 1957.

18  Mary Ann Anderson, *Mr. Adams & Eve*, Albany, Georgia: Bear Manor Media, 2011, 71.

19  Wally George, "Strictly off the Record," *Los Angeles Times*, March 8, 1958.

20  "Full Speed Anywhere," Telepix Reviews, *Variety*, September 15, 1960.

21  David Weddle, *If They Move . . . Kill 'Em! The Life and Times of Sam Peckinpah*, New York: Grove Press, 1994, 170.

22  Christopher Knopf, *Will the Real Me Please Stand Up*, Albany, Georgia: Bear Manor Media, 2010, 47.

23  "We Start with the Character," *TV Guide*, April 25, 1959.

24  Mark Goddard, *To Space and Back: A Memoir*, New York: iUniverse, Inc., 2008, 46.

25 Dave Kaufman, "On All Channels," *Variety*, February 6, 1959.

26 Hal Humphrey, "All Those TV Buckskin Heroes Did Wrong by Jane Russell," *Detroit Free Press*, January 25, 1959.

27 Hal Humphrey, "Powell A Reluctant Host," *Los Angeles Mirror-News*, November 9, 1956.

28 Aaron Spelling with Jefferson Graham, *A Prime-Time Life: An Autobiography*, New York: St. Martin's Press, 1996, 37.

29 Bill Davidson, "Deadeye Dick from Little Rock," Part 1, *TV Guide*, March 24, 1962, 8.

30 David Weddle, *If They Move . . . Kill 'Em!*, 147.

31 "Trouble at Tres Cruces," Telepix Reviews, *Variety*, March 30, 1959.

32 "President Powell of Four Star," CBS Television Press Release, November 11, 1958.

33 "Four Star Entering Syndication Field," *Variety*, November 1, 1958.

34 Knopf, *Will the Real Me*, 59.

35 "Wanted – Dead or Alive," Television Reviews, *Variety*, September 10, 1958.

36 Ibid.

37 Quoted in J. Fred MacDonald, *Who Shot the Sheriff? The Rise and Fall of the Television Western*, New York: Praeger, 1987, 52.

38 James Best with Jim Clark, *Best in Hollywood: The Good, the Bad, and the Beautiful*, Albany, Georgia: Bear Manor Media, 2009, 80.

39 Frank Rose, *The Agency: William Morris and The Hidden History of Show Business*, New York: Harper Business, 1995, 216.

40 Sherry Van Meter, Private communication with author, January 23, 2018.

41 David Weddle, *If They Move . . . Kill 'Em!*, 137.

42 Ibid., 168.

43 The Gigi Perreau character is called "Vicki" in the pilot but the end credits list the character's first name as "Carrie."

44 Jack Hellman, "Light and Airy," *Variety*, June 22, 1959.

45 Mark Goddard, *To Space and Back*, 31.

46 Richard Levinson and William Link, *Stay Tuned: An Inside Look at The Making of Prime-Time Television*, New York: St. Martin's Press, 1981, 15.

47 Bob Chandler, "You Think It's Easy to Turn Out a Bad TV Show? H'wood's Got the Formula," *Variety*, January 6, 1960.

48 David Weddloe, *If They Move . . . Kill 'Em*, 175.

49 Ibid., 182.

50 Jack Hellman, "Light and Airy," *Variety*, November 14, 1960.

51 "Stagecoach West," Telepix Followup, *Variety*, March 16, 1961.

52 "An Actor-Turned Producer," *Broadcasting*, July 22, 1957.

53 "Goodyear Theatre – A Turn of Fate," Television Reviews, *Variety*, October 2, 1957.

54 "The Vengeance," Telepix Review, *Variety*, July 2, 1959.

55 "Miss Allyson Was Not Amused," *TV Guide*, September 17, 1960, 18.

56 "Format for *Dogs Courageous!*," McGreevey Papers, Lilly Library, Indiana University, Bloomington, Indiana.

57  Jack Hellman, "Light and Airy," *Variety*, November 21, 1960.

58  "McDermott's 'Hey, Pay Attention'," *Variety*, May 31, 1961.

59  Harold Stern, "Shayne's Creator Blasts TV Show," *Press and Sun-Bulletin* (Binghamton, New York), October 22, 1960.

60  Gary Clarke, *How It Happened*, Albany, Georgia: Bear Manor Media, 2016, 96.

61  Jack Hellman, "Light and Airy," *Variety*, October 6, 1960.

62  Dave Kaufman, "On All Channels," *Variety*, November 22, 1961.

63  Larry Tubelle, "Out of the Tube," *Variety*, August 19, 1960.

64  Dave Kaufman, "On All Channels," *Variety*, February 13, 1962.

65  Martin Berkeley, "The River: Presentation," undated, Martin Berkeley Papers, UCLA Library Special Collections.

66  Hal Humphrey, "Viewing TV," *Beckley Post-Herald* (Beckley, West Virginia), December 15, 1962.

67  Sherry Van Meter, Private communication.

68  Cynthia Lowry, "Peter Lind Hayes Pretty Wife Mary; Don't' Love Lucy," *The Greenwood Commonwealth* (Greenwood, Mississippi), August 4, 1960.

69  Forrest Powers, "Molly Won't Watch Her New Series," *The Minneapolis Star*, October 4, 1961.

70  S.L. Remark, "Preparation for TV Series," undated, Shirley Jones Papers 1942-1980, UCLA Library Special Collections. Since the treatment for the *Esther Williams Show* was part of the Shirley Jones Papers, one can conclude that Ms. Jones was considered for a role on the proposed series probably as the sister-in-law.

71  John Eimen, Private communication with author, February 7, 2018.

72  John Eimen, Private communication with author, June 24, 2018.

73  Jack Hellman, "Light and Airy," *Variety*, May 28, 1962.

74  June Allyson with Frances Spatz Leighton, *June Allyson*, New York: Berkley Books, 1982, 222.

75  "More on How Pilots Get Long Pants of Their Own by 'Audition' on Series," *Variety*, August 13, 1958.

76  "Look for a Flock of TV Spinoffs to Ease Pilot Loses," *Variety*, November 22, 1961.

77  Bill Davidson, "Deadeye Dick from Little Rock," Part 3, *TV Guide*, April 7, 1962, 16.

78  "4 Star Freezout on a Successor Show to Powell," *Variety*, February 6, 1963.

79  Frank D. Gilroy, "Who Killed Julie Greer?," Frank Gilroy papers, Rauner Special Collections Library, Dartmouth College.

80  Knopf, *Will the Real Me*, 61.

81  Hank Grant, "TV Time: Lloyd Bridges Show Has Uncertain Future," *The Troy Record* (Troy, New York), March 12, 1963.

82  William Donati, *Ida Lupino: A Biography*, Lexington, Kentucky: The University Press of Kentucky, 1996, 229.

83  Jack Hellman, "Light and Airy," *Variety*, July 23, 1962.

84  George Segal, Private communication with author, February 8, 2018.

85  Ibid.

86  "Burke's Law," Telepix Reviews, *Variety*, September 23, 1963.

87 Spelling, *A Prime-Time Life*, 48.

88 Stephen Kandel, Private communication with author, December 9, 2017.

89 Cecil Smith, "Four Star's 'Rogues,'" *Detroit Free Press*, June 21, 1964.

90 Kandel, Private communication.

91 Eve Starr, "Inside Television," *The Mercury* (Pottstown, PA), May 22, 1963.

92 Marion Purcelli, "Bob Can't Beat 'em – He Joins 'em," *Chicago Tribune*, January 17, 1965.

93 Spelling, *A Prime-Time Life*, 55.

94 Dave Kaufman, "On All Channels," *Variety*, October 5, 1965.

95 Alex Gottlieb, "The Boss Who Came to Breakfast, Lunch and Dinner" script, *The Smothers Brothers Show*, January 31, 1966.

96 Marlyn Mason, Private communication with author, December 10, 2017.

97 Daniel Bubbeo, "A Sweet and Sour Memoir of the Pickle Brothers Comedy Team," *Newsday*, May 21, 2016.

98 Walt Dalton, "Out of Mouth of His Dummies," *The Los Angeles Times*, June 4, 1965.

99 "Malibu U," Tele Follow-Up, *Variety*, August 2, 1967.

100 Mortimer Adler Papers, Special Collections, University of Chicago Library.

101 J. Fred MacDonald, *Who Shot the Sheriff? The Rise and Fall of the Television Western*, 95.

102 Knopf, *Will the Real Me*, 75.

103 Dwight Whitney, "The Queen Goes West," *TV Guide*, Febuary 26, 1966, 7.

104 "Four Star Begins the Long Road Back," *Broadcasting*, November 17, 1969.

105 Jack Hellman, "Light and Airy," *Variety*, March 12, 1970.

106 "Psychic Phenomena as 'Substance' for 4 Star," *Variety*, March 27, 1968.

107 "Program Notes," *Broadcasting*, July 1, 1968, 50A.

108 Dave Kaufman, "It's Four Star 'Intl.' Now; Charnay Spells Out Plans on Programming," *Variety*, November 15, 1967.

109 Donald L. Barlett and James B. Steele, "If Hughes Wants Secrecy, Uncle Sam Will Oblige," *Chicago Tribune*, December 20, 1975.

110 "In the Syndication Marketplace," *Broadcasting*, May 13, 1985.

111 Vernon Scott, "News from Hollywood," *The Logansport Press* (Logansport, Indiana), September 16, 1971.

112 Harold V. Cohen, "At Random: The Stars Fall on Four Star," *Pittsburgh Post-Gazette*, May 8, 1968.

113 "Tom," Film Review, *Variety*, September 21, 1973.

114 Jack Hellman, "Light and Airy," *Variety*, October 8, 1970.

115 Max Evans as told to Robert Nott, *Goin' Crazy with Sam Peckinpah and All Our Friends*, Albuquerque, New Mexico: University of New Mexico Press, 2014, 12.

116 Cathleen Decker, "Multimillionaire Solved His Own Killing, L.A. Jury Told," *The Los Angeles Times*, March 23, 1985.

# Index

168-69, 174, 180-81, 186, 188, 190,
199, 201, 207-08, 216, 219, 224,
246, 250
McQueen, Steve   67-70, 110, 252,
259
N
Niven, David   xv, 3-13, 15-16, 30, 34,
39, 49, 51, 65, 94-97, 100, 123, 130,
147-48, 174, 176, 178-79, 216, 241,
250
O
Official Films   1, 7, 15-16
P
Peckinpah, Sam   39, 57, 60, 66,
72-73, 87, 89-90, 158, 183, 256-57
Powell, Dick   xv, 1, 3-11, 15-16, 22,
30-31, 34, 39-40, 42-43, 47, 50-52,
60, 63-65, 72, 87, 95, 99-100, 106,
108, 112, 114, 122-25, 129, 135,
145-48, 150-52, 162, 174, 195, 208,
216, 250
Powell, Jane   94-95, 140
Q-S
Sharpe, Don   xv, 1, 3, 6-7, 13, 15, 21,
25-28, 108
Spelling, Aaron   39, 52, 54, 57, 59-60,
81, 83-85, 92, 111, 145-47, 163,
174, 176, 189, 191, 195, 197, 203,
264
Stanwyck, Barbara   56, 95, 183, 217,
219-20, 241
T
Taylor, Don   22, 38, 40, 193
Taylor, Robert   40, 42-45, 173-74,
188-89, 220
Toomey, Regis   11, 40, 97, 174, 176
U-W
Whitmore, James   22, 61, 112

Printed in Great Britain
by Amazon